Praise for *Taxonomies: Practical Approaches to Developing and Managing Vocabularies for Digital Information*

'Helen Lippell's new book is a treasure trove of taxonomy practical best practices for any digital transformation initiative. Spanning a variety of use cases and industry applications of taxonomy, there are many nuggets to get you started on your taxonomy program, from business use cases, to taxonomy development and management, and integration into the user experience. Her book pulls from a wide variety of industry experts who have preserved their wisdom in these pragmatic case studies, real stories from the frontline. Many of the scenarios definitely resonated with me in my own experiences in information architecture and taxonomy development. I also appreciated the wealth of tips and tools provided, so be sure to also peruse the appendix for jumpstarting your taxonomy development work.'
**Madonnalisa Chan, Product Management Director – Content and Taxonomy Services, Salesforce, USA**

'Helen has done a brilliant job (as you'd expect) curating a wonderfully written, informative and useful set of essays on how to make better decisions to structure your taxonomies.

Her enthusiasm for the subject is palpable from page one. Whether you're starting out in your career, have embarked on a major project, or want to refresh your ontological knowledge, this book will help you organise your thoughts and your content. I can see myself using this as a point of reference for many years to come.'
**Lisa Riemers, Content and Digital Strategist, Lisa Riemers Ltd, UK**

'There is something in this book for everyone, from the novice taxonomist to the experienced consultant. Particularly useful are the sections dealing with identifying the benefits and getting buy-in from senior management, always tricky subjects, but very clearly discussed here. Another welcome aspect is the emphasis on understanding and working with your users to make sure your taxonomy is actually fit for purpose.'
**Judi Vernau, Information Architect, Metataxis, New Zealand**

'Bringing together this collection of contributions on a wide range of taxonomy-related issues from highly experienced practitioners into a seamless and authoritative book is a major achievement by Helen Lippell. The diversity of approaches to taxonomy strategy, development, implementation and management will be of immense value both to organisations that are starting to appreciate the value of metadata and taxonomies and also to those who have started on a taxonomy journey and are looking for inspiration and advice on how to maximise the return on their investment.'
**Martin White, Managing Director, Intranet Focus Ltd, UK and Visiting Professor, Information School, University of Sheffield, UK**

'All the meticulously edited chapters in this book will become your default reference when you are trying to explain why taxonomies are becoming so essential in this ever-changing digital content transformation landscape that we are currently living in. The case studies and the knowledge shared by these taxonomy practitioners will guide and inspire your information architecture, content management or any metadata related taxonomy project you might be developing right now. So many good references and best practices that I guarantee you will be re-reading the chapters more than once. I highly recommend it!'

**Leslie Santibanez, Information Architect, DataElix, Inc., Canada**

'Excellent and comprehensive book to start off your taxonomy project, but also to review a project that is ongoing. With a practical approach and plenty of examples, the book helps ensure all bases are covered, from buying-in to design to execution.

Personally, I found the indications on building a successful business case extremely useful and insightful since it guides you to consider all the important elements providing tips and practical ideas. It made me rethink my initial approach to the benefits of my own taxonomy project.

Rich with practical examples, the book provided suggestions for metrics, which helped to frame the project and monitor its developments - essential to demonstrate its value over time.

Despite not being a textbook, it is an extremely comprehensive work covering all aspects of taxonomies, from the project initiation to the actual design of the taxonomy, to all possible applications and its governance. The chapter on interoperability and the wider metadata ecosystem was particularly insightful and contributed to place the taxonomy project in the right context, while reading about corporate search engines also helped me to critically assess the project I am working on and to complement my initial knowledge.

Insightful and practical, the book guides the reader throughout the whole journey of a taxonomy project, helping to reflect critically on all the aspects that need to be considered from the start. Upon reading, you will feel that you will have considered all the elements and chosen the right approach tailored to your specific case.'

**Ivan Donadello, Information Management Officer, European External Action Service (EEAS), Belgium**

# Taxonomies

Every purchase of a Facet book helps to fund CILIP's advocacy, awareness and accreditation programmes for information professionals.

# Taxonomies
**Practical Approaches to Developing and Managing Vocabularies for Digital Information**

Edited by
Helen Lippell

facet
publishing

© This compilation: Helen Lippell 2022
The chapters: The contributors 2022

Published by Facet Publishing
7 Ridgmount Street, London WC1E 7AE
www.facetpublishing.co.uk

Facet Publishing is wholly owned by CILIP: the Library and Information Association.

*British Library Cataloguing in Publication Data*
A catalogue record for this book is available from the British Library.

ISBN 978-1-78330-481-3 (paperback)
ISBN 978-1-78330-482-0 (hardback)
ISBN 978-1-78330-483-7 (PDF)
ISBN 978-1-78330-525-4 (EPUB)

First published 2022

Text printed on FSC accredited material.

Typeset from contributors' files in 10.5/13pt University Old Style and Myriad Pro by Flagholme Publishing Services.
Printed and made in Great Britain by CPI Group (UK) Ltd, Croydon, CR0 4YY.

For Simon Turmaine and Liz Marley
I miss your wisdom, generosity and friendship

# Contents

# Figures and Tables

## Figures

## Tables

# Notes on Contributors

## Editor

**Helen Lippell** is a taxonomy consultant with over 15 years' experience of helping clients make the most of their content and data, whether by improving findability, content production efficiency or by exploiting reuse opportunities. (Or, as she sometimes puts it, helping them sort out messy stuff.) Her clients include Electronic Arts, Pearson, the BBC, Department for International Trade, Financial Times, Philips and the Metropolitan Police. She has been the programme chair of Taxonomy Boot Camp London since its inception in 2016, contributes articles to The Search Network, and speaks and writes regularly for taxonomy practitioners. She lives in London with her husband Simon and two cats.

## Contributors

**Tom Alexander** is a taxonomy professional who first cut his classification teeth in 1999 at major visual media company Getty Images. Since then, he has developed his classification capabilities and now works as Taxonomy Manager at Cancer Research UK. He is particularly interested in understanding how good classification can support, and be supported by, other disciplines within a digital environment, such as user experience, Search Engine Optimisation and content design. He believes that good taxonomy management doesn't come from on high – it comes from talking to the people who need it to find the content and assets they are looking for.

**Rahel Anne Bailie** is a consultant, university instructor, speaker and author. She is well known in the content industry, with books, awards and other accolades to her name. More importantly, Rahel is passionate about content and has spent almost three decades helping organisations make sense of their content operations, taking on increasingly complex problems in the areas of content strategy, content operations, knowledge management and related areas of content production. She looks at content, seriously, in ways that help companies leverage their content as valuable assets.

**Jeremy Bright** is a Global Operations Manager and a member of Practice Leadership for Managed Services at ICP in North America. He has been in the digital asset management and metadata/taxonomy space for about a decade. Jeremy has spent most of his professional career ensuring content on any platform is searchable and usable for end-user needs and always works to improve internal processes and find efficiencies through technology. Jeremy lives in Atlanta with his partners Cliff and Adam and their little bub (a Shih Tzu named Pita).

**Helen Challinor** has over 30 years of experience as a librarian in central government departments. She has held roles that have included cataloguing, library stock acquisitions, answering enquiries, service management and information standards. Since 2014, she has been the departmental taxonomist at the Department for Education.

**Jonathan Engel** specialises in digital information management and content tagging to improve navigation, search and delivery. He has built and implemented content classification and information management systems for UK government agencies, global companies and influential charities. He spent nearly half his 45-year media career at Reuters, where he devised the classification and metadata scheme for the news agency's multimedia news and data products. He now runs his own information architecture consultancy, InfoArk. Jonathan regularly speaks and conducts workshops on information architecture, focusing on taxonomy design, content classification and enterprise search. He'll never let taxonomy get in the way of a good joke.

**Annette Feldman** has been part of the Metadata Technology team at The Associated Press for over 15 years. At AP, Annette is responsible for creating and shepherding metadata for news content from its creation to its successful delivery. She works with AP editorial colleagues spanning every media type and with those who curate news products for every kind of customer, using ancient and modern technologies and standards. Annette holds an MLIS from Rutgers University and an MBA from Simmons College, as well as a BA in Linguistics from Brandeis University.

**Mags Hanley** is a career and information architect who has worked in digital for over 25 years. Her work focuses on helping retailers make their products findable online and helping designers find and plan their right career. She has worked across three continents for organisations such as Telstra and JB Hi-Fi in Australia, Argus Associates in the US, and the BBC and Time Out in the UK. She is the author of *Career Architecture*, a book for designers on how to plan and structure their careers using the tools of UX design. She can be contacted via her website www.magshanley.com.

**Heather Hedden** is the author of *The Accidental Taxonomist* (Information Today, 2010; 2016; 2022), which has become the most popular book on how to build taxonomies. Heather has worked as a taxonomist since 1995 in various organisations, and as an independent consultant. In 2020 she joined the professional services team of Semantic Web Company, vendor of PoolParty taxonomy/ontology management software. Heather continues to teach online workshops on taxonomy creation through Hedden Information Management (www.hedden-information.com), where she also blogs, and is a frequent conference speaker and taxonomy workshop instructor.

**Sara James** is the Strategy and Implementation Director and Practice Lead for ICP in North America. She has been in the content and taxonomy space for over 20 years. Sara is passionate about creating a user-friendly and intuitive user experience and ensuring that processes, technology solutions, taxonomy and metadata are serving the people who use them. Sara lives in Atlanta with her husband Scott and their two dogs.

**Michele Jenkins** is an information management consultant specialising in taxonomy-driven content strategy. She has more than 20 years' experience working with organisations across industries, including Harvard Business Publishing, EA Games and the Office of the High Commissioner on Human Rights (OHCHR). Michele draws from her multidisciplinary background in programming, information architecture/UX design, information science and publishing for a holistic approach to information and content management. She helps clients align their business goals, content requirements and technical functionality to engineer usable, sustainable architectures. She holds a BA in Linguistics from University of California at Santa Cruz and a MLIS from McGill University.

**Bob Kasenchak** is a taxonomist and information architect at Factor, an information architecture and human experience consultancy. A frequent writer, speaker and presenter on taxonomies, ontologies and knowledge graphs, Bob has been helping organisations design and implement taxonomy programmes for the past ten years. His current research interests include graph-based knowledge management and novel semantic applications. Bob holds degrees from St John's College, Santa Fe, and the New England Conservatory of Music. He lives in Albuquerque, New Mexico, with his wife and elderly cat.

**Jo Kent** is a self-described 'massive data geek' who has been working with BBC metadata for over ten years in news, online, television and radio and is showing no signs of getting bored. She has presented papers and talks at semantic linked data and taxonomy conferences nationally and internationally and is always happy to talk and learn more about data and its many uses. She is currently Data Architect on the BBC News Labs team, an innovation unit that aims to use new technology to bring the news to people in new and innovative ways.

**Cynthia Knowles** is a professional taxonomist, librarian and information manager with experience in a variety of industries including legal, healthcare, logistics and supply chain, energy and gaming. Currently, she is part of a team of passionate information science professionals at Electronic Arts, working together to create an intelligent content ecosystem for 450 million players around the world.

**Yonah Levenson** is a metadata strategist and taxonomy consultant. She is the co-founder, co-director and instructor of Rutgers University's Digital Asset Management (DAM) Certificate Program. In 2020–2021, she was awarded the Rutgers Professional Development Instructor of the Year. She is the founder and co-chair of the Language Metadata Table (LMT), an industry standard for language codes sponsored by MESAOnline.org (Media Entertainment Support Alliance) and SMPTE.org (Society for Motion Pictures and Television Engineers). Formerly, Yonah was the Manager of Metadata Strategy and Taxonomy Governance at WarnerMedia and HBO, as well as the Senior Metadata Analyst at Pearson Education.

**Maura Moran** has over 20 years' experience helping organisations meet their goals through improving their taxonomy, information architecture, content systems and workflows. She has a particularly strong background in commercial publishing, having worked for world-leading firms including Pearson, Elsevier and Oxford University Press. She is currently a Senior Content Consultant at Mekon Ltd, solving complex content challenges for clients particularly in the pharma, education and manufacturing sectors. Maura understands that changing an organisation's working practices can be a messy business, so she balances finding the right technical solution with a focus on practical implementation, including a solid approach to change management and content governance.

**Bharat Dayal Sharma** is an Information Architect, SEO Lead and 'accidental taxonomist' with 16 years' experience in the NHS. He has worked on information standards for Leeds Council, applying diverse taxonomy to their LOOP service directory using OpenReferral across the city and currently on NHS Digital's website. Dedicated to making the complex world of health and care understandable to all, he specialises in using the semantic web and taxonomies to enable this. As a British Indian and passionate anti-racism campaigner, he aims to make the NHS more diverse and inclusive as communications lead for NHS Digital's race equality network.

**Ed Vald** is a metadata, taxonomy and search professional, having spent far too many years entranced and/or confused by digital asset management, website and e-commerce projects for companies such as Getty Images, Bridgeman Images and the Chartered Institute of Personnel and Development (CIPD). He has contributed to papers on Machine Learning for the EU and is a past winner of Taxonomy Practitioner of the Year. When not creating, implementing and governing metadata frameworks and taxonomies, he can be found muttering profanities about metadata frameworks and taxonomies.

**Joyce van Aalten** is an independent taxonomy consultant and trainer. She has over 15 years' experience with taxonomy, thesaurus, ontology and knowledge graph projects for a broad range of customers. Her customers include KLM, Philips, Thesaurus for Health Care and Welfare and the Thesaurus for the Dutch House of Representatives. Joyce specialises in taxonomy management software and the possibilities of metadata/taxonomy within information management systems, like Office365/SharePoint. She frequently shares her knowledge via workshops, conferences and articles, and is co-author of *Maak het vindbaar* (*Make it Findable*) (2017).

# Acknowledgements

I'm so grateful to all the contributors for their enthusiasm for this project. Over the course of the development of the chapters, I had many enjoyable video calls, which livened up many samey days during the global lockdowns of 2021, when we could step away from day-to-day workloads and focus on getting great ideas onto paper/screen. Most importantly, thanks one and all for the fantastic quality of content. I hope this book will be a useful way for all of you to continue to promote your skills and expertise, inside and outside organisations.

Thanks to Val Skelton, who made invaluable editing and thematic suggestions, especially at points where I had long since stopped being able to see the wood for the trees.

Thanks to Pete Baker at Facet Publishing for his support and encouragement throughout the project, and to the early reviewers who helped shape a vague idea into a coherent proposition.

Finally, thanks to my husband Simon, who has put up with the long hours of me being on calls or bashing at a keyboard and has supported this project all the way. Thanks to you, no cats were neglected in the making of this book.

Helen Lippell
August 2021

# Foreword

*Heather Hedden*

Taxonomies for digital information management are no longer new, but their adoption is becoming more widespread. Taxonomy uses have expanded beyond traditional information publishing and e-commerce to include managing internal knowledge bases, intranets, marketplace and matchmaking services, technical documentation and help pages, regulated content for compliance, digital assets or media, user community content and customisable and reusable content for document creation, among others.

When I started giving conference presentations and workshops on taxonomies more than 15 years ago, I explained how taxonomies were versatile in supporting both search and browse for information retrieval in addition to enabling consistent tagging at the back-end. Over the years, this list of taxonomy uses has grown to also include information discovery, filtering and sorting of results, workflow management of content, metadata consistency for comparison and analysis, visualisation of topics, curated content in feeds or info boxes, sentiment analysis, personalised information, recommendation systems and question answering systems. Some of these also involve taxonomy support of knowledge graphs.

As the uses of taxonomies increase, more people are becoming involved in them. Furthermore, people who become involved in taxonomies are in increasingly varied roles. Taxonomies have diverse stakeholders, during both the taxonomy creation project and ongoing maintenance phase. These stakeholders include knowledge managers, information architects, user experience professionals, solution architects, search experts, digital asset managers, content managers, content strategists, product managers, text analytics linguists, data scientists, ontologists, etc. These people need a solid understanding of what is involved in creating, adapting and implementing a taxonomy, even if they do very little or no editing of the taxonomy themselves.

My own book, *The Accidental Taxonomist*, is targeted at those who need to build taxonomies, whether they want to start work as taxonomists or need to improve their existing taxonomy skills. This book, *Taxonomies*, is suitable for a broader audience that also includes taxonomy project managers and owners and those in the aforementioned related roles, while serving as an excellent resource for all taxonomists. It provides information needed to be a taxonomy manager or to manage taxonomies from any job role.

Some chapters address particular issues in taxonomy creation, others are dedicated to different aspects of taxonomy management and their implementations. This includes taxonomies and search engines, content management, digital asset management, metadata, e-commerce, taxonomy governance, maintenance, user testing and taxonomy software selection.

The opening chapter on business buy-in and scoping addresses a taxonomy management issue that is just as important as taxonomy creation. Taxonomy projects are rarely initiated in the upper levels of an organisation that control strategy and budget (and if they are, they are probably not well thought out). What is more common is that someone responsible for content management or user experience learns about taxonomies, or those who already know the benefits of taxonomies are in a position without organisational authority, and they need to obtain buy-in and budget from above. The fact that there is rarely a single, obvious department within an organisation that clearly oversees taxonomies leads to additional challenges and opportunities.

Despite standards and best practices for taxonomies, the applications and uses of taxonomies are so varied that diverse approaches are often needed. Taxonomies are also multi-disciplinary (knowledge management, content management, information architecture, information technology, etc.). This book features contributions from a number of taxonomy practitioners and others who represent different specialisations, such as digital asset management (DAM) and structured content.

Case studies and other real-life examples add a lot when explaining taxonomies and that is another benefit of having contributed authors sharing their varied experiences. No single author would have so many informative case studies to share. Even then, the information presented can be generalised and is thus valuable.

Well-constructed and well implemented taxonomies are at the core of successful information and knowledge management systems and services. It is important that more professionals in a wider variety of roles realise this. So, I am very pleased that this book will serve that end, helping more people understand, implement and manage taxonomies better. I commend Helen Lippell on both her selection of taxonomy management topics and her recruitment of knowledgeable colleagues who have shared their expertise with the rest of us. I am pleased to learn new things, too.

# Introduction

Quite early in my career, one of the interaction designers I was in a team with turned to me and the other taxonomists in the office and, mostly tongue-in-cheek, called us 'list-makers'. The remark was intended to belittle the work we were doing on a complex content modelling project, where accurate tagging was crucial to the right content being delivered to the right place at the right time.

Even when I had only worked on a few taxonomy projects, instead of the dozens I have done since, I knew that characterising taxonomists as 'list-makers' was silly. Taxonomies are more important in the world of digital information than they have ever been. Hopefully, the fact that you are reading this text means, on some level, you agree.

First, to get the dictionary definition out of the way: a taxonomy is a list of words and phrases, most often organised into a hierarchy. It is used to classify, categorise or tag just about anything, but this book is concerned with digital content, data and information.

What elevates a mere list of words and phrases to being a live taxonomy is how it is used. I love the sheer versatility of taxonomies and how they have become a core component of so many types of digital products and services. Here are some examples:

- content delivery
- content classification
- search relevancy
- search facets and filters
- recommender systems
- digital asset management (DAM)
- knowledge base systems
- training machine learning
- product information for e-commerce
- process flow management
- enhanced navigation
- analytics and insights.

All of these, and more, are mentioned in the book. It is worth noting that the intended application for a taxonomy will likely shape how the taxonomy is structured. For example, a taxonomy for e-commerce search may have multiple facets because of the many ways a product can be described or searched for. In contrast, a taxonomy for tagging web documents may only have a few dozen terms, as only broad categories are needed and the set of terms needs to be manageable for taggers.

## Who is this book for?

This book had its genesis in a snatched conversation with Pete Baker at the drinks reception at Taxonomy Boot Camp London. Did I want to write/produce a book for Facet Publishing on the subject of taxonomies? There are some superb books in the 'canon' already, and many books on topics such as digital asset management, search, library and information science, semantic technologies and digital design, that touch on the importance of taxonomies. However, the area where I thought a new book could make a difference was in helping people understand what you need to do in order to make a taxonomy project successful.

Right from the start, I wanted this book to have a wide ranging appeal for anyone who comes into contact with taxonomies as part of their jobs. You might be an intranet manager who uses a taxonomy to improve search, a product manager who needs high quality data to optimise their product or a developer who is interested in doing more with vocabularies and semantics, to name but three. You might be a student of library science, information science, computer science or some other information-related discipline.

You might also be one of the many people who has come to taxonomies from some other direction, in which case you went down a similar path to me. I had studied Latin and Economics at university without much idea of what I wanted to do afterwards. Because of the Economics qualification, I got an entry-level job at the *Financial Times*, a leading business newspaper in the UK. Once I started working on indexing news sources from around the world and saw how this tagging helped create targeted news feeds for all kinds of customers, I was hooked. I loved the work of trying to understand what content was about, what concepts were relevant to a particular domain and how to structure those concepts in a meaningful way.

I hope, above all, that this book will be useful for the people who work closely with taxonomies every single day. There is no equivalent to the PRINCE2 methodology of project management when it comes to seeing a taxonomy project from beginning to completion, but you will find plenty of best practices, tips and tricks, and cautionary tales in this book.

## Themes and skills

According to Austin Kleon's excellent book about creativity, *Steal Like An Artist*, people who give you advice are really just talking to themselves in the past. I think that may be a little harsh; on the other hand, I would love to have been clutching this book when I started out.

I always had a natural affinity for organising information. I recently found a sheet of paper from when I was 8 years old, on which I had categorised the 88 constellations according to whether they represented animals, objects or people, usually figures from classical mythology. (I was an only child and there were a lot fewer TV channels in the 1980s.) But a love of classifying information, on its own, will not make you a successful taxonomist – although I do think it is essential to have an appreciation of the connections, differences and characteristics of things. If you have that, then it is not hard to learn the language of taxonomy development and start applying it to real projects.

As I read through and edited all the chapters, there were three main thematic areas that kept coming up for me again and again:

1 **Mindset**, or the mental approach that taxonomists bring to their work. I do not mean this in a nebulous self-help, pop psychology sense. I mean the ways that taxonomists can work effectively when organisations (regardless of sector) are undergoing change. They need to be flexible, proactive and reflective, and to try to keep their taxonomy work aligned with the organisation's strategic objectives. A taxonomy is never 'finished' in the sense of 'never needing to be looked at again', so keeping an emphasis of sustainability beyond the immediate life of a development project is also helpful. This is as true for someone working in-house as it is for a taxonomy consultant like me (even for a short project, I always want to leave good documentation about ongoing governance and maintenance).
2 **Communicating effectively** is a non-negotiable part of doing taxonomy work. I cannot lie; there have been times on projects when I just wanted to be left alone to review content, play with words and structures, and come up with synonyms and other semantic relationships. But all of this thoughtfulness and skill is wasted if colleagues do not appreciate the value of the end product. Several chapters discuss strategies for communicating, whether this is with senior managers who have budgets, or team mates who will be loading your taxonomy into a new system, or content authors who need to be convinced of the benefit of the extra work of tagging, or the colleagues working on other systems that will need to use your taxonomy.

Crafting the right messages is important for these groups; tailoring the language and call to action depending on what you might need from them. Less formal communication techniques can pay off in terms of awareness-raising too; when it comes to selling the benefits of a taxonomy, a chat over a coffee could be as useful as a data-filled report to the senior management team.

3  **Relationships** – not the ones inside a taxonomy, but the human ones. Whether the taxonomy users are inside the organisation, or outside, a strong focus on user satisfaction is something I cultivate in myself and encourage in others. A user-centred mindset is even more salient when working on taxonomies that need to account for diverse perspectives and/or shifting language. There are many ways to build connections with users, using a range of qualitative and quantitative approaches, including analytics, interviews, surveys, social media and publishing taxonomies for feedback. Rather than being the owner of a taxonomy, I like to think of it more as being a steward of the organisation's knowledge (which is used in products and services that make life easier for users and, for external applications, make money for the organisation). That responsibility means it is important to build active partnerships with others.

## Introducing the chapters

The chapters in this book have been written by expert practitioners with over 400 years of experience between them. There are many excellent communicators in the taxonomy community and I selected each contributor based on my knowledge of their work, their conference talks or their writing. The chapters are a mix of organisation-specific case studies and information synthesised from multiple projects (even including the odd one that did not quite go to plan!). I think the book can be used in a variety of ways. It can work as a cover-to-cover read, a reference for specific phases of a project and a refresher for even the most experienced practitioner.

**Part 1: Getting Started** deals with getting the foundations right. I have seen first-hand how a taxonomy project can get off to a bad start, with the consequence that the finalised taxonomy never really meets the organisation's and the users' needs. **Chapter 1** covers the work needed to get buy-in from the stakeholders who will support your project not just with strategic direction, but also resources. Expectation setting is vital at this stage, so that everybody involved has a realistic vision of what the taxonomy will achieve. The ideal position is the 'Goldilocks' one, where people understand the taxonomy as a key component but do not get carried away with how the taxonomy will fix any underlying problems in content production or business processes. The topic of **Chapter 2** is also fundamental. A taxonomy that is being developed or substantially revised needs to be stored somewhere, such that it can be worked on and then used. There is a range of options, from the humble spreadsheet to the commercially available tools, and the chapter covers the various considerations to weigh up.

Part 2: Building Taxonomies deep dives into many aspects of the development process. **Chapter 3** discusses first principles of structuring – as mentioned earlier, the way the taxonomy is intended to be used should shape how it is built so that it is fit for purpose. Choosing the right structure will also inform how the taxonomy should be extended over the project and beyond. Getting this right will save a lot of refactoring pain later on. **Chapter 4** deals with an area I am particularly keen to see become more prominent in this field, that is, the ways that taxonomists (or indeed, anyone working in digital technology) can ensure their output captures the full perspectives of their audiences and is as free from biases as possible. We all have our own life experiences and biases, but there are ways to ensure that diversity is represented throughout a taxonomy, for example, consulting a wide selection of users or capturing diversity notes, such as definitions or usage restrictions with each taxonomy term.

**Chapter 5** is a crash course in the technical language and practice of industry-standard taxonomy construction. It is a great place to start for people with no experience and includes numerous examples of real-world things that bring to life the design decisions a taxonomist makes. **Chapter 6** provides a truly user-centred approach to making taxonomies work well for their audiences. Different techniques are covered, from the formal to the informal. (One of my favourite projects was doing guerrilla interviews at a home improvement show on behalf of an architecture organisation. Five-minute chats with people interested in doing up their homes, with a few open questions, elicited a huge volume of feedback for a new search product.) It also addresses how to balance users' mental models with your own when these diverge.

**Chapter 7** is another crash course, this time in making taxonomies and vocabularies work with multiple systems. It can be hard enough working with taxonomies inside one system, never mind more than one, but there is groundwork that can be done. This work is both technical (analysing data flows between different systems) and people-focused (building relationships with colleagues to improve mutual understanding of requirements). **Chapter 8** has a tongue-in-cheek title that belies its serious message. There are many ways a taxonomy implementation can go wrong. Even a seemingly minor blip in the taxonomy hierarchy could cause an infinite loop, meaning an application that uses that hierarchy cannot read it correctly. This could cause content to stop being tagged, or content to be automatically tagged incorrectly, or stop tags being available to human taggers, or search quality to deteriorate. And so on. Taxonomy errors are similar to software bugs in this respect.

**Part 3: Applications** covers four important areas where taxonomies can make a big impact. **Chapter 9** deals with enterprise search, that is, search engines for intranets, knowledge bases and other internal tools. It can be very satisfying to see how changes you make in the search engine back-end positively affect the quality of results for users. **Chapter 10** packs in a lot of invaluable information about taxonomies and digital asset management. Images, video, audio, etc., have different metadata needs from text-based content and are often stored in the hope of future reuse, maybe for content marketing or e-commerce purposes. Therefore, good taxonomy design and implementation is a must, as is understanding the entire asset lifecycle from commissioning to archiving.

**Chapter 11** covers the burgeoning area of structured content, an idea that has been around for a long time but is now gaining traction as an efficient way of managing multichannel content operations. Siloed content management systems and processes hold organisations back. Creating structured content, and harnessing the power of taxonomies to describe and deliver it, is more efficient and opens up new opportunities. **Chapter 12** is an introduction to designing navigation, search and content for e-commerce. The principles of good taxonomy design can be applied to navigation models, search facets, product category labels and more; findability is integral to the success of any e-commerce offering.

**Part 4: Business Adoption** presents four in-depth case studies from practitioners. **Chapter 13** is the pragmatic story of implementing taxonomies and metadata in a global news organisation, where timeliness and accuracy are at a premium and journalists need tagging to be as frictionless as possible. **Chapter 14** is a blend of best practice advice about taxonomy governance and the journey that a video games giant took to make their own governance framework happen. **Chapter 15** is also a goldmine of best practice, this time on taxonomy maintenance. Too often, governance and maintenance get forgotten in the push to get a taxonomy project delivered, but these are essential so that the taxonomy delivers value for years to come. **Chapter 16** is more focused on taxonomists than taxonomies; it covers strategies and opportunities for those working in a development team. Learning to draw on the knowledge and skills of colleagues, such as developers, product managers, etc., and, conversely, being able to evangelise and educate about taxonomies, can be tremendously energising and help with building a career.

There are three appendices containing useful extra resources for use in project work. These are: a template to capture taxonomy term diversity; an introduction to ontologies; and a metadata model template. Finally, there is a detailed glossary of technical and business terminology used throughout the book.

# Part 1
# Getting Started

# 1 Business Buy-in and Scoping

*Maura Moran*

*Editor's note*: I asked Maura to write this chapter because I've seen how good she is in action, working with clients to set the scope of a taxonomy project, making it meaningful, measurable and, most of all, realistic. As is true for any technology project, a good foundation and plan is essential (even if the plan evolves along the way). A taxonomy is a business artefact that will, with the right care and attention, deliver value to an organisation for years to come.

## Introduction

As an information professional, you understand that improving your organisation's use of taxonomies can solve some of its challenges. Maybe you've got a problem with search, or you need to improve navigation options. Maybe you need to support a recommendation engine or a chatbot. Or maybe you just need to classify your content accurately in order to get a handle on managing your content at scale. Better use of taxonomy will help, but how do you persuade your stakeholders to invest the time and money required? And where do you start with your taxonomy project?

Whether your organisation is large or small, commercial or non-commercial, the need to secure business buy-in and scope the project correctly is the same. In this chapter I'll share best practices and case studies that offer insight into:

- how to secure (and maintain) buy-in for your taxonomy project
- how to scope and prioritise your taxonomy development and investment
- how to maintain this investment and support in the future.

Throughout this chapter, I talk about 'adding a taxonomy' or 'your taxonomy approach'. I'm using this to cover a multitude of scenarios, including starting from scratch, improving the taxonomies you've got or expanding the scope or use of taxonomy. The approach outlined below is relevant to many different scenarios.

## Getting started

First, you need to have a clear view of what the project will deliver, the challenges you're trying to address and how you think the taxonomy project will help address these challenges. This whole process will be iterative, and you'll have a chance to adapt your hypotheses and refine your plan as you go along. As a first step:

1  Think about the benefits that the taxonomy project will bring, being as specific as you can:
   • If you're looking for efficiency gains, define which specific changes to your workflow will create these efficiencies, and how.
   • Identify the real, underlying benefit. Improving the findability of your content is a noble goal, but what tangible benefits does it bring? Will it lead to an increase in revenue or influence? Will it lead to lower costs, perhaps through increased content re-use?
   • Remember that simply introducing a taxonomy or a taxonomy management system is not in itself a benefit.
   The work you do at this stage will feed into your planning and business case:
   • The changes necessary to the workflow are good candidates for metrics to measure the benefits.
   • The benefits you identify will feed directly into your benefit planning and the cost/benefit analysis portion of your business case.
2  Think about what processes and systems need to change to deliver the benefits, for example:
   • Do you need to change how content is keyworded?
   • Do you need to align and govern disparate taxonomies in your organisation?
   • Do you need to change your website or search index to allow the taxonomy to improve the navigation or search?
   By identifying processes and systems that need to change, you identify tasks or dependencies for your project. You can also add the people and departments who are responsible for these processes and systems to your stakeholder analysis. You are also identifying users who will be impacted by your project and who will need support with change.

3  Think about what tasks need to be done in the project. You need to source a taxonomy, of course, which probably entails creating one from scratch or modifying an existing one. You may also be selecting and implementing software, keywording content or improving the search indexing.

4  Finally, think about the people and skills you need to carry out these tasks. In terms of roles, you will probably need taxonomists, subject matter experts and keyworders. A larger project, particularly one involving new software, may also need IT people, testers, user researchers, etc. As well as your colleagues, you may also need to involve suppliers, partners and perhaps key customers. You may also need to hire into new roles or bring in contractors or consultants for additional expertise. Identifying tasks, people and skills feeds into your project planning and the cost element of your business case.

As a result of this overall thinking phase, you will gain an understanding of the general shape of the project, what the organisation will gain and what needs to be done, as well as some analysis that will help you to identify stakeholders, roles and budget.

## Getting buy-in
### Align to organisational goals

By now you should have identified one or more goals for your taxonomy initiative. Perhaps it's classifying information or content more accurately, or perhaps you want to improve findability or support personalisation. In order to get business buy-in, you now need to position those goals, and your project, in terms of what your organisation is trying to achieve.

First, align your project to the organisation's current objectives. Typically, these are described in the strategy or mission statement and may include:

- increased revenue (for commercial organisations)
- increased reach, influence or awareness (for non-commercial organisations)
- increased efficiency (both costs and effort)
- improved time to market
- improved products
- better user experience or customer journeys
- better data stewardship
- increased innovation.

A taxonomy project can deliver against any of these areas, so you can position your project accordingly to make it clear that the taxonomy project is worth investing in for your organisation.

## Managing stakeholders

Identify all the stakeholders you need to influence in order to get buy-in. This includes people who will give you the go-ahead and budget, of course, but also a wider group of people who could be a help or a hindrance to your project. Stakeholders could:

- be directly involved in approving your business case
- provide you with the budget or people for your project
- be involved in the technical side – hosting, security checking, etc.
- be directly involved in creating the taxonomy or using it to tag content
- be responsible for products, services, websites, etc., that will benefit from the taxonomy
- be involved in quality control or regulatory compliance
- be accountable for the benefits you're trying to achieve, for instance, improved revenue or fewer errors
- be a key customer or partner.

You should carry out stakeholder analysis to map your project to each person's goals or concerns. Then, develop your messaging and plan how best to communicate with and influence your stakeholders.

Remember that different stakeholders may respond to different goals or cultural values. For instance, one may be excited by innovation while another wants to secure cost savings and a third may be focused on maintaining quality. Make sure you are able to frame your project in the right way for the right person or occasion.

Review the stakeholder list as you move through the project, especially after you have drafted the costs and benefits for your business case. This activity may reveal stakeholders you didn't identify earlier. You should also keep a look out for allies. These are people who are not directly impacted by your project, but who may be able to help you frame the business case or influence the organisation.

## Look for influence and budget

There are two more activities that can help you secure the organisation's approval for your project:

1   If your organisation is large enough to have decision-making bodies that control strategy, investment or content governance, you should try to join them if you can, or influence them through your manager or allies.
2   Identify any existing initiatives or projects that you could join forces with. This can be a really effective way of securing budget and attention. Often it's easier to justify the investment in the business case too, because you can talk about the combined benefits of a whole set of activities rather than taxonomy alone. Efficiency drives, new digital products, a quality focus, customer focus or website re-development are all good projects to align your taxonomy project with.

## Effective communication

Take every opportunity to communicate. Some of the channels available to you might be face-to-face briefings, an intranet campaign, email newsletters, blogging and physical artefacts, such as posters, as well as formal reports to senior management. Remember most people won't be interested in the technical details of a taxonomy project. Focus instead on how the project benefits the organisation and customers or users.

Ensure you can quickly explain the goals of the project in a meaningful way to stakeholders. Come up with a few sentences that can be used in slides or documents. Your first sentence should explain what you are doing and why. For example: 'This project will improve how we classify our content so that customers can more easily find and purchase our services.' You may also want to come up with an even shorter, memorable tagline that describes the benefits, for instance, 'smarter content', 'next generation delivery', 'the right content at the right time', etc. You can use this on all communications to reinforce your message.

Create a communication plan that will run throughout the project to maintain your visibility and which allows you to report progress or key achievements such as Proof of Concept (POC) or budget sign-off. Use the work you did in your initial stakeholder analysis (described above) to think about which messages and communications channels to use for each stakeholder and the wider organisation.

---

### Case study:  Educational publisher
The product management team of a leading educational publisher had some exciting ideas for their online services. They wanted to link teaching, learning

and assessment materials to each other using a curriculum framework. For instance, a textbook lesson about learning fractions would link to the teacher's notes, which would link to a quiz on the material.

Unfortunately, they underestimated the effort involved in creating a curriculum framework that would link the various materials together. The metadata manager could see that a set of taxonomies would be required, but needed to make a business case to secure the budget and people to create and maintain them. To make this case, she:

- linked the taxonomy project to larger initiatives in product development, gaining access to some of their budget, project management resource and visibility
- sought out advice from other divisions and sought allies across teams
- highlighted similar initiatives in competitors, underlining the message: 'We don't want to be left behind'
- softened decision-makers up before key decision-making meetings to make sure that they had a chance to ask questions and express concerns privately before key meetings
- made sure she could explain the purpose of taxonomies quickly and could explicitly link them to new product development.

This resulted in approval for her curriculum taxonomy project.

## Drafting your business case

How formal the business case needs to be depends on your organisation's practices and your own role in it. If you have some budget that you can allocate with minimum fuss, you may be able to do some or all of the project with a relatively informal justification. Conversely, you may be asked for a formal justification of every stage, even for the smallest steps. Whatever your situation, you will certainly need to justify your expenditure and predict benefits at each stage of the project.

### Costs

Costs vary enormously depending on the scope of your taxonomy project and what you already have available in terms of people and technology. Therefore, every business case is different, but some typical costs to consider include:

- taxonomists – you and your existing team, additional staff, consultants

- additional internal/external effort – e.g., testing, project management, user research, IT
- software licensing
- infrastructure (e.g., servers) or hosting (note that most software is now hosted in the cloud, unless your organisation has security policies that prevent that)
- training
- support.

Note that some organisations will also require you to account for the value of staff time in the business case.

## Benefits
### Financial benefits
You will probably need to include some hard financial benefits in your business case. These might include:

- Efficiency: Reducing costs or effort or avoiding new costs. Remember that reducing effort has a financial impact, even when you are considering internal staff rather than suppliers. Also, look for efficiencies in the wider workflow, not just directly in taxonomy and tagging.
- Increased revenue through:
  - Improved products (e.g., more functionality) leading to new customers or increased customer retention.
  - Better findability or content recommendations leading to increased sales.
  - Reduced time to market for new products, particularly where timing against competitors' offerings is key to gaining market share.
- Faster revenue: Reduced time to market leading to revenue coming in more quickly.

You may also want to focus on other benefits that are not directly financial, such as benefits to customers from improved services, or the benefits to staff of a system that is easier to use. But if you're building a financial case, remember to always bring the argument back to how these improvements will increase revenue or save money.

For instance, replacing a system that is difficult to use with one that is better should increase productivity, which results in efficiency or faster revenue. Similarly, making content more findable isn't a financial benefit, but it should lead to increased revenue. Or it may lead to lower costs, for instance, if customers can find the answer to their questions on the website instead of contacting Customer Services.

## Non-financial justifications

You may also want to add non-financial benefits to your business case, especially if your organisation is non-commercial or has a mission to help its users or members, or if the financial case isn't persuasive on its own. Some non-financial justifications include:

- legal or regulatory compliance
- increase in quality, for instance, improved data quality
- risk reduction, for instance, reducing the risk of publishing inaccurate information or disruption from fragile systems
- increased reach or visibility for your organisation
- influencing the behaviour of your users
- happier staff.

Review your thinking about how to align the project against the organisation's goals for ideas.

## Metrics

While you're planning your benefits, think about how you will provide evidence later that your project has been a success. You will probably need to justify the project at different stages, for instance, after you have done some initial work, after you've completed the project and even in future years to justify the maintenance costs.

There are always many potential benefits, but you need to prioritise measuring a few. Less is more for metrics. Remember you have to collect, analyse and act on them, and tracking too many can be a burden. So focus on the ones that are key to your business case or most persuasive to your organisation.

### How to collect metrics

Plan how you will measure each benefit, including who will take the measurement, what the specific measure is and how and when it will be collected.

Make sure you baseline before introducing any changes, so you can better see the effect of your project.

To minimise the work for yourself, collect metrics automatically where possible, or use ones that the organisation is already collecting for another purpose. For instance, revenue or usage figures are almost certainly being produced already and you may find that other key indicators are as well.

If you have to gather metrics specifically for your project, think about:

- automated reporting
- bespoke testing, e.g., usability testing or focus groups
- gathering user feedback through surveys (either internal or external users)
- a case study approach with a small team recording your key metrics such as time. It's most persuasive if you can compare their experience with a control group that has not made a change, though this can be a lot of work.

Remember that measuring the wrong thing can lead to unintended consequences. Metrics can become de facto objectives and using them wrongly can distract from the real goal or, even worse, entrench undesirable behaviour.

There are a few other pitfalls:

- It's hard to untangle the project's impact from other changes happening at the same time.
- Some benefits are not apparent straight away. If the new workflow or system requires effort to learn, productivity and satisfaction can even drop initially.
- Some measures can be ambiguous. For instance, what does it mean if your taxonomy project causes searches on your website to increase? Are people using the search more because it's more useful or are they finding it harder to find what they want?

*Example metrics*
Some of the quantitative metrics you could consider include:

- specific task comparison:
  - search - time and quality of results
  - tag, load or check data or content
  - ease of re-using content (including creating new services or publications from existing content)

- usability testing: Are relevant results returned? Can users find what they need?
- percentage of positive or negative feedback from users
- increased usage of your site or product
- increased sales
- number of new customers registering
- data quality measures.

*Qualitative metrics*

You may also want to gather some qualitative metrics as you roll out your project. For instance, you can run regular surveys asking colleagues how they feel about the project and how well they understand it. You can also ask your end-users how they feel about any improvements to your services. This feedback is useful because it allows you to adjust your approach as you continue to roll out. It can also be shared in communications with stakeholders. Often a well-written quote is more memorable and more persuasive than the dry statistics in your reporting.

## Planning for the future

Naturally, at the start of a project you are focused on getting your project approved and making it a success. Remember though that all the components of your taxonomy project will require investment in the future, from the maintenance of the taxonomies themselves to software licensing and support costs. Of course, your benefits will also continue in subsequent years; in fact, they may even grow. So you may want to do a multi-year business case from the beginning or, at least, be prepared with your figures for next year's maintenance business case.

## Early trials: Proof of Concept and pilot

Taking your first practical steps is exciting and you have a number of options depending on your circumstances. If you are planning significant changes in taxonomies, process or technology, it's best to take an iterative approach to your project. An iterative approach is lower risk and it gives you a chance to try out and adjust an approach before committing to it. The focus below is on a Proof of Concept and piloting approach, although you may also want to use another iterative framework, such as an agile approach.

## Proof of Concept (POC)

A POC is a low stakes, low cost way of exploring a new way of working. This is more than an opportunity to 'play' with taxonomies or new software; instead it is a structured phase of the project. You don't need to have all your processes and infrastructure in place. In fact, costs and disruption should be kept low:

- Keep the impact on a small scale – a small amount of content, a small taxonomy or set of taxonomies, a small set of products or services.
- Use a small, committed team that is forgiving of any teething problems.
- Usually, a POC does not mean making a real change to your process or services. It's something you can learn from but throw away.

This keeps the cost of infrastructure, training and support low. You can often prove your concepts without spending much at all. For instance, you may be able to manually improve a bit of your search index or manually produce content recommendations to demonstrate the improvements you could make with a taxonomy.

If you want to use the POC to explore new software, the major software vendors are often open to low cost trials. If you've got the budget to put such a trial in place, you should find it easier to get approval for the software later.

## Pilot

The next phase in this approach is a pilot. This should be bigger in scope than the POC, but still small enough to be manageable, for instance, one facet, or one set of content, or one website or set of products. You also need to make it more real, testing your new processes with the real users in your organisation.

You should have a better view of your requirements for software now. You will also want to start piloting with software you are really considering, if you didn't before. Again, software vendors should be open to low cost, low commitment trials for this phase.

## Further trials

Depending on your circumstances, you may wish to conduct both a POC and a pilot, or indeed repeated POCs and pilots, particularly if you want to try out different software. (Though be aware, each trial requires both cost and internal effort, so only do as many as you really need.)

Structure all your trials properly so that you know what concepts and assumptions you're testing at each stage. You should expect both the POC and pilot to flag up some initial issues, so that you can adjust your approach and avoid them in the full rollout phase.

Use your initial trials to build buy-in:

- Each of these initial phases provides a communication opportunity for you to build buy-in and visibility within the organisation.
- If you can, ask the teams who work on the POC or pilot to champion it to their teams and managers, and use them as part of your communications. They may be more authentic and persuasive with their teams than you are.
- Use the trials to gather metrics for your business case and check to see whether your costs and benefits are in line with your expectations. If they are, then use the real data in your business case and also in your communications to build buy-in. If they're not, then you have an early chance to re-adjust your plans.

Of course, you may be in a position where you are making less substantial changes to your workflow and a POC or pilot is not required. Perhaps you are just modifying a taxonomy or extending its use. Or perhaps your organisation already has software in place, so you don't need to run pilots to select the correct one. In that case, select the approach to trialling that suits your circumstances. Remember to structure any trials on what you need to learn to make the rollout a success and on gathering evidence of benefits and costs that you need for the business case.

## Rollout in stages

When the trials are completed, you'll need to move on to future rollouts until your entire vision is complete. Throughout the rollout stages and even once your project is complete, remember to keep managing your stakeholders, keep promoting successes via your communications channels and keep updating your key metrics. Make sure that you can continue to explain and demonstrate the value to the organisation in order to retain the investment and buy-in.

**Case study: Health Education England Technology Enhanced Learning (HEE TEL)**

HEE TEL, a national provider of online training resources for healthcare workers, had a challenge with the findability of content on its Learning Hub website. This was partly because of the complexity of the health domain itself, but also because the content was sourced from a large number of contributors in the healthcare community, which resulted in inconsistent keywording.

The website manager knew that he could improve the findability of content by sourcing a set of taxonomies. He also needed a taxonomy management tool and a new search engine, as well as some consultancy. He set about securing approval by first doing a short, cheap POC, working with the software vendors for the taxonomy and search tools to create a small, working prototype containing real content.

He used the prototype to demonstrate to stakeholders the improvements the taxonomy could bring, directly comparing searches on the current website (without the taxonomy) and in the prototype using the taxonomy. The search using the taxonomy found many more relevant results. People could see for themselves the benefits that the website manager was promising. It was a lightbulb moment for stakeholders and they went on to approve the investment.

## Choosing and scoping your taxonomy

When you are planning  your initial taxonomy or taxonomies, try to start with those that will generate the most impact, but will also be manageable. Consider which ones would be most helpful to your flagship product or content, solve your biggest problem or help your biggest set of users.

Then you need to define the scope of this taxonomy. (The singular term is used here for convenience, but, of course, you will probably have multiple taxonomies to wrestle with.) You need to understand the context of your taxonomy work:

- **Purpose:** What is the taxonomy for? What features will it underpin (for instance, findability, personalisation, recommendations)? What problems are you trying to solve?
- **Audience:** Who will benefit from the taxonomy?
- **Content:** What content is being described by the taxonomy?

Next, you need to do some research on language usage and the current taxonomy landscape:

- Current taxonomy landscape: Do any relevant taxonomies or vocabularies already exist? These could be in your organisation or in the industry more widely. Can you adopt them as is, or do they need modification?
- Content analysis: Look at a representative sample of content and think about the facets and terms you would use to describe it. Look at the content and metadata itself, including titles, keywords and descriptions. You may also want to look at navigational structures, such as folder names, or navigation or search filters on the website.
- How do users describe the content? Review the search logs from your website if you have any. This is an excellent source of the language users are really using to describe the content and will give you concepts, synonyms and even misspellings that you may want to include in your taxonomy.
- You may also benefit from some user research and brainstorming. Card sorting is a typical technique for structuring a session during which users brainstorm and group potential terms. This is covered in more depth in the User Testing and Validation chapter.

This research will give you a large pool of candidate concepts that you can start to sense check and expand. You should then be able to group the candidates into facets and taxonomies. This activity, and your thinking on purpose, audience and content, will help you decide what is in scope and out of scope.

Remember to get real data from users or work with real users whenever possible. Your taxonomy has a purpose and an audience and you need to stay focused on whether it will meet those needs.

---

**Case study: Software provider**

An international provider of consumer software services was looking to improve its approach to keywording content. Content was already being keyworded extensively, but the keywords were not consistent between teams working in different sectors, or between its historic core business and recent acquisitions. While consistency was a key goal, the organisation still needed to support market-specific terms, local dialects and multiple languages. It therefore decided to review and improve its use of terms. With such a large number of vocabularies to review, the problem was where to start.

The Content Management team decided to structure the project so that it aligned with the business' priorities. They focused on the highest revenue-generating services in the US and UK, which were their most profitable markets. They focused the first phase of their project on developing taxonomies to support the functionality for the end-users of these digital services. The functionality in scope included search, navigation, reporting and recommendations. This gave them an explicit scope, which was to support certain features for end-users, in high priority digital services, in the UK and US markets, and in American and British English.

This gave them a manageable focus for the project, one that was aligned to the organisation's goals of increasing revenue and producing innovative services.

Having an explicit scope allowed them to make decisions about requests for additional taxonomy support during the first phase. Many requests were clearly not in scope and could be declined. However, one request was to standardise the keywords needed for internal content administration and copyright management. The product teams needed these keywords in place to add new content to the flagship services and to support content re-use. Supporting development of the flagship services was one of the agreed purposes of the taxonomy project. The organisation also had a goal of increasing content re-use. Therefore, in this case the scope was widened to accommodate the request.

## Conclusion

It can be challenging to get business buy-in when any investment or change to working practices is required. Budgets are generally tight and it's difficult to persuade people of the necessity of change. This is perhaps even more true when it comes to a taxonomy project, since taxonomies may feel a little abstract for most people. What taxonomies are and the benefits they bring are not widely understood by non-specialists.

No matter what kind of organisation you work for, you might have your work cut out to make a convincing case for your taxonomy project. To secure buy-in, you need to:

1  Align your project with the organisation's vision and goals.
2  Identify and manage your stakeholders and frame the project in a way that resonates with their hopes or concerns.
3  Try to join or influence decision-making bodies.
4  Look for people or programmes that have budget already and try to join your project to theirs to take advantage of their budget, resources and approvals.
5  Be able to explain your project and its benefits in a meaningful way to non-specialists. Write a short project description and consider writing an even shorter tagline. You can repeat these in all your communications to reinforce your message.

6   Communicate repeatedly to stakeholders and the wider organisation, incorporating lessons learned as you move through your trialling phases. As more people come on board during the project, try to get them involved in your communications too.

7   Make a financial business case if you can. Remember to align any proposed benefit to the specific financial gain it will bring. You may also want to supplement your business case with a non-financial justification, if that is particularly compelling for your organisation.

8   Plan how you will collect metrics, focusing on those that are key to your business case or most persuasive to your organisation. Make collecting metrics manageable by automating the collection or using KPIs that are already being gathered, where possible. You may also want to collect some qualitative metrics, such as feedback from users or colleagues, to add colour to your case.

9   Adopt an iterative approach to trialling and rollout, perhaps using a POC/pilot framework or an agile methodology. The earliest trials (such as the POC) should be low cost and low risk. Gradually expand the scope of the work as you move through later iterations.

10  Use your trials to gather evidence that will underpin your business case, and also to try to build enthusiasm within the organisation.

11  Create an explicit scope for your taxonomy project by agreeing which purposes, audiences and content it will serve. An explicit scope helps you make decisions about what to focus on and how to justify the project to the organisation.

12  Explore what language is being used already in your subject area by analysing the content, finding out what existing taxonomies are available and looking at search logs if you have them. This gives you candidate concepts and facets that you can use to scope the taxonomies.

Above all, keep making a case for your taxonomies throughout your rollout and then beyond into business as usual. Your taxonomy work will always need a budget, resources and stakeholder engagement to continue to be a priority for the business.

# 2 Choosing Taxonomy Software

*Joyce van Aalten*

*Editor's note*: I always advocate for getting hold of the best possible tool you can for the job of storing and managing a taxonomy. This is a good thing to get right from early in the project, as it is a hassle to move a taxonomy from one system to another later on. Joyce brings a wealth of experience of helping clients make the right selection for their particular needs. We taxonomists can be sniffy about using spreadsheets to manage a taxonomy, but Joyce argues that they can have their place in the toolbox. Other options discussed in detail are built-in modules, such as within SharePoint, and dedicated taxonomy tools.

## Introduction

When it comes to creating and maintaining a taxonomy, you need some kind of tooling to store the taxonomy terms and relationships between these terms. In this chapter, 'tooling' is used in the broadest sense of the word, meaning the file or systems where you store taxonomy terms, relations and other attributes. In my work as a taxonomy consultant, I've created many taxonomies from scratch, but I've also worked with taxonomies and thesauri that have been around for some time. These taxonomies range from 50 up to 20,000 terms, and they vary from flat lists to complex knowledge graphs, being used by small local NGOs and large multinationals. Despite their differences there is always one question that arises: what is the best option to store and maintain this taxonomy? The answer is: it depends. In this chapter, I will describe these dependencies.

Taxonomy tools can be divided into three high-level groups: spreadsheets, built-in modules and dedicated taxonomy tooling. They differ from each other in terms of specific taxonomy functionalities, ease of use and integration with other systems, costs and more. I will elaborate on the different options and explain which option might be best for what situation. Also, I will describe what to take into account when choosing a dedicated taxonomy tool.

## Spreadsheets

Although spreadsheets are of course not a taxonomy tooling by nature, they are used as such by many organisations. A spreadsheet is often a starting point for creating the first drafts of a taxonomy. The main benefit of using spreadsheets for your taxonomy is that spreadsheet tooling is available within every organisation and it comes without additional license fees. The possibilities of structuring data make spreadsheets a logical candidate for taxonomies. The hierarchical structure of taxonomies can be captured in columns. For instance, a concept in column A is the parent of the concept in column B. And this concept in column B is therefore the child term of the concept in column A. Apart from hierarchical relationships, additional term information like synonyms and notes, can be included. Add to that the fact that almost all built-in modules and dedicated taxonomy tooling have the option to import a taxonomy in a spreadsheet, and it won't be a surprise that a large number of organisations consider a spreadsheet as their main taxonomy tool.

Of course, needless to say, a spreadsheet, although used as such, is not a taxonomy management tool. One of the main disadvantages is that it does not truly understand the way a taxonomy is structured. In a spreadsheet, the relationships between taxonomy terms are implicit, the relationships between concepts depend on the structure of the spreadsheet and naming of columns in that spreadsheet. If we make the relations explicit, the relations become much more meaningful. For instance, if we say term A is the parent term of term B, term B is automatically a child of term A. A spreadsheet can't make relationships reciprocal and is therefore more labour intensive and more prone to human error.

## Built-in modules

Content, documents and data can be stored and structured in an information system, like a content management system (CMS), document management system (DMS), record management application (RMA), Digital Asset Management (DAM) system or library system. To tag content in that system, some of these tools have a module for storing and maintaining taxonomies. Examples are the Managed Metadata Store of Microsoft 365/SharePoint and the Drupal Taxonomy Manager. Built-in modules offer functionalities for taxonomy term maintenance, like the structuring of terms in an explicitly hierarchical way, where the parent-child relationship between terms is stored as such. Another commonly seen functionality is storing synonyms. However, it depends on the specific module how basic or advanced these taxonomy functionalities are. For example, some, but not all, built-in modules include multilingual support or the ability to store specific notes or definitions with the taxonomy terms. Sometimes it's questionable if these modules can be called taxonomy modules. I've come across some that weren't much more than a spreadsheet in a nice user interface.

Even though the options and quality of these modules may differ, the key idea behind them all is simply this: to store and maintain a controlled list of terms (taxonomy) that can be used for tagging content in that system. Because the taxonomy is part of the content system, there is a flawless integration with that system. By which I mean that it doesn't take any technical effort to have the taxonomy terms available for tagging (applying to) the content. But being an integral part of the system is also the main pitfall: the intention of these modules is that the taxonomy will be used only for content that is stored within that system. If you come to a point where you want to use your taxonomy in other systems (which is a realistic scenario, especially if your taxonomy is successful), this might be a big challenge. Export options are rarely available in these modules and connecting the taxonomy module to other systems is almost impossible.

## Dedicated taxonomy tools

Dedicated taxonomy tools are specifically developed for creating and maintaining controlled vocabularies, taxonomies, thesauri and ontologies. Although there is a wide range of tooling, varying from pretty straightforward to more sophisticated, all of these tools offer the commonly needed taxonomy functionalities. Among these are the automatic prevention of term duplicates (disambiguation) and circular references, automatic detection of orphan terms and creation of reciprocal relationships.

The idea of a dedicated taxonomy tool is that you have one specific, dedicated tool for taxonomy management that can be used for one or more taxonomies. Once stored in the taxonomy tool, the taxonomy can then be synced with all the external content systems the taxonomy is needed in (see Figure 2.1 on the next page). This can be done via export/import files or via API (application programming interface) connection/webservices. The underlying idea of having a central repository for taxonomy terms makes a dedicated taxonomy tool the go-to option if you want a central, organisation-wide taxonomy.

If we want to classify the different types of taxonomy tools (and we taxonomists do love to classify), we can distinguish the following groups:

- thesaurus focus vs ontology focus
- stand-alone tool (taxonomy management only) vs part of a suite (additional modules for semantic enrichment)
- open source vs closed source.

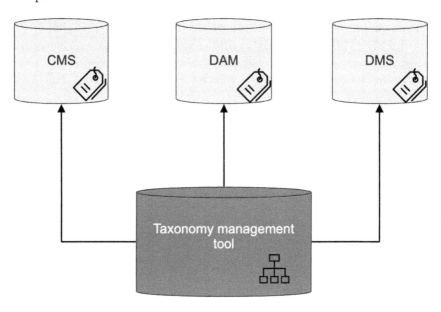

**Figure 2.1** *The taxonomy management tool as a central repository, connected to other content management systems*

The first distinction in taxonomy tooling, a thesaurus or ontology focus, is the one that most affects the work of a taxonomist. By thesaurus focus I mean that, following the Simple Knowledge Organization System (SKOS) standard, the most important relationships of the taxonomy are the basic relationships. Broader, narrower, related, concept schemes are the heart of a thesaurus; custom relationships and attributes are optional. An ontology, on the other hand, starts with defining classes, subclasses, custom relations and attributes for these classes, in line with the OWL (Web Ontology Language) standard. So, although thesauri and ontologies are both semantic knowledge models (i.e., knowledge organisation systems), the approaches to building are different. That might be the explanation why, for a taxonomist, an ontology tool might have a much steeper learning curve compared to a thesaurus tool. For the taxonomists that want to build an ontology, luckily some of the taxonomy tools have the option to start with building a taxonomy that can be expanded and make use of an ontology in due course.

Some taxonomy tools are stand-alone tools. Taxonomy tools can also be part of an application suite. By that I mean that next to a module for taxonomy management, other related applications are offered. For instance, semantic search, auto-tagging or text mining options can be part of the suite. The applications vary by suite and vendor, but they all offer semantic enrichment. The user interface of applications in a suite is shared and, obviously, they integrate smoothly. Although the taxonomy functionalities are not influenced by whether or not the taxonomy module is part of a suite, I recommend you investigate whether or not your organisation needs semantic enrichment. Be aware, these extra applications, obviously, come with a price tag.

The pricing of taxonomy tools varies and can depend on, amongst other things, license fees, number of users, degree of support and required add-ons. They can become very costly. I often get the question: 'Aren't there any free or cheap taxonomy tools available? Could open source be an option?'. There are indeed some open source taxonomy tools available on the market. And although open source means that you don't have to pay any license fees, that doesn't mean that these types of tools are cheap or completely cost-free. Costs are much more diffuse. Additionally, open source tools often lack official support (since there is no real vendor that is accountable for support). It goes without saying that open source tools are not by default the holy grail that they seem to be.

## The options compared and which option to choose
### When and how to use a spreadsheet
Over the years, I've met people who told me that you must be insane to use a spreadsheet for taxonomy management. I don't agree. In some cases, spreadsheets can do the job – for example, if you are at the beginning of your taxonomy adventure and your taxonomy is still small. Every taxonomy I build starts in a spreadsheet, even though I sometimes prefer mindmaps for their visual representation and structuring. If your taxonomy is rather static and doesn't change that often, a spreadsheet might be a good option, especially if the expectation is that the taxonomy will stay small over time. And sometimes another tool just isn't an option, for example, if there's no budget or the content system doesn't have a built-in module. Another reason to stick to the spreadsheet might be that there is a lack of stakeholder/IT-involvement and you don't get any technical or business support for your taxonomy tool.

But you should be aware of the caveat: know when it's time to stop and say goodbye to the taxonomy spreadsheet. Indicators are that your taxonomy starts growing, both in types of relationships and in number of terms. Or when your taxonomist (or you as a taxonomist) gets overwhelmed, frustrated and says, 'I can't do my job properly'. Then you know it is time to look into either a built-in module or a dedicated taxonomy tool.

A best practice for building a taxonomy in a spreadsheet is using a logical format. To indicate hierarchical relationships put every term on a single row. So, the parent term in cell B3 and the child term in columns C4, C5, etc. Most of the taxonomy tools, both built-in modules and dedicated tools, require this structure for their import files. By using this structure, you make the spreadsheet as ready as possible for importing into other systems, regardless of whether that system has additional requirements for the import files.

## When and how to use a built-in module

Despite the fact that built-in modules might have their flaws when it comes to (sophisticated) taxonomy management functionalities, there might be situations where a built-in module can do the trick. There are two preconditions/indicators where a built-in module could be a good choice:

1  The taxonomy will be used in one content system only AND
2  That content system fits your taxonomy functionalities' needs.

Let's dive a little bit deeper into this. First, verify with stakeholders that the taxonomy will be used within one single content system and it is expected that this situation won't change in the short term (i.e., not within two years). Then, match the taxonomy functionalities of the built-in module with your and your organisation's taxonomies' needs. Decide if and how you want the tool to support polyhierarchy, multilingual, associative relationships. This will answer the question of whether the built-in module is sufficient for your needs.

When using a built-in module, find the right balance between making a taxonomy given the constraints of the built-in module on one hand, and considering what you might need to make the taxonomy as futureproof as possible on the other. In practice, this will mean you might have to make concessions. For instance, not having synonyms in the taxonomy since the module doesn't allow you to do so. Document the concessions you have made, so you can reconsider implementing them when moving to another or dedicated tooling in the future.

Also, keep in mind to tailor the taxonomy in order to optimise its value for the users who are interacting with it on the front-end. This way the built-in module could work as a trigger point to let the organisation get familiar with the use and benefits of a taxonomy. Over the years, I've created a number of taxonomies in SharePoint's Managed Metadata Store, for a variety of customers. In these projects, I've not only focused on the creation of the taxonomy but I've also used it as a playground for the taxonomy getting 'landed' in the organisation. I've shown them how a taxonomy could improve the findability of content, and how it can enhance the search engine and let users get familiar with tagging of content. It will be a good learning experience for you and your users. But again, document the decisions you've taken in this and any concessions you might have made.

## When and how to use a dedicated taxonomy tool

Of course, a dedicated taxonomy tool is the go-to solution if a spreadsheet or built-in module is not sufficient (anymore) for your taxonomy maintenance functionality needs. Also, when your taxonomy is growing in the number of terms and/or relations to maintain and/or the number of taxonomists, I recommend looking into dedicated taxonomy tooling.

A taxonomy does not have to be comprehensive to use a dedicated taxonomy tool. If you're aiming for a centralised, company-wide taxonomy and want your taxonomy to be the single point of truth, I would also recommend a dedicated taxonomy tool. Recently, I've developed a relatively small taxonomy for a client. Within that organisation there was a lot of discussion and disagreement on what terms/words to use for their topics and themes. Standardisation of terminology was a hot topic across all levels of the organisation, from the top level management to content managers and web analytics managers. The list of terms was not huge, but I still recommended that they acquire a dedicated taxonomy tool, which we made easily accessible and searchable for all employees. With this taxonomy being available in a real tool, instead of another spreadsheet, we gave the taxonomy more prestige.

If you want to connect the taxonomy to more than one content repository system, a dedicated taxonomy tool is the best option. It gives you the opportunity to maintain your taxonomy in one centralised way. However, there is one major precondition: you need to have the adequate technical skills (in house or budget to hire) for connecting the tool. Connecting the tool is no sinecure. The technical implementation can be a struggle sometimes: you need to connect to other systems and therefore you must rely on the 'connectivity friendliness' of those systems.

In summary, indicators that you may require a taxonomy tool are:

- the taxonomy is outgrowing your spreadsheet
- a built-in module doesn't have the adequate tooling/doesn't fit your requirements (anymore)
- you need to store more sophisticated relations between terms (synonyms, hierarchy and other semantic relations, notes)
- there are multiple taxonomists that want to collaborate on the taxonomy and they have specific governance needs
- you're aiming for a centralised, company-wide taxonomy (single source of truth)
- multiple systems need to use (part of) the taxonomy.

Also, alarm bells should go off when you hear that your IT department wants to build their own taxonomy management tool. How hard can it be, right? Well, it can be. A taxonomy tool is a highly specialised application with some nitty-gritty functionalities. Talk them away from this idea as soon as possible. It might help to give them a list of your requirements for a taxonomy tool.

Some would say that a dedicated taxonomy tool is your preferred choice when it comes to building and managing a taxonomy. I don't necessarily agree with that. First of all, we need to be realistic: not all organisations have the budget and/or technical skills to acquire such a tool. You're fortunate if budget, skills and stakeholder support are available. But even if they are available, when a spreadsheet or built-in module meets your needs, then there is less urgency to get a taxonomy tool. A dedicated tool is not a perquisite for your taxonomy to be successful. However, it might be needed to take your taxonomy to the next level.

## Selecting a dedicated taxonomy tool

How do you choose a dedicated taxonomy tool that fits your organisation? Make sure you have clarity on the available budget and technical support and an overview of relevant internal stakeholders. They define the framework in which you can operate for the tool and vendor selection process. Selecting a taxonomy tool roughly follows the same procedure as the selection of any other software content tool.

Start by making an inventory of what you want from your taxonomy tool: how fancy do you want the quality checking, version history, user rights management or the ability to create your own custom relationships? This list of requirements has to be as clear as possible. See the next section for some high-level requirements that you need to think of. If you're the taxonomist, your input for the needed requirements is of course important, but make sure to involve other (direct and indirect) users of the tool as well. Their wishes need to be taken into account. I would recommend doing a workshop with the relevant stakeholders to discuss the list of requirements so that they are involved in this process. You will also probably hear that one of the most important criteria is the ease of use, especially if non-taxonomists have to use the tool.

For the actual selection process, I take the list of requirements, prioritise each requirement (nice to have, must have, knock out criterium) and ask a selection of vendors to respond to these requirements. Can they meet each requirement and, if so, how does their tool meet this requirement? Based on their responses, I select the top three tools/vendors and ask for a pricing/proposal and a demo of their tool. Preferably, this demo is tailored to include input you can give them upfront: what would you like to see, what is your specific use case for a taxonomy? Provide them with a small demo taxonomy if possible. I would also advise setting up a test environment/proof of concept: the best way to get to know the tool is by using it yourself. Also, make sure you involve your stakeholders in this. How intuitive is the tool, even for non-taxonomists?

Although I've done many tool selection projects, there is no tool that is better than others. Each taxonomy and each organisation are different and therefore there is no one-size-fits-all. The final decision will probably be based on the mix of requirements that can be met, user friendliness of the tool, support and responsiveness of the vendor and a little bit of gut feeling.

Sometimes the decision is made for you. One of the organisations I advised to look into dedicated taxonomy tools turned out to have already acquired a tool. Even though it was purchased by another department, we could share the license fee and contract agreement. That shortened the selection process significantly.

## Taxonomy functionality requirements

Most, but not all, dedicated taxonomy management tools offer the following functionalities:

- term management (create terms according to standards, automatic reciprocal relationships, bulk editing, drag and drop, support of polyhierarchy, multilingual support, full text search)
- term validation (automatic prevention of term duplicates (disambiguation), circular references and non-preferred terms from hierarchical and associative relationships)
- quality checking and set rules for custom quality checking

- compliance with industry standards (International Organisation for Standardization (ISO), SKOS, SKOS eXtension for Labels (SKOS-XL), OWL)
- integration with other systems: provision of APIs/webservices and out-of-the box connectors to other systems
- collaboration: check history, audit trail, workflow, user permissions, versioning and ability for end-users to suggest candidate terms
- relationship management: customise relationships and attributes; moving towards an ontology
- end-user interface and making visualisations
- import and export, generate reports
- connect to other Linked Open Data (LOD) resources
- full text search and browse hierarchically or alphabetically, ability to filter on status, etc.
- advanced semantic functionalities: (auto-)indexing, (semantic) search, corpus analysis, text mining
- linked data management, make taxonomy available as LOD.

---

**Case study: Local authority**

Some time ago, I was asked by a customer to help them select a taxonomy tool. This customer, an autonomous administrative authority, wanted to build and use a central company-wide taxonomy. That taxonomy was expected to be used and implemented in at least three information management systems: Microsoft SharePoint as their collaboration tool, Microsoft Dynamics as their customer relationship management (CRM) tool and a new, yet to-be selected CMS for their website. With this desire to connect the taxonomy to three systems, the decision for a dedicated taxonomy tool seemed obvious. Also, the taxonomy would (partly) be based on an external thesaurus. That thesaurus had rich semantic relations that the organisation wanted to capture and retain.

We did have a look at the SharePoint Managed Metadata Store but found it too limited in functionality, since we couldn't store associative relationships. Another big drawback was that the updates of the external thesaurus couldn't easily be imported into the Managed Metadata Store: a new import was considered as a new taxonomy and not as an update of the existing taxonomy. With a frequently changing thesaurus, that would mean a lot of manual labour for my customer, precisely something we wanted to avoid by using (parts of) an external third party thesaurus.

We shifted our focus to the selection of a dedicated taxonomy tool and made sure we got sufficient budget for acquiring a tool. The IT department, although limited in available time and skills, could take care of the installation. So, we were good to go on the taxonomy tool selection process. First, we set the high level technical requirements. Open source was not an option in the organisation's IT landscape, so that was a given fact. Another knock out criterium was that the taxonomy tool had an out-of-the-box SharePoint connector, since (at that time) the technical skills and knowledge of the IT department were too limited on this point. These criteria led to a long list of ten taxonomy tools and their vendors.

Based on the input of taxonomy stakeholders, I created a more detailed list of 'real taxonomy' requirements. Among them, the ability to create semantic relationships and the ability to import and export thesauri/taxonomies. We also covered 'supplier and support' criteria, like a vendor's support team being available during customers' working hours. Via desk research (vendor's websites, taxonomy discussion boards), we shortened our long list to four vendors. These four vendors were asked to respond to our requirements list.

Based on their responses, we invited two vendors to demo their product and answer some specific questions (importing data, etc.). Pricing was also requested. Since both tools offered quite similar functionalities, best value for money and the user-friendliness of the tool were deciding factors in our choice.

## Conclusion

Just as every organisation or environment in which a taxonomy will be used is different, so no two taxonomies are the same. Therefore, there is no single best choice when it comes to a taxonomy tool. It all depends on how you want to leverage your taxonomy, the size and complexity of it and the content system(s) your taxonomy will be used for.

In this chapter, I've described which type of taxonomy tool could be the best fit for which situation. But please bear in mind that your decision might not be in line with the thoughts I've described. The most important take away I want you to remember is that your decision should be a well thought-out and considered one. It might be tempting to go for an easy to implement solution, or perhaps you think that a taxonomy can only be successful in a dedicated taxonomy tool. Neither are a solid basis for a sustainable decision. You should have a clear vision on the characteristic of the taxonomy, how it will be leveraged, in what content system(s) it will live and how people within the organisation will probably respond to that.

Remember: the taxonomy tool is the technical aspect, but it's the quality of the taxonomy itself that will determine if it's successful or not.

# Part 2
# Building Taxonomies

# 3 Taxonomy Structuring and Scaling: A Standardised Approach

*Jonathan Engel*

*Editor's note*: Jonathan has a gift for explaining the complex world of taxonomy development and for making it relevant to the goals of the organisation. His chapter is a detailed case study that will be useful no matter what type of information you are working with. It will make the sometimes daunting question of 'how do we expand this taxonomy to do more?' feel answerable.

## Introduction

An author needs to establish credibility, so here goes: I've been a consultant Information Architect for 18 years, extending a longer career in journalism and digital publishing. In more than 30 projects to build and implement content classification and information management systems, I've worked for UK government agencies, global blue-chip companies and influential charities. My projects have covered financial services, law, health care, social services, international development, media, IT, telecoms and consumer products.

In this chapter, I present a case study that incorporates a range of proven techniques and demonstrates how a controlled vocabulary answers many information management challenges. You'll learn how to:

- set goals focused on user benefits, not IT demands
- instigate an information audit – identify what content descriptions are available, what's needed and your key stakeholders
- understand the main structural elements of a controlled vocabulary and how best to use them
- build a multi-faceted taxonomy, comprising entities, subject areas and content types
- extend that taxonomy with synonyms, related topics and contextual keywords

- explore multiple uses of your taxonomy, from building better web navigation to improving search, and from increasing publication efficiency to managing a document's lifecycle
- leverage your taxonomy to improve content classification and drive automatic classification with rule-based and machine-learning solutions.

## Background to the case study

This chapter describes the content management challenges faced by the Institute of Chartered Accountants in England and Wales (ICAEW) and the solutions it employed. Although its area of knowledge was specialised and its needs specific, I introduced a standardised approach to taxonomy building to improve content classification, navigation and search.

While that approach, described below, featured many best-practice techniques, the success of the project owed much to top-level management support, plus the expertise of the group's library and information staff, represented on the project by the invaluable Alice Laird.

The ICAEW is a standards body and member organisation for accountancy. It serves practising professionals, students and members of the public. In 2012 it needed to restructure and unify its content classification system to improve information retrieval and delivery, both internally and externally.

A wealth of specialist content needed to be categorised accurately and consistently, in an efficient workflow, using standard, logical and unique descriptions. The aim was to help staff, Institute members, students and members of the public find relevant information, especially through a revamped ICAEW website.

The user-centred goals of the Corporate Taxonomy and Metadata Project included:

- create a comprehensive, consistent corporate taxonomy
- improve information retrieval
- revamp content management and publishing processes with better use of metadata
- devise a better structured and more easily searchable website, especially to support faculty members and communities
- develop metadata guidelines for a digital document archive
- support new publishing channels for intellectual property.

As with most taxonomy projects, the work began with an information audit. These preliminary tasks, taking a user-centric approach, started with reviewing the current sources and structure of internal and external information. Employing surveys and workshops, we collected and analysed information needs, subject topics, search terms and user preferences. At this stage, taxonomists often use card sorting to identify, prioritise and link key topics.

The outcome of this work produced a preliminary list of preferred terms, with synonyms and related topics. For instance, *Accounting standards* became the preferred term, but a successful search would recognise the synonyms of *Accounting rules, Generally Accepted Accounting Principles* and its acronym *GAAP*. Related topics would include the following regulatory entities and their acronyms: *International Accounting Standards Board (IASB), Financial Accounting Standards Board (FASB)* and the *Accounting Standards Board (ASB)*.

At this early point, we also identified subject matter specialists from ICAEW faculties and special interest groups with a keen interest in the project to join a representative body to advise on consistent terms for retrieving and delivering information. This group would eventually feature in the representative governance structure to approve the taxonomy and develop it via a transparent change management process.

We then summarised the audit results for senior management and agreed core issues that would feature in a taxonomy implementation plan. For instance, we needed to agree our high-level taxonomy categories and the balance between using internal vocabularies and external standards, such as the Dublin Core.

We also determined the scope of the project, for example, whether our taxonomy work would inform webpage re-design or document lifecycle management.

While we recommended a review of useful taxonomy/ontology management tools and automated classification software, the main requirement was to produce a best-practice taxonomy structure that could be represented either in a simple Excel spreadsheet or in more sophisticated software.

At this stage, it was also important to identify whether the relevant content management and search systems could accommodate a controlled vocabulary featuring nested hierarchical topics, synonyms and related topics. InfoArk was once asked to develop a detailed hierarchy for a major UK government agency, only to discover that its content management system could not recognise Tanzania as a constituent of the broader terms East Africa or Africa.

Successful implementation of the taxonomy project also requires senior management support, secured through high-level presentations, a strategic plan for top stakeholders, plus development of communications materials and tactics to engage key users.

## Building the taxonomy – basic definitions

To ensure project discussions go smoothly, it helps to define terms. Therefore, we need a word or two about metadata types and management.
    Metadata can usefully be defined by three types:

1 Administrative metadata – often system-generated and includes Creator, Date, Publisher. The Dublin Core metadata designed for online use is mostly administrative.
2 Descriptive metadata – tells users what content is about or who needs it. Most of our content classification efforts are devoted to descriptive metadata.
3 Structural metadata – defines chapters, series or media packages.

But why stop there? We can also define two types of metadata management:

4 Controlled vocabularies – someone is in charge, defining preferred terms, synonyms and related terms.
5 Folksonomies – no one is in charge! Users are free to tag content with personally meaningful keywords.

Luckily, these last two approaches are no longer mutually exclusive. Most organisations that successfully manage information realise the importance of a controlled vocabulary, but understand it needs to be flexible and responsive to user needs. Today's keyword that adds context might be tomorrow's preferred term defining a new domain.
    Once these basic definitions were agreed, we started to build a multi-faceted taxonomy, focusing on descriptive metadata within a controlled vocabulary.

## The multi-faceted taxonomy (vertical view)

As a vertical structure, a taxonomy provides the benefit of logical navigation and metadata inheritance, where any selection of a lower-level heading should automatically invoke the parent metadata above it.

If I select *Inheritance tax* as a document tag, I would expect the higher-level tags of *Personal taxation* and *Taxation* to be included.

However, to reflect the reality that users enter the 'information pool' from a variety of directions, any taxonomy should be 'multi-faceted', that is, it should cover more than subject matter and answer a variety of questions about the organisation, such as 'Who' and 'Where are we', 'Who we work with and for', 'What do we do', 'Why do we do it', and, finally, 'How we do it'.

The answers to these questions will suggest different facets of the taxonomy. There are three useful components under which the resulting facets can be grouped, as we did initially with the ICAEW. They are summarised in Figure 3.1. *All components the highest level in a structure?*

| Entities | 1. Geographic location and infrastructure<br>2. ICAEW structure<br>3. Organisations<br>4. Statutes, regulations, standards and qualifications |
|---|---|
| Subjects | 5. Accounting, business and economics<br>6. Government finance, taxation and law |
| Focused filters | 7. Events, projects and initiatives<br>8. Content types<br>9. Audience and stakeholders |

**Figure 3.1** *Example of a multi-faceted taxonomy*

**Entities** – proper nouns, like Organisations, Company departments, Geographic locations, People or Statutes. To help describe these entities, it is useful to capture relevant attributes, e.g., Properties and values, such as the location or subject expertise of staff members.

**Subject matter** – largely generic topics like Business activities and Business sectors, including domain-specific topics like Accounting standards, Law and Corporate finance.

**Focused filters** – descriptions of useful filters for finding specific information, such as Content types, Event types and Language. Many of these filters can be applied automatically using templates, as SharePoint does by adding metadata and workflow paths to Content types.

The ICAEW recognised the importance of such distinctions and maintained Entities and Focused filters in what it called 'managed lists'. These were nested hierarchies and flat lists. What I would call Entities included such lists as:

- Locations
- ICAEW department
- Organisations.

While my designation of Focused filters covered:

- Content type
- Media format
- Publication
- Language
- Audience.

The remaining topics were structured in a subject-oriented taxonomy, with cascading hierarchies under such top-level concepts as:

- Accountancy training and regulation
- Business management and strategy
- Business operations
- Business sectors
- Corporate finance
- Economics
- Financial reporting and accounting standards
- Financial services and markets
- Law
- Taxation.

The ICAEW traditionally had staff manually select metadata tags for easily identified Entities and Focused filters. However, it decided that automated content classification could assist staff in accurately and consistently choosing the more problematic subject metadata.

Normally, I'd suggest that specific statutes be treated as Entities, listed as preferred terms, with their associated subject matter referenced as related topics from the Subject matter hierarchy. Using that approach, I'd list a statute such as The Bribery Act 2010 among other laws relevant to the organisation. It could then additionally be defined by a related taxonomy topic of *Bribery*, under the parent subject topic of *Crime and misconduct*, and ultimately, *Law*.

Because the ICAEW decided that its priority was to identify and automatically classify subjects, it employed such statutory references to identify *Bribery* and other subjects, using the specific law as a contextual keyword. This decision was helped by the operation of the SmartLogic classification engine, which favoured keywords rather than related preferred terms.

For accurate content classification of *Bribery*, it didn't make much difference – the taxonomy could be altered, or a classification rule modified, to treat candidate taxonomy topics as if they were contextual keywords. However, for organisations needing to retrieve content about specific laws or other entities, listing them as preferred terms in their own right would be the logical choice.

The ICAEW took that latter approach to long lists of specific financial reporting and accounting standards, compiling them near similar subject topics such as *Going concern* and *Earnings per share*.

The foregoing options demonstrate that taxonomy discussions often reflect different approaches and that there are several ways to deliver the benefits users require.

Within this vertical structure outlined above, we can employ the 'top down, bottom up' approach to refine the taxonomy. The facets above provide the 'top down' categories. Existing vocabularies, glossaries, websites, databases, library catalogues, etc., supply the 'bottom up' terms to populate these top-level categories.

The key element in this vertical, multi-faceted structure is the Preferred term – the word or phrase we select to describe the topic. Once the Preferred term is established, we can extend the taxonomy with further information on the topic, for example, by adding appropriate columns along its horizontal axis, as we would in a spreadsheet or database.

## Extending the taxonomy (horizontal view)

For the ICAEW, as with all InfoArk's projects, we utilised a hybrid approach to create a horizontally 'extended taxonomy', combining the structural elements of a Taxonomy (nested hierarchy of preferred terms), Thesaurus (their synonyms) and an Ontology (related topics among the preferred terms and their stated relationships). A properly structured ontology will sometimes be called a Knowledge Graph, adding greater levels of meaning to legacy content and data structures.

We can even add contextual keywords from our old friend the folksonomy, treating them as additional 'clues' to meaning. These associated descriptions are neither equivalent nor related terms from the taxonomy, but reflect detailed knowledge derived from domain specialists and relevant documents. They are also candidates for elevation to preferred term or synonym status. Figure 3.2 below provides an example of an extended taxonomy topic.

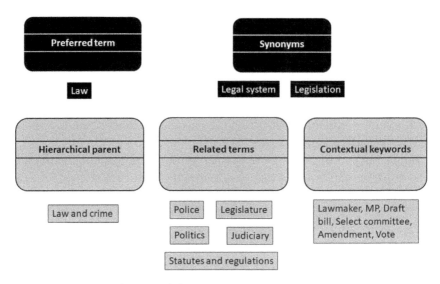

**Figure 3.2** *Example of an extended taxonomy topic*

As we noted above, the ICAEW preferred to treat potential related topics as contextual keywords, partly because the managed lists of Entities that might furnish related topics were excluded from the automated classification initiative. In defining a standardised approach to taxonomy design and classification, however, I will continue to highlight the useful role of related topics.

This horizontal extension of the taxonomy can be displayed usefully in a spreadsheet, with additional columns for synonyms, related taxonomy terms and relationships, and for contextual keywords.

There are several **sources for extended taxonomy elements**:

- 'Runners up' to preferred term
- Acronyms
- Search queries
- Subject specialists
- Domain-specific documents
- Text-mining software
- Faceted-classification or search software (especially if employed when building taxonomy, not after).

By design, these elements of an extended taxonomy comply with British Standard 8723 (ISO 25964) for structured vocabularies, by representing three types of relationship – hierarchical (Preferred term and Hierarchical parent), equivalent (Synonyms) and Associative (Related terms, Contextual keywords and Properties). They are also comparable to the information structure guidelines from the National Information Standards Organization (NISO). Here is an example of **an extended topic**, taken from the ICAEW taxonomy structure, with its emphasis on associated keywords rather than related taxonomy topics:

Preferred term = *Business ethics*
Synonym = *Corporate ethics*

**Contextual keywords**, representing three types:

1 A keyword, preferably unique to that topic within the taxonomy, also called High Evidence Terms. Examples in this case would be *Appropriate business practices, Ethical behaviour, Ethical conduct, Ethical guidelines.*
2 A keyword common to more than one taxonomy topic, also called Low Evidence Terms. Examples would be *Codes of conduct, Integrity, Professional behaviour.*
3 A keyword that should NOT be considered evidence for a topic, where its ambiguity usually demands a negative classification weight, rather than an outright ban on the preferred term. Here's a classic example, used by a fellow taxonomist working on the ICAEW project, of two terms you would not want to confuse: *Asset management* (relating to financial services) and *Digital asset management* (a branch of information technology).

There are helpful international formatting standards to ensure that taxonomy structures and extensions support initiatives in Big, Open and Linked Data. A useful starting point is the World Wide Web consortium (W3C) standards. These include the Resource Description Framework (RDF) to define related topics, and two complementary, machine-readable syntaxes for controlled vocabularies – the Simple Knowledge Organization System (SKOS) and the Web Ontology Language (OWL).

It is also best practice to ensure alignment with an organisation's data structures. While it was not necessary for the ICAEW project, in other engagements I have noted the helpful similarity in structure between a taxonomy and a conceptual data model, and between an ontology and a logical data model.

Such alignment opens up wider uses for a central controlled vocabulary. While a taxonomy might be required initially for a single purpose or project, once it is established, multiple uses are possible. Obvious benefits are better web navigation and improved search. However, a taxonomy that uniquely identifies relevant entities, subject matter, events and content types could readily be employed to streamline publication processes and enable more effective document lifecycle management.

## Taxonomy-generated rules for classification and search

It is a major step to devise a consistent, comprehensive, organisation-wide extended taxonomy. Unfortunately, such a controlled vocabulary is not sufficient by itself to improve information retrieval. While consistent in structure, the vocabulary also needs to be consistently applied.

Even experienced subject matter specialists vary in their knowledge and interpretation of a taxonomy when it comes to tagging content.

InfoArk analysed around 500 news stories for an international news agency and discovered that the tagging accuracy of its specialist editors ranged from 40% to 100%, with nearly half of the 500 sample stories failing to hit the 80% accuracy target.

Fortunately, the ICAEW was alert to this problem and embraced automated content classification to assist its metadata taggers, to ensure content reached its webpages more accurately, consistently and quickly. To that end, we ensured that the extended taxonomy structure would support the classification methods used by the major vendors in this sector.

By understanding the relationships among the terms from the extended taxonomy, we can exploit its structure to create effective rules for automated content classification. Those same rules can help select relevant documents into well-curated repositories for two other important purposes: (1) to build training and test sets for assessing the accuracy of the rules; and (2) to refine the rule results using Natural Language Processing and machine learning.

This approach means that a well-structured taxonomy will align closely with the capabilities of most automated content classification providers, such as SmartLogic, Expert System and open source systems like GATE.

The same rules that produce focused metadata can be leveraged for similarly structured and stored search queries. These queries supplement dynamic search results initially filtered by taxonomy facets and related topics.

To take advantage of modern search methods, a successful user must combine knowledge of the correct terminology, including synonyms and associated terms, the correct Boolean logic to link them and the proper syntax to run the search effectively. As an alternative, rule-driven search queries turn all users into search specialists.

So, how can users exploit the taxonomy structure to improve rule-based classification and search?

The rules can be generated via simple formulas, based on the contents of the taxonomy rows and columns, much like a mail-merge application creates address labels from feeding a list of contacts into a template structure. Once such a system is established and tested, the taxonomy manager need only ensure the relevant taxonomy data fields are updated correctly.

Ultimately, the rule structures may vary by organisation, vocabulary and classification software. For example, some elements of the rules described below were already embedded in the SmartLogic classification process selected by the ICAEW. But the following example will illustrate the generic approach we took at the ICAEW and for other clients, to employ classification rules that leverage the taxonomy structure.

In automatically suggesting metadata tags to content creators or editors, we are trying to identify the topics that are most important - or salient - to the content. The aim is that well-tagged content will then prove relevant to users retrieving the information via navigation, search or profile-driven delivery.

At InfoArk, we've identified three core elements to any rule and two supplemental tests.

The three core elements (as shown in Figure 3.3 on the next page) are:

1 **Frequency** - how often a preferred term or synonym appears in the text.
2 **Prominence** - how often a preferred term or synonym appears in priority locations, such as the content title, URL, first paragraph or sections marked as Introduction, Summary, Conclusion, etc.
3 **Proximity** - how many preferred terms (or synonyms) appear near their hierarchical parents, their child terms, related topics or contextual keywords. At the ICAEW, we gave greater weight to unique keywords compared with keywords that were common to more than one preferred term.

The supplemental tests give greater weight based on:

• **Taxonomy facet** - where for instance a subject matter heading would be more salient than a named entity that could appear in several contexts, such as an organisation or country.

- **Taxonomy depth** – where a topic appearing lower in the general-to-specific hierarchy would usually be more salient.

**Frequency test:**

Relative number of references to Preferred term OR Synonyms

**Prominent location test:**

Preferred term OR Synonyms in Title OR in URL OR in prominent Content section, e.g. Summary, Conclusion, etc.

**Concurrent proximity test:**

Preferred term OR Synonyms within 10 words of Hierarchical parent, Related terms and Contextual keywords OR within same paragraph OR same Content section OR same five rows of text

**Figure 3.3** *Useful 'combo' classification elements for rules-based automatic classification*

## Post-weighting adjustments

In practice, we also need to employ two other adjustments to classification results:

1　A **parricide rule**, which stops a parent term from ranking – through hierarchical relationships alone – as an equally salient concept alongside its more detailed child term. Such a rule will elevate metadata tags that accurately reflect the specific content, rather than tags that are added only through upward topic expansion.
2　A **blocked concept** list to exclude several legitimately classified and weighted terms that are too general to be of help; often these are organisational headings, e.g., *Government bodies*. These topics could be marked up in a taxonomy tool as 'Do not extract'.

On the following page is a sample classification rule using the three core elements for the preferred term topic of *Strategy*. We have included synonyms such as *Long-range plan* and contextual keywords such as *Leadership*, *Direction* and *Objectives*.

The use of wildcards, if supported, expands the following classification rule to include 'strategic', 'strategise', etc., as it looks for:

1  Frequent instances of the following preferred term and synonym variations: (Strateg*, vision, long range plan*, long term plan*, business plan, mission statement, vision statement).
2  The above terms in the Title, URL, Introduction, Summary, Conclusion, etc.
3  The above terms near (say within ten words of) the following list, usually containing the preferred term's parent and child terms, as well as related terms and contextual keywords: (business management, plan, leadership, direction, policy, review, goals, objectives, aims, priorities, roadmap, future state, transform*, CEO, board of directors, senior manag*, corporat*, develop*).

To prove the usefulness of this approach, some successfully tagged content made no mention of 'strategy', but did include 'business plan', 'vision' and 'mission'.

It helps to select the synonyms, related terms and contextual keywords carefully and limit their number. The advantage of limiting these elements is to keep the classification rules roughly balanced between the dual accuracy measures of precision and recall. For every term we employ in our rules, the scope widens and the recall increases; limiting the number of terms generates the most precise topics available.

While the production of these consistent rules depends on a clear understanding of the extended taxonomy, prolonged success requires a representative and transparent governance procedure for keeping the vocabulary up to date.

## Testing classification accuracy

The accuracy of content classification improves over time, through iterative testing to improve both the taxonomy and the classification rules themselves.

An out-of-the-box classification engine, equipped with a few simple rules applied to a small training set of documents, would normally generate accuracy between 65% and 75%.

Further taxonomy extensions, a larger and more-selective set of training documents, and increasingly sophisticated rules should push accuracy into the 75% to 85% range.

At the ICAEW, we targeted at least 85% accuracy, initially to place relevant and dynamic content on a revamped website. However, we expected that further refinements after the website relaunch could produce accuracy in the range of 85% to 95%.

Machine learning or artificial intelligence (AI) alone can now reach accuracy of around 70%, using algorithms and a large corpus of curated documents. However, collecting well-curated documents for each taxonomy topic can be difficult and time-consuming.

That's why for quicker and more accurate performance we recommend a hybrid approach – additionally using the classification rules to find those relevant documents, so machine learning can refine the rules-based results.

The ICAEW considered three potential suppliers of content classification software, each with a built-in taxonomy management tool. The vendors responded to detailed requirement specifications and were also judged on their classification results for the same set of test documents.

The winning vendor was SmartLogic, a rules-based classifier. Its technical specialists helped train ICAEW staff and two temporary contractors to fine-tune the classification engine. Work focused on generating repeatable and transparent results using four template rules, optimised for:

1  short documents
2  normal/medium-length documents
3  long documents
4  Adobe's Portable Document Format (PDF).

Plugging extended taxonomy terms into each template structure produced consistent rules for around 600 taxonomy terms, populating the template's field variables with rows of taxonomy data comprising preferred terms, synonyms and related terms/contextual keywords. Because the rules employed a consistent structure, wholesale changes or weighting adjustments could improve results from ALL the rules, a much more effective and efficient approach than testing and re-writing rules for each taxonomy term.

To improve results for an individual rule, we could simply add or delete synonyms, related terms and contextual keywords that were selected from documents or proposed by subject experts.

To measure this classification accuracy, we devised a spreadsheet matrix, with columns for each of the potential metadata tags being tested and rows for each document being assessed.

Expected tags, based on prior analysis of the test set, were marked as 'hits' and validated against the results of the tagging engine. Any tags the engine failed to attach were overwritten as 'misses', while any tags attached in error were marked as 'noise'. This consistent process – and the tagging guidelines agreed by three assessors – built a large degree of objectivity into what otherwise could have been a subjective exercise.

Industry standard accuracy formulas were embedded in the spreadsheet, producing separate scores for recall and precision and an evenly balanced composite rating for accuracy.

Table 3.1 below summarises the measures used.

| Table 3.1 *Measures used to determine the accuracy of automatic classification rules* | |
|---|---|
| **Hits** | Correctly appended taxonomy topic |
| **Misses** | Incorrectly missed taxonomy topic |
| **Noise/ Over tagging** | Incorrectly appended taxonomy topic |
| **Recall** | Proportion of all *relevant* terms actually *applied*, avoiding 'under tagging'. Expressed as a percentage. |
| **Precision** | Proportion of *applied* terms that are actually *relevant*, avoiding 'over tagging'. Expressed as a percentage. |
| **Accuracy** | Percentage equally balancing Recall and Precision scores |

The actual formulae to determine Recall, Precision and Accuracy are as follows, with the '\*' symbol standing for multiplication and '/' for division:

**Recall** = Hits / (Hits + Misses)
**Precision** = Hits / (Hits + Noise)
**Accuracy** = (2 \* Precision \* Recall) / (Precision + Recall)

Achieving optimal accuracy is an iterative process, involving the key information management tools described in this chapter. For example, you can tweak results by creating a new preferred term or by adding more synonyms or contextual keywords to a taxonomy topic description. At the same time, you can adjust classification rules and weightings and refine the focus of training and test documents.

## Conclusion

The process all begins with a multi-faceted taxonomy, comprising entities, subject areas and content types, that can be expanded to lower levels of detail and extended with equivalent or associated topic descriptions. The taxonomy will improve information navigation, search and delivery, and support other information management activities, from efficient publication to document lifecycle management. It's the Swiss Army Knife of information management - you'll wonder how you survived without one.

### Best practice in action – five taxonomy-building guidelines

1 Refine ambiguous or overly general terms for clarity and consistency across the taxonomy.
2 Consolidate and remove duplicate or overlapping terms, including any synonyms repeated for different preferred terms. For example, *CDs* should not be a synonym for *Compact discs* AND *Certificates of deposit*.
3 Replace an unneeded compound topic by using new or existing terms as dual descriptors; for instance, in many cases the term *Real Estate tax* could be replaced by the reusable dual descriptors of *Real Estate* and *Tax*. (There are three exceptions to the 'building-block' approach above. First is the need to find a home for lower-level terms, which would validate compound topics like *Construction law*. Second, if you have a large volume of documents requiring the precision of the compound term. Third, if the combined description matches a job function, allowing you to deliver relevant content electronically and highlight staff expertise alongside displays of documents.)
4 Aim to nest a child term under one parent term only (a monohierarchy rather than a polyhierarchy) and use Related Topics to reflect the other connections within the taxonomy. This guideline helps avoid the over-application of tangentially related metadata through hierarchical inheritance, which dilutes search accuracy by expanding recall over precision. There can be exceptions – at the ICAEW, documents categorised as *Private Finance Initiatives* generated the dual parents of *Project finance* (under *Corporate finance*) and *Government finance* (under *Economics*).
5 Convert a term to a synonym or 'contextual keyword' of a more comprehensive preferred term, especially if it is an 'orphan', that is, the only term under a heading.

# 4 The Diversity of Terms: Respecting Culture and Avoiding Bias

*Bharat Dayal Sharma*

*Editor's note*: When I first met Bharat a few years ago, I was struck by his willingness to question standard narratives of how knowledge and language should be modelled. This was especially true when it came to representing diverse perspectives in a taxonomy. Language is rarely neutral and this chapter is intended to challenge all of us who work with taxonomies to make sure we don't disregard any groups of users in our quest to produce the 'perfect' taxonomy.

## Introduction

The first step in looking at how your taxonomy will work for everyone is to acknowledge that all users are different and that every user's needs should be considered.

Understanding culture, diversity and bias is not an optional step, but a necessary one, because negative bias is something that can affect anyone at some point in their lives. If you ignore these perspectives, then your taxonomy may not be viewed as a success by the end-users of the terms you publish.

In this chapter, I will be using my experience of working in the National Health Service (NHS) in England and for my local city of Leeds. I explain how you can measure the success of your taxonomy by demonstrating how much you understand the end-users who will experience it. I also share practical tips and ideas on how you can try to be aware of culture, diversity and bias in the taxonomy authoring process.

## What are terms in a cultural context?

Terms are words, phrases or labels applied to a concept that taxonomists wish to describe. Ideally, a single concept can have many different terms that can be understood by as many different people as possible. Most taxonomies, however, use a single preferred term as an attempt to be as close to the words that are used by a majority of their audience. This is so that they are recognised by as many people as possible.

Cultures can be defined as a way that a group of people understands their past, present and future. Every person born and brought up in a culture will experience what terms mean. This is because of the friends and family they talk to every day, the use of those terms in school and in government and how these terms are used to influence thinking in media like newspapers and adverts.

Terms are connected to history, time, emotions, intent and thoughts. It is our job as taxonomists to understand the terms that our audience will recognise, but also where the terms came from, what they were designed to do and what the impact will be of using them. I use the term **users** in this chapter.

## What are diverse users?

Diverse users are people who will **use** the taxonomies we create and the terms we select. **All users are diverse**, because there is something unique about them. But at the same time there will be one or more characteristics that they have in common with other users who use your taxonomies, such as age, gender, sexuality, religion, disability and ethnicity among others.

As taxonomists, we have to understand there are many users who are not the same as us. We must think about them when we select terms because we have the power to make their lives easier or harder.

Some of your users may not even know they are using the taxonomy or what one is! But if they are using it, it is our duty to include them in the research, design and authoring processes to better understand and meet their needs.

Considering all users and including their needs in a product, service or decision is known as being **inclusive**.

### Overcoming bias

As a taxonomist, you are sometimes distanced from the users who will benefit from the taxonomy and this can introduce bias.

Bias is when the decisions you make are based more on your personal experiences than those of your users. Naturally, your lived experiences, which are different from other people's, can cloud your judgement and make you believe you understand your users and what they need. However, being aware of bias means realising that it is less likely for yourself or colleagues, who may be from a similar background to each other, to equally consider all your users and their needs, no matter how different they might be to you.

Once you acknowledge this, it is recommended you try to discover who your users are and attempt to understand them better.

## Understanding your users

To be more inclusive, you must try to include as diverse a sample of people as possible, to ensure a taxonomy that your users will understand. One way to do this is to ask questions or request feedback via user testing tools. You can make these available on a website that displays your taxonomy or ask volunteers to meet with you to view your work.

### How to reach diverse users

When trying to approach users to ask questions or request feedback it is recommended to follow design justice principles (https://designjustice.org/read-the-principles). Design justice is where you ensure that from the very start of your design process, you consider and respect the lived experiences and needs of a diverse community. The principles help to ensure all users can contribute equally, not be stereotyped solely based on major diversity characteristics, not exploited just to fill a quota or even consulted then ignored later on.

### *Use social media*

There are many communities on social media that bring together people from underrepresented areas.

You may want to consider sharing information with these groups, particularly if they cover a set of people that are affected by your taxonomy. Because social media is live and rapidly changing, it can help you to understand the current cultural context, ask questions and get clarification from users.

On 16 April 2021, I approached my organisation's deaf awareness network via the internal social networking platform. I explained that 'I manage the list of topics used to categorise content on the NHS Digital website. I saw this on Twitter and wanted to ask whether this was appropriate language.' I then shared with them the following tweet:

> Did you know that 'hearing impairment' is not appropriate terminology?
> (@NadiaNadarajah, https://twitter.com/NadiaNadarajah/
> status/1382612948573696007)

At the time, the NHS Digital website taxonomy classified deafness data as:

- data and information
-- conditions
--- sensory impairment
---- hearing impairment
----- deaf

One response I received helped to plan a change request to improve the hierarchy and provide a more inclusive choice:

> Yes, hearing impaired can be offensive. It indicates we are impaired in some way, and this is not the case. We just have hearing loss, there are different levels. Some say they are HoH (hard of hearing), partially deaf, severe hearing loss or profoundly deaf.

### The good

To be more inclusive, going out to your users gives them a chance to provide their feedback and share information you may not be aware of. It brings lived experience and understanding directly to you, so you can make better decisions as to what terms will be understood and accepted by your users.

### The not so good

Social media can often amplify the voice of an individual and this may not be representative of the communities they belong to or characteristics they may have. If, for example, 99% of your users agree with one term and 1% of users use an alternative, it is important to be practical in deciding which action to take.

If your taxonomy can support synonyms, you may consider adding the 1% of user's suggestions as synonyms or alternative labels.

If any term is described as offensive by a user, it is recommended to do extensive research to validate whether this is actually offensive and why. Some terms over time can be no longer considered acceptable or have been replaced historically as awareness has grown about the origin of that term.

An example of this is the outdated phrase 'third world', which was replaced in the media and other public discourse with the term 'developing country'.

## Online resources

Within the NHS and social care, users tend to make do with the tooling at their disposal, often productivity software like Microsoft Office. In search engine results, you may find these documents published as PDFs, full of knowledge from diverse or specialist communities, that were published on a website without due consideration for how they might be useful to someone else in the future.

If you use popular search engines, the following query allows you to retrieve PDF files that likely contain lists of terms and their full form and definitions: '**Filetype:pdf taxonomy**'.

If you cannot find taxonomies online, you can also look for 'glossaries', which are lists of terms without hierarchy. This way you can retrieve terms and then add hierarchy to them, especially where these terms are hard to find.

When looking at local terms for common medical conditions using the query '**Filetype:pdf yorkshire medical slang**', I explored PDFs and found an example that displayed phrases used in Yorkshire, UK, (Doncaster West PCT, 2004, www.pennine-gp-training.co.uk/res/yorkshire_slang_glossary. pdf). These terms could then be used as alternative labels or synonyms of common medical terms. For example:

Ay up – Hello
Badly – Feeling ill
Barking – Cough

## Online surveys via websites

If you have access to websites that you know your users visit, you can place surveys on them.

A useful tip from my experience as a Search Engine Optimisation (SEO) professional was to use this feature to intercept a user when they are having difficulty. A feedback tool like Hotjar could pop up a survey after a specific set of actions, such as the user performing an unsuccessful search and then trying to close the website.

From this point, I asked the user what they were expecting to find from the search query entered. This helped to inform the taxonomy as to what topics and terms should ideally be associated with content to improve the search.

### Community organisations

There are organisations, like charities, that aim to protect and give a voice to minorities of a certain background, cause or situation. There are many barriers we can inadvertently introduce to these users if we do not consider the terms we use and how they affect users.

An example of this was in the Leeds Council LOOP service directory. We knew that if it was not clearly tagged that a weekly elderly community group spoke languages like Hindi, there would be a significant lack of interest from those from an Indian background who wanted to meet others who spoke the same language and understood their culture. I know this as my own grandfather hesitates to register and attend these same community groups! Most service directories do not have a diverse enough taxonomy behind them, often relying on a sentence in the description rather than being clearly searchable and filterable for the languages spoken or cultures they specialise in, for example.

If they are representative of your users, these organisations will often welcome the chance to influence and provide feedback on the taxonomy you are using or are considering using.

Including these organisations at the start of your taxonomy creation, instead of later, will also increase the level of interest, investment and help they can provide. This is known as co-designing.

## Being open, transparent and inclusive

Imagine that the next version of your taxonomy will be online and anyone in the world could comment on it. Would they understand the words being used? Could they suggest improvements?

In an ideal world, being inclusive means everyone can contribute. This means giving enough information for anyone to have an equal understanding, whether they are young, old, an expert or new to the subject.

The first step to being open, however, is to consider publishing your taxonomy with an open license, so it can be viewed and reused by anyone. This can vary from simply making a file available for download, to hosting it on a website.

Being open to feedback by providing contact details means if a user has an issue with your taxonomy they can get in touch. Recently a member of the public contacted us about the label used to represent the ethnic grouping term of Irish, displayed as 'White Irish'. The user found that, on forms within the NHS, the only option available to describe themselves as Irish was under the parent taxonomy term of White. However, the user, while considering themselves Irish, did not consider themselves White.

This is why there needs to be consideration for diversity, which provides a high level of choice for all your users. In this case, White Irish joins what are two concepts together into one term, in this case skin colour and ethnicity, which while suiting some users, removes any suitable choice from others.

## Making taxonomies accessible

In the UK alone, one in five people classify themselves as having an illness, impairment or disease and may require the use of accessibility features to equally access web content. In the UK, 2018 accessibility guidelines say that all public sector organisations must ensure their internal and external web content is accessible (Gov.uk, 2018, https://www.gov.uk/guidance/accessibility-requirements-for-public-sector-websites-and-apps). Just like web content, a taxonomy should be accessible. This is so the content can be reused confidently, in a format that accessibility tools like screen readers for visually impaired people can recognise, and that can be visually adjusted for ease of reading, such as being responsive to different resolutions and text sizes.

When thinking about publishing your taxonomy, try to provide content in an accessible format, such as Hypertext Markup Language (HTML) on a website. Publishing in an inaccessible format like PDF can present difficulties for users to access and read the content.

Consider including additional supporting metadata around your term. This can range from labels or synonyms in multiple languages, alternative formats like easy-read descriptions that avoid complex language or even the use of images that could support visual definitions.

An example of this is how Microsoft integrates a picture dictionary using its immersive reader in products like Teams (Microsoft, 2020, https://support.microsoft.com/en-us/topic/define-words-using-immersive-reader-picture-dictionary-a584d219-2028-4d92-a403-3ec8ea5113af), offering images instead of term definitions.

## Publishing your taxonomy

### Exporting your taxonomy as a file for download

- Comma separated values (csv)
- Spreadsheets – Excel (xlsx) or open document spreadsheet (ods)
- JavaScript object notation syntax (JSON)
- Human-readable data-serialization language (YAML)
- Extensible markup language (XML)
- Resource Description Framework (RDF) turtle (ttl).

### Publishing on GitHub

GitHub is a popular repository for open source files, code and issue reporting.

Open source can be described as content being made available for reuse, comment and visibility on the internet.

You can publish on GitHub by uploading files containing your taxonomy onto GitHub for the public to download. More detailed options include uploading individual files or code for each term.

GitHub has the ability to host 'issues', a request for information or action, which allow users to contribute queries and suggestions on the GitHub 'repo' to give direct feedback. The site tracks requests and, as the taxonomy is updated, a detailed change history can be captured so users can see changes over time and you can acknowledge who has contributed to your taxonomy.

Being inclusive means openly acknowledging who has contributed to your taxonomy. Highlighting your contributors and demonstrating actions you have taken from issues raised provides a visible record.

Writing a new taxonomy gives you the opportunity to listen to voices that may never have been heard before, or ones that traditionally have never reached taxonomists before. A platform like GitHub allows anyone to make their voice heard. In the example of the Self-Defined dictionary (www.selfdefined.app), it is a website created from user suggestions about what language is appropriate or inappropriate to use. This uses the issues feature of GitHub to collect these suggestions in the forms of requests (GitHub, 2018, https://github.com/selfdefined/Web-app).

### Publishing a taxonomy as web content

Some taxonomy management systems provide features to import and/or publish directly as a set of webpages. This way, your live taxonomy can be exported into a web accessible form that can be browsed, searched and even visualised as a diagram.

## Making your taxonomy open and understandable

There are many different ways to publish your taxonomy. However, making something available is of no use if the content is not **open and understandable** to all, demonstrated in the following example:

    - Condition
    -- Pain
    --- Acute

A user viewing each term in isolation may have questions about exactly what each means, if not seen alongside a definition and its parent and child terms in a hierarchy or tree.

'Condition' - does this refer to whether something is in good condition or bad? Does this refer to health conditions?

'Pain' - does this refer to a level of pain a person is feeling? Is it emotional or physical pain?

'Acute' - does this refer to sudden pain or refer to secondary care such as hospitals?

**Ontologies**, however, provide the opportunity for a taxonomy to contain infinite additional information about each term so that they can be fully understood on their own. And this can be exported later as a taxonomy for use in other applications.

## Writing your taxonomy like an ontology

Ontologies have the capability to include additional knowledge in the form of metadata that provides you with background, intelligence, properties and relationships around a term that could exist in a taxonomy.

This can be used to capture the diversity of a term's origin, alternative labels, use, misuse (to indicate it is inappropriate to a specific community, for example) and context that otherwise could be lost. Taxonomy management systems typically only store and publish taxonomies as terms in a hierarchy of other terms, without the ability to contain lots of metadata.

An ontological approach means picking and choosing from a selection of properties to describe the term in detail. As an example, I use a template that allows for just enough information for both a taxonomist or user to understand what the term is and information about its provenance to explain:

- where the term comes from
- what the term means
- why the term was included in the ontology
- how the term was supposed to be used or not to be used.

This template is designed to be simple enough for anyone to contribute to it, but it can also be converted into an ontological data format for export, such as Resource Description Framework (RDF), JavaScript object notation syntax (JSON) or human-readable data-serialisation language (YAML).

The properties displayed come from a combination of established open standards that specialise in capturing knowledge and metadata about an object.

In this case, a lot of the properties come from an ontology known as SKOS – the Simple Knowledge Organization System. By using properties that already exist in the world, we can also be confident that we are providing clear metadata around a taxonomy term that conforms to a standard everyone can understand, access information about and will not misunderstand.

The template that I used in the NHS (in the absence of a taxonomy management tool) could be made into a spreadsheet, but just as easily could be made into a form that users can fill out on a collaborative system like SharePoint, Confluence or Mural. The columns and descriptions can be found in Appendix A and aim to provide a wide variety of established properties that, if populated, help to capture and recognise the diversity around a term.

## Designing taxonomies without limits

Taxonomies should not be designed to fit the technology, but technology should adapt to fit your taxonomy. This may be an issue when considering reusing or incorporating taxonomies or terms you find elsewhere.

When considering building your own taxonomy, or reusing terms from other sources, it is recommended to define a standard of metadata completion. This can be a target set to ensure that as many metadata properties as you wish to collect about a term get populated.

A lot of taxonomies start life as a way of categorising or tagging content in content management systems (CMS). The problem with most CMS systems is that they offer poor methods of maintaining a taxonomy because it is not their primary purpose. There is also often an inability for search results pages or webpages to visualise multiple levels of hierarchies for fear of complexity or system restrictions.

These restrictions can cause difficulties when trying to represent diversity in, for example, only three levels of hierarchy of your system. When deciding what to do, it is always better to design for the future and ensure you capture as many levels of hierarchy as appropriate in your documentation. This ensures that when your system is capable, you can provide a wider variety of choice to users. The more choice, the more chance the term will be recognised by a diverse set of users.

By capturing more than the minimum information than you actually need in order to address your main use case (e.g., a category facet in a CMS), the extra detailed metadata gives you flexibility to change and adapt as your system becomes more capable. It could also support more advanced uses of your taxonomy, such as using it as a corpus for natural language processing or for conversion into a knowledge graph. Even if some of the metadata fields are optional, treating them as required information is best practice.

The more information you document around a term, the more easily a future taxonomist who looks at your taxonomy can understand the history and decisions made around it.

## Do you have to choose a single preferred label?

Part of the challenge of expressing diversity in taxonomies is that there is often a requirement that a taxonomist must select only one 'preferred label'.

This means you may be forced to choose one label that suits most of your users. But for this very reason, while some users may be happy and recognise this term, others may not. Often, the others who do not are the minority of your users, who you have just excluded from using language they prefer and that may be commonplace within a community of people.

## *Technical restrictions*

This restriction of only one 'preferred label' can often be a reason that a taxonomy becomes less inclusive, as you must choose only one label that can be displayed on the screen or in a dropdown to express a term. For example, if the taxonomy will be implemented in a simple tool/system, it may not allow the display of any synonyms.

Most information systems support a variety of different input methods to select one or more terms from a taxonomy.

### Dropdowns

Taxonomies are likely to be the kind of information that has a large selection of terms to choose from. You may find that dropdowns are the most common selection method, as they can be scrolled and only show the large quantity of choice following a click.

However, the default and basic behaviour of dropdowns is that you are presented with a list of values and must select one. This 'control' often only supports a single label, and often no metadata, as the width available is too small to display all the possible information.

In addition, when a keyboard is used in an attempt to avoid repetitive scrolling of a long list, the basic feature of a dropdown is to press a key that matches the first character of the preferred label. In the NHS, a lot of our services are named with 'NHS' in the title, for example, 'NHS Mail'. To select the service, most dropdown controls will only support you typing 'N' to scroll you down to the letter of the alphabet the label starts with. Try pressing 'M' for mail, or searching for mail or email, and the functionality is unlikely to be available.

### Tree selectors

Taxonomies rely on being displayed as a tree and often only support one label. Again, as with dropdowns, simple implementations may not have a search function or display any other metadata about the term. The preferred label becomes the only visible label to make a decision about whether it is the term you are looking for, backed up with terms above, alongside and below it in the hierarchy to understand the context.

## Possible solutions

Design like you can, not like you can't.

There are ways to capture the diverse synonyms of a label, and this could include a technical solution or by ensuring you have published your taxonomy openly with these documented.

### SKOS-XL

SKOS-XL is a variation of the SKOS ontology model that allows a label to be a separate resource with its own resolvable Uniform Resource Identifier (URI). A label representing an abbreviation of a term, or an alternate term used locally, for example, can exist in a taxonomy as if it was a term on its own. With SKOS-XL, therefore, a label can exist as a term, with its own metadata, history and relationships to define it in context.

SKOS-XL enables you to respect the different ways a term is recognised by your users, by keeping information about who uses this label, why it is used, what situations it shouldn't be used in and who contributed to it, that would otherwise be lost. Taxonomy labels typically support ISO 639-1 languages (https://en.wikipedia.org/wiki/List_of_ISO_639-1_codes) – for example, my label@en – but with SKOS-XL you can define a label in the cultural context of a local language, region or dialect.

*Smart dropdowns*
When working to represent the sheer diversity of a citizen of Leeds in the UK, I knew that a normal dropdown would cause a significant burden to the user, in selecting so many different properties of a service in the Leeds LOOP service directory. Therefore, it was extremely important to find a solution that, while looking like a simple dropdown, supported features like partial searching, filtering and a tree.

This allowed multiple classes of the taxonomy to be present in a single view. So, it would be simple for a user to pick a service that catered for one or more certain ages, gender, language speakers, life experience or locations. There are many technical solutions available and the one implemented in Leeds was vue-treeselect (https://vue-treeselect.js.org), as it met all the requirements necessary.

## How do I show I have been diverse and inclusive?
Assumption is a large part of why we think diversity and inclusion is present in products and services we use every day. We assume big organisations were inclusive from the start and we don't believe they could have missed the needs of some of their user base.

But they often do, due to a lack of recognising all their users, not just the majority of them, and not empowering all users to collaborate and feedback into their products and services. How do we prove that we have done things differently?

## Collaborative editing of the taxonomy
Demonstrate the origin of the terms you use. When providing reference data in your taxonomy, such as ethnicity, look for terms that will allow people the maximum choice possible to express themselves. These can

always be placed under more common groupings so that collaborating users can be as specific as they wish.

When editing collaboratively, store records of contribution in metadata fields like useful background notes, or better yet, have the contribution recorded by using repositories such as GitHub.

## User feedback

Keep your user feedback summaries as evidence to show you have been inclusive. As your taxonomy changes, you can then approach users for updated feedback. If you have surveys, it is recommended that they be a permanent feature of the website on which you host your taxonomy, so feedback can continually be received. Test your decisions against users so you know they are acceptable and understood.

## Diversity completion score

Consider measuring how much metadata has been completed for your taxonomy content when documenting it like an ontology and use this as a scoring system (e.g., 50% complete). The more you fill out metadata about the term, the more you are likely to capture diversity about the term's meaning, origin and how it could be used.

## Keep checking for changes and usage

It is important to recognise that language changes over time. While you believe your taxonomy is diverse, there may be users who find it does not work for them.

Use tools like Google Search Console (https://search.google.com/search-console/about) or AnswerThePublic (https://answerthepublic.com) to analyse search terms and keywords and you might discover new terms and labels.

If your taxonomy is present as a facet or filter on a website's search results page, often the selection of a taxonomy term by the website user can be seen in the web address of the page. For example, https://yourwebsite.com/search/category=your-taxonomy-term. Therefore, you can discover through web analytic tools how often those terms have been clicked on by users by analysing its page views and track how it assisted a user to get to their destination.

## Conclusion

As taxonomists, we have an opportunity to reflect the whole of society that uses products that have our taxonomy within them. It is easy to assume we have thought of everyone, but it is only natural for bias to occur where we have thought more about a section of our users that is like us or our lived experience.

Building new taxonomies gives us the chance to demonstrate we are aware of this. It proves that effort has been made to identify all the types of users of a taxonomy and to recognise the terms they need and the synonyms that they use that may differ from what we think is the preferred term.

We must be prepared to be wrong, but adaptable and open to feedback, placing taxonomies in the open ready to receive contributions and queries so we can measure success and hear out any criticism. Users who have difficulty finding terms that represent their own diversity in our taxonomy should have routes to contribute these, if we have made ourselves inclusive and open to change. This way we empower products and services to express details about them that currently users would struggle to find, that describes their diversity and what they are looking for.

In conclusion, you must understand your own culture, diversity and bias and acknowledge this. Acknowledge you do not know and have not experienced everything. Whilst you author the taxonomy, it is owned by those who use it – if we are inclusive and allow it to be!

# 5 Relationships, Hierarchies and Semantics

*Bob Kasenchak*

*Editor's note*: This book was never intended to be a textbook on how to build taxonomies. But if you need a crash course or refresher, Bob's chapter introduces all the key points, using examples of everyday things like beverages and dog food. Sometimes the jargon of taxonomies can seem esoteric, yet it exists to make taxonomies make sense and thus work for their users. Semantics is about understanding the underlying meanings of the words in a taxonomy so that they can be organised logically - few people other than Bob can make this understandable as well as fun.

## Introduction

The topic of 'Taxonomy' is both strictly *and* loosely defined. This is recursive (being the category of things about categories), which is a pleasure.

Taxonomy, broadly speaking, is the art and science of categorisation. Many controlled vocabularies that fall under the topic of 'Taxonomy' are not taxonomies: authority files, which are flat lists (that is, they have no hierarchy), such as countries, people or organisations, are closely related to taxonomies and are often included in the discussion. On the other extreme, ontologies (which are *seriously* beyond the scope of this chapter), which may include taxonomies as a part of their structure, have become part of the world of taxonomy.

Frequently, taxonomies are used to structure groups of subjects, topics or categories: organising products on a website or structures of topics to organise content (think the Dewey Decimal System or a topical browse on a website) into broader and narrower categories so that people can find things in large repositories of information. These categories are objects in an information system.

A taxonomist is therefore a kind of Gorgon. Like the mythical beast from Greek mythology that turned people into stone, a taxonomist turns *subjects* into *objects*.

The problem, of course, is that language is fluid and the meaning of words changes over time (and in contexts!). The science of taxonomy is, correspondingly, an inexact and tricky one. Deciding which categories are relevant and what they are called has practical (what are the branches of science?), philosophical (what does it mean to name something?) and ethical implications (who gets to say how many genders are included on your web form?).

An important part of the taxonomist's job is to negotiate between the ideal-state rules for taxonomies (as outlined in the standards) and the real-world context and constraints for implementing the taxonomy.

To understand these issues it's crucial, of course, to learn the basics.

## Standard taxonomic relationships – the basics
### Hierarchies – broader and narrower terms
A taxonomy is, strictly speaking, a hierarchy of *terms* – words or strings of words representing *concepts*.

Hierarchical organisation (borrowed by information science from the concept of Linnean taxonomy in biology) is familiar from browsing websites for content or products as well as from the way file folders are presented in desktop applications.

The basic units of a taxonomic hierarchy are these *terms* and their *relationships*.

The most important relationship is between *Broader Terms* and *Narrower Terms*. A Narrower term (NT) is the reciprocal of a Broader Term (BT), which means that if A is the BT of B, B is an NT of A. For example:

- Beverages
-- Alcoholic Beverages
--- Wine

In this small example, Beverages is the Broader Term of Alcoholic Beverages, and the inverse is also true: Alcoholic Beverages is the Narrower term of Beverages. This is often expressed (outside of the hierarchy itself, which does a marvellous job of visually presenting this information at a glance) in the forms such as:

Beverages *has NT* Alcoholic Beverages
Alcoholic Beverages *has BT* Beverages

Or, in the case of a print thesaurus (once common, now largely supplanted by electronic versions) or another organisation of a vocabulary based on a *term record* (a summary of all information about a term and its relationships):

Alcoholic beverages
  BT Beverages
  NT Wine

It is also common to say that Beverages is the *Parent Term* (or simply *Parent*) of Wine, and, once again to reflect their reciprocity, that Wine is the *Child* of Beverages.

In most cases, terms *must have unique labels*. The label of the term is the unique identifier for that term (although most taxonomy software will assign and/or allow you to designate some unique code as well). Accordingly, circular relationships are not allowed; a term cannot be its own grandparent and a term also cannot have the same BT as an NT. The following structure is therefore disallowed:

-- Pets
--- Dogs
---- Pets

This implies that the second 'Pets' also has NT 'Dogs' and so on to infinity. This is rightly deemed not desirable; in both print and electronic formats, representing infinite loops is rather inconvenient. Further, it is illogical if, as discussed below, this structure implies that all Dogs are Pets and all Pets are Dogs as we are both making contradictory claims and asserting something illogical.

Fortunately, again, most taxonomy software will not permit this kind of illegal relationship. Enforcing these kinds of rules is one good reason to use a dedicated taxonomy application instead of, say, a spreadsheet to manage a taxonomy of any significant size or complexity. (Full disclosure: I have worked for several companies that provide such software, but I'm not just saying this; I have horror stories.)

Although we think of taxonomies primarily as hierarchies (as the hierarchical structure is the primary feature), from another point of view a taxonomy is a *directed acyclic graph*. We can envision a hierarchical structure like this:

  - Alcoholic beverages
  – Beer
  -- Wine

. . . as a graph (Figure 5.1) in which the terms are nodes and the relation-ships are edges:
  This may not seem helpful right now, but it's important.

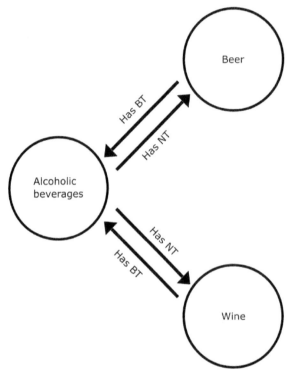

**Figure 5.1** *Taxonomy fragment expressed as a simple graph. Terms in the vocabulary are expressed as nodes and relationships as edges*

## The All–Some Rule

The Parent-Child, or BT-NT, relationship is the unit on which taxonomic structures are constructed. This analogy of familial relationships is extended to the idea of *Sibling Terms*, which are terms with the same parent. In the structure below, the terms Beer and Wine are siblings:

  - Beverages
  – Alcoholic beverages
  --- Beer
  -- Wine

One further extension of the family unit analogy is also used in taxonomy practice: an *Orphan* term is a term that has no parents. (Orphan terms may or may not be problematic depending on your taxonomy, but in most cases they are not desirable.)

In most instances (with notable exceptions), the basic principle of hierarchical organisation is that *All* of the NTs belong to the category of the BT. This principle is called the *All–Some Rule*. The idea is that any child term inherits the characteristics of its parent (or parents; more on this shortly).

Therefore, the structure:

- Animals
-- Cats

. . . is correct (or, rather, standards compliant), since **all** Cats are Animals. The counterexample:

- Pets
-- Cats

. . . is therefore incorrect (i.e., not standards compliant), as **some** Cats are not Pets (or, rather, not **all** Cats are Pets) as they may be stray cats, feral cats, unadopted cats, and so forth.

This simple rule has, in practice, many exceptions (e.g., in the context of a pet store, all cats are probably pets), but for now let us take it as a given.


## Polyhierarchy

It is possible, and even likely, that some terms will have more than one parent, or BT. This is known as *polyhierarchy* and it is exceedingly common in many kinds of taxonomies. Polyhierarchy is straightforward: the rule is that for a given term, all of its BTs must be valid according to the All–Some Rule. For example, in conceptual taxonomies used to index content for retrieval - which is common in publishing contexts - many domains are transdisciplinary, which can be represented in a hierarchy outlining fields of study:

- Science
-- Biology
--- Biological chemistry
-- Chemistry
--- Biological chemistry

A different and instructive example from the realm of e-commerce presents a similar solution:

- Clothing
-- Shoes
--- Women's shoes
-- Women's clothing
--- Women's shoes

The only real problem with polyhierarchy is taking care of reciprocal relationships, but all commercial taxonomy management software will do this automatically.

Polyhierarchy is extremely useful (I think it's essential) but can be overused, especially when strict hierarchical protocols are not enforced.

### Types and subtypes of BT–NT relationships

The ANSI/NISO Z.39.19 standard for constructing controlled vocabularies allows specific subtypes of the BT–NT relationship. I mention this here because even if you don't use these subtypes as labels in your data (and you very likely won't), it's crucial to understand the concepts they outline.

The three types of permitted BT–NT relationships are *Instantive*, *Partitive* and *Generic*. (The standards allow for the labelling of BT–NT relationships (BTI–NTI, BTP–NTP and BTG–NTG), but these are rarely used.)

**Instantive** BT–NT relationships describe the NT as an *instance* of a BT: a specific exemplar. In this way, Ghana is an instance of a country. Instances are often called 'classes of one' since they do not by definition (well, usually, more on this below) have any narrower terms of their own (they are 'leaf nodes' in some taxonomic parlances).

- Countries
-- Ghana

**Partitive** BT–NT relationships describe whole-part relationships between *terms*. Virginia is *a part of* the United States; an engine *is part of* a car; the heart *is part of* the circulatory system.

Perhaps it's already occurred to astute readers that mixing BT–NT types can be troublesome. Since Ghana is divided into ten regions, we can use the Partitive rule to assign these as NTs of Ghana:

- Countries
-- Ghana
--- Ashanti

So, although, in theory, Instantive NTs are childless terms (leaf nodes), it's often the case that they are not - if they have Partitive NTs of their own.

**Generic** (as in *genre*, not describing some default case) BT-NT relationships describe sub-*genres* of things: subtopics, subclasses, subkinds, subconcepts. This is easily the most used (and abused) category of BT-NT relationship as it can be invoked to broadly gather loosely related terms under a single parent by appealing to the idea that they're all subconcepts of the same thing.

Some examples of Generic BT-NTs include:

*Fields and subfields*
- Chemistry
-- Analytical chemistry

- Linguistics
-- Grammar

*Subclasses or subgenres*
- Chairs
-- Desk chairs

- Comedy
-- Romantic comedy

- Pens
-- Ballpoint pens

*Subtopics*
- Golf
-- Golf equipment
-- Golf courses

These last examples are actually a problem: they seem to follow the logic of the Generic BT-NT relationship (the topic of Golf includes subtopics about equipment and courses) but in fact this seemingly innocuous structure breaks the All-Some Rule: *Golf equipment is not a golf.*

Accordingly, Generic BT-NT relationships should be carefully considered, as mixing concepts and topics can create confusing and not-very-useful hierarchies, especially if they are intended for any kind of inference or machine learning. However, this organisational principle – which might be described as 'let's just put all the golf stuff under Golf' – is very common in public-facing taxonomies; endless exemplars can be found in website navigation and e-commerce taxonomies.

## Topics vs concepts

Consider the following structure:

- Skiing
-- Cross-country skiing
-- Downhill skiing
-- Ski apparel
-- Ski equipment
-- Ski resorts

The structure as shown is intuitive: all of the NTs are definitely *associated* with Skiing; they are all properly subtopics of the topic of Skiing.

Clustering all of the related concepts under a single BT (Skiing) is a common way to organise product taxonomies, which are designed to allow users to quickly find what they're looking for. This organisation is predicated around *Skiing as a Topic*.

Within this small structure the terms 'Cross-country skiing' and 'Downhill skiing' are in fact types of Skiing: subclasses (or sub-genres) of Skiing. You might say, obtusely, that 'Downhill skiing *IS A* Skiing' to denote that in fact Downhill and Cross-Country skiing are subclasses of Skiing: they treat *Skiing as a Concept*.

On the other hand, Ski Equipment and Ski Resorts are not, strictly speaking, types (genres) of Skiing; we might (just as obtusely) say that 'Ski Resorts *IS NOT A* Skiing'.

So, there are two things going on here: the terms 'Downhill Skiing' and 'Cross-country skiing' treat Skiing as a concept while the terms describing apparel, equipment and resorts treat Skiing as a topic.

The problem of conflating (or mixing and matching) topics and concepts is one of the subtlest and most confusing in the field. Many taxonomies can risk becoming unwieldy, and therefore less useful, because of this.

To be clear: this kind of structure is useful in some kinds of taxonomies, like website navigation and product taxonomies. Although it's true that 'Dog food IS NOT A Dog', if you're building a taxonomy for a pet store website, you will probably make 'Dog food' an NT of 'Dogs' (as a subtopic) since in context it makes sense (i.e., people looking for products for their dog will easily locate what they're looking for if 'all dog stuff is under "Dogs"').

In other, stricter kinds of taxonomies – specifically (but not exclusively) those used as the basis for ontologies or for machine learning and other kinds of inferencing – this is highly problematic.

This illustrates a basic tension encountered when constructing a taxonomy: Do I categorise this term according to *what it is*? Or should I put it *where people can find it*? The answer is usually guided by context.

## Thesauri and thesaural relationships

A *thesaurus* is a taxonomy that includes other information about each term as well as other, non-hierarchical relationships between terms. Most importantly, this includes synonyms (or non-preferred terms (NPTs)) and related terms (RTs). The inclusion of synonyms (and, less frequently, antonyms or other types of linguistic relationships) is what ties the term *thesaurus* to the common desktop reference books of the same name. (To add to the confusion about naming things in taxonomy: it is absolutely the case that in the vast majority of situations, when people say taxonomy, they really mean thesaurus.)

### *Attributes*

Information about terms (often called fields or attributes) store other information about a term *that does not relate to other terms.*

Common fields include dictionary-like descriptions of a term (definition) and how the term is understood in the context of the taxonomy (scope note), metadata about the term (who created it or edited it and when), codes or other unique identifiers, indication of the status of the term (Candidate or Approved, Withdrawn or Deprecated), and any other information useful to know about the term. Some taxonomies have lots of fields, while others have few or none.

Attributes are often restricted by data type (free text, number, URL, email address, time, date, string) to restrict the values entered. In some cases, values in fields may be restricted to a given list of terms, a picklist (like a dropdown menu of choices) or even another taxonomy. In this way, it is possible to connect taxonomies into a single connected semantic structure; you can use a taxonomy of countries to populate a field in a taxonomy about colleges and universities, specifying the location of each.

## NPTs

Non-preferred terms (NPTs) are often called 'synonyms' but in practice they cover a broader range of *alternative labels* for terms. NPTs can and often do include:

- actual synonyms: alternative names for terms – Beverages NPT Drinks
- adjectival or adverbial forms of terms (which tend to be nouns and noun phrases) – Philosophy NPT Philosophical, Philosophically
- other alternative forms of a term, such as practitioners of a discipline – Gymnastics NPT Gymnasts
- alternative spellings, such as British or American variants (depending on your perspective) – Honor NPT Honour
- narrower concepts that did not warrant inclusion in your taxonomy – Beer NPT Lager, Stout, Ale, etc.
- abbreviations and acronyms (or, occasionally, spelled-out acronyms): it is good practice to use the acronym for the Preferred Term or Preferred Label for a concept when it has supplanted the word in common usage – Boston Symphony Orchestra NPT BSO, LED NPT Light-emitting diode
- punctuation variants – Long-lost brother NPT Long lost brother.

Sometimes, foreign language versions of terms are used as NPTs – although these can be treated specially in some cases and given a label to indicate their language of origin. In many European Union thesauri, language variants of terms have their own corresponding definitions, scope notes and other fields.

Often, NPTs are useful not just for lookups and *See* references (think about the old physical card catalogues (*Drinks*: see Beverages)) but as hooks for natural language processing (NPT: NLP) to classify content (automatically assign indexing terms) and to leverage in search engines for query expansion. For this reason, you may also find NPTs that are common misspellings or other strange-looking near-words (Dog food NPT Dogfood).

## Related terms (RTs): uses and abuses

The standard related term (RT) relationship is the other primary thesaural relationship. Since RTs connect two terms but do not affect the hierarchy, they are also called *non-hierarchical* or *associative relationships*.

If NPTs are *See* references, RTs are *See Also*. RTs are useful for directing someone who is interested in a topic (or, more likely, the content or data connected to that topic) to other topics they are probably interested in.

RTs are, in truth, pretty subjective. In their simplest form, RTs point terms at one another as related but *make no assertion about the strength or nature of the relationship.*

So, while perhaps [Dogs RT Dog food] and [Stethoscopes RT Physicians] are both valid (they are), the relationship is not the same – nor does it assert similarity. While it is possible to declare and assign custom RTs in a thesaurus describing specific relationships [Dogs EAT Dog Food], in practice this is mostly the domain of ontologies.

RTs are best used exactly as described above: as *See Also* references to gently guide a user to related topics *not represented in the hierarchy as related.* Too many RTs become cumbersome and, at a certain point, totally useless: connecting every topic to every other topic is unhelpful.

Finally, in most cases RTs (like BTs/NTs) are reciprocal: if A is RT to B, B is also RT to A. In theory (and according to the standards), RTs can be *unidirectional* (one-way) but this is less common.

### RT or NT?

Novice taxonomists often struggle with assigning RTs versus NTs. This is because, as discussed above in the example about Skiing, it is easy to mix topics and concepts.

Skiing
    NT Cross-country skiing
    NT Downhill skiing
    NT? RT? Ski apparel
    NT? RT?  Ski equipment
    NT? RT? Ski resorts

Should 'Ski equipment' be included here as an NT, or in a branch of 'Sporting goods' and made an RT? The answer, again, is to examine the context. A sporting goods store probably doesn't need a hierarchy of sports separate from the one organising sporting goods; it makes more sense to organise the sporting goods *under* the sports – so make it an NT. In another context, sports and sporting goods may be in different branches and the terms require an RT relationship.

## Advanced hierarchical concepts
### Size, depth and breadth

A taxonomy organises the concepts in a field or topical area to describe or tag, for example, content or products for a particular task. This can be organising the content on a website or categorising (for filing physical copies) all of the books in a library.

The *size* of a taxonomy is generally measured in the number of preferred terms in the hierarchy. When scoping a taxonomy project, consider the universe of objects that needs to be organised. Using the entire Dewey Decimal System to tag 30 blog posts is overkill, while ten categories is insufficient to browse a content set numbering in the hundreds of thousands of objects. Display space can also be a consideration; the design challenge of surfacing a few dozen terms in a browsable interface is very different for thousands of terms.

The *depth* of a taxonomy describes the granularity to which the topic is covered and, to a lesser extent (but often as a shorthand), the number of levels in the hierarchical tree in the deepest branch. The depth of a taxonomy should be sufficient to reflect the objects (content, products, etc.) to be labelled. If you have some content about food, how many terms describing specific foods are required? Do you really need to list every type of apple? On the other hand, if most of your content is about food (say, on a recipe website), a single tag 'food' is probably not sufficient to aid in content discovery.

The *breadth* of a taxonomy describes the topical area(s) covered by the taxonomy. A publisher with articles about all kinds of science will need a broader taxonomy than one publishing exclusively on topics in physics. The breadth of a vocabulary is the subset of All Things That Are with which the taxonomy is concerned.

### Alphabetical vs notation or forced sort

By default (according to the standards), taxonomies are arranged alphabetically. The top layer of terms is alphabetised as is every branch underneath:

- Dairy
- Fruits
-- Apples
--- Fuji apples
--- Gala apples
--- Granny Smith apples
-- Bananas
-- Lemons
-- Limes
-- Oranges

- Grains
- Vegetables

This is fine in most situations, but there are good reasons to want to organise - or display - your taxonomy in some other order. Various methods exist: a *sort field* holds a string that forces the display order out of alphabetical using some sequence of numbers or letters. One example of this is a notation system, like that used by the librarian and mathematician S. R. Ranganathan (1892-1972), a fragment of which is below:

z Generalia
1 Universe of Knowledge
2 Library Science
3 Book science
4 Journalism
A Natural science
B Mathematics
C Physics
D Engineering
E Chemistry I

Each of these has a subheading: B2 is Algebra, under B Mathematics, and so on.

Reasons to use notation - that is, to force a non-alphabetical sort - might be to mirror the importance of subjects, for display on a website to promote or highlight certain product categories, to reflect a process in order, or to make sure definite articles or other strings in the term name are not used for sorting, for example, you don't alphabetise *Le Nozze di Figaro* under 'L'.

### Top-down versus bottom-up hierarchical construction

When constructing hierarchies, it is useful to consider the difference between *top-down* and *bottom-up* thinking as two methodological strategies, both with useful features. These methodologies are best seen as complementary approaches.

Let's say you have a set of 1,000 candidate terms to organise into a taxonomy. How should you go about getting started?

**Top-down** thinking takes the highest level categories as a given, under which the rest of the terms are sorted (see Figure 5.2 on the next page). So, if, for example, your taxonomy is organising products for a shopping website, it may be pre-determined that the top-level terms (probably the

# Top-down technique

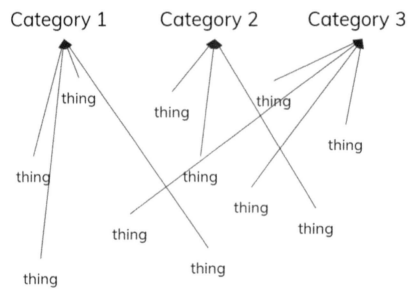

**Figure 5.2** *Top-down construction provides categories as a starting point and assigns terms to branches as appropriate*

first level categories displayed on the website) will be Clothing, Furniture, Appliances, and so forth – either based on mirroring the departments or organisation of products in the physical store or for some other reason. The remaining terms can be grouped together into the appropriate branch(es) and then further refined into a hierarchy using the BT–NT guidelines discussed above. Top-down hierarchical construction is straightforward: simply sort everything into the appropriate branch. The rigidity of the structure, however, can cause problems (or, thought of another way: identify outliers) when terms cannot be usefully sorted into any of the given branches.

**Bottom-up** thinking designs the hierarchy by arranging terms into whatever broader categories (and so on up to the top terms) suggested by the terms themselves and without reference to a pre-determined set of top categories (see Figure 5.3 opposite). Bottom-up thinking is more flexible but can be more chaotic, with an overall top-level structure slowly emerging rather than driving the construction.

# Bottom-up technique

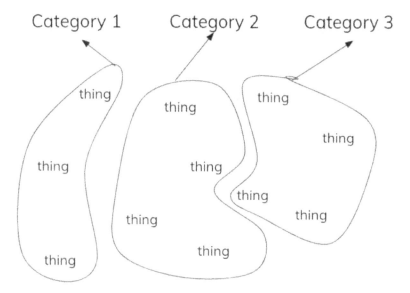

**Figure 5.3** *Bottom-up construction allows categories to emerge from the concepts rather than pre-defining them*

In practice, most taxonomy construction uses a combination of top-down and bottom-up approaches. Understanding the distinction as well as the advantages of both methods is useful for practical taxonomy construction (and maintenance).

## Stricter and looser hierarchies

As noted, the principles of taxonomy construction (as outlined in the standards) when applied to real-world situations must be somewhat flexible and take into account the context in which the vocabulary will be implemented. Accordingly, there are stricter and looser taxonomies depending on their use and deployment. A pet store website might reasonably make 'Dogs' the BT of 'Dog food' with the justification that this arrangement facilitates customers easily finding what they're looking for. A stricter taxonomy used to, say, tag images to train a machine learning algorithm to recognise dogs in pictures would want to keep 'Dog food' hierarchically separate from (but probably RT related to) 'Dogs' as it is undesirable to have the artificial intelligence (AI) identify a bag of kibble as an animal.

Accordingly, various types of taxonomies have common underlying features.

### Dictionaries

Alphabetical lists of topics grouped for browsing under the first letters in the terms are taxonomies in name only: the hierarchy exists merely to group things by letter to collapse the number of browsable categories to 26 (in English). The BT–NT relationships of such tree structures do not imply any actual relationship between terms.

### Web navigation taxonomies

Website navigation taxonomies hierarchically organise the pages on a website for browsing and easy access. Such taxonomies tend to be small, narrow and shallow, dictated by display and user interface (UI) design considerations. The logic of web navigation hierarchies tends to be loose: BT–NT relationships are dictated by convenience of browsing (often discovered via user research, such as card sorting activities) instead of the standards.

As with several other types of taxonomies, the user-facing web navigation taxonomy may be a small, reorganised version of a larger, stricter taxonomy in the background.

### E-commerce

Taxonomies designed to offer discovery of products on a website are necessarily focused in breadth (the world of things to be classified is restricted to the products in question) but can be quite large and very deep. Since the goal of e-commerce taxonomies is to connect users with products, a user-facing organisational logic is required. The 'where will people find what they're looking for?' rule applies here, which is to say that you may very well be mixing concepts and topics: 'Dog food' may very well make sense as an NT of 'Dogs'. Product taxonomies are also commonly polyhierarchical, as it makes sense to place terms into multiple branches for easy discovery; it makes sense to put a category 'Children's shoes' in both the 'Shoes' and 'Children's clothing' branches so users can find it in either place. Examples of product taxonomies can be found on any retailer's website.

*Content indexing and retrieval taxonomies*

Publishers and other managers of large repositories of content maintain taxonomies to index (or 'tag') the content for retrieval. In sufficiently large content sets, free-text searches (searches literally just looking for whatever string you enter in the search box) are insufficient for retrieving content as they do not look for variations or synonyms, so searching for 'drinks' will not return 'beverages', nor will searching for 'drones' or 'UAVs' return 'unmanned aerial vehicles'.

Content indexing taxonomies therefore often contain robust NPTs to aid in search and discovery of content. The depth, breadth and size of these taxonomies reflects the size and breadth of the content set to be indexed. Since (for example, in scholarly publishing) such content repositories can have hundreds of thousands to millions of objects, the taxonomies constructed to index them can be very large indeed, often with thousands or even tens of thousands of terms.

The logic governing the organisation of content indexing taxonomies is stricter (closer to the standards) than product taxonomies but topics and subjects are often mixed, as the subfields of a field of study:

- Economics
-- Applied economics
-- Econometrics
-- Macroeconomics
-- Microeconomics

. . . become intermixed with the topics covered by a discipline:

- Microeconomics
-- Competition
-- Consumer demand
-- Monopolies
-- Opportunity cost

Since, as discussed above, the All–Some Rule breaks down along topical lines, the operative question should be: would I expect to find all papers on *term B* if I searched for *term A*? In other words, would I expect to find all papers about 'Monopolies' if I do a search for all papers about 'Micro-economics'? Generally, this corresponds to which topics are covered in a department teaching about a discipline (or a business unit, for example).

Once again, since many topics are interdisciplinary, polyhierarchy is common in structures of this type. Consider 'Chemical biology', which is a topic in the field of chemistry as well as biology; it would not make sense to select only one of these as the BT, but rather to place it in both branches:

- Biology
-- Chemical biology
- Chemistry
-- Chemical biology

Content indexing taxonomies are often rich in synonyms and other NPTs, including variants and other types discussed above. In addition to being used for browsing and tagging, this additional information is often (but not often enough) included in the search logic to explode queries. That is to say, the consumers of content indexing taxonomies include both humans and other systems.

### Taxonomies for machine learning

Taxonomies used to tag content as exemplars for machine learning (and related activities) must be constructed strictly to prevent the 'machine' (an algorithm making inferences based on tagged sample data) from drawing false conclusions. This is not a good place to implement our fictional taxonomy for a pet store; treating 'Dogs' as a topic and collecting all of the terms/products related to Dogs as NTs is essentially saying that 'dog food is a dog'.

Imagine, again, that a set of photographs is being tagged (most likely by humans) to teach a computer vision program how to recognise various objects. Users tag every photo of a dog with the term 'Dogs' as well as some other common objects (whatever is relevant to the project). The computer doesn't really learn what a Dog is, but by feeding it many, many images of dogs tagged with the term 'Dogs' it generalises about (for example) the outline, colour and other features of pictures that include dogs. The taggers have instructions to tag specific breeds of dog if they recognise them, but otherwise to use the tag 'Dogs'. This is possible if the taxonomy behind the tags organises breeds of dogs as NTs of the term Dogs, so that any term tagged with a specific breed of dog will also be understood to be a Dog: *all pictures of German Shepherds are pictures of dogs*. If 'Dog food' is also an NT of 'Dogs' the algorithm will 'learn' that *all pictures of dog food are pictures of dogs*, which is not helpful to the desired result.

In this case, lumping 'Dog food' as an NT of 'Dogs' is misrepresenting information used by the computer in a way that our pet store taxonomy does not (as it is intended to be consumed and used by people).

Machine learning data sets are in practice unlikely to use taxonomies to organise their tags; instead, they employ related structures called *ontologies*.

## Conclusion

Presented with a sufficient number (say, more than seven or ten) of things of any kind, humans tend to arrange them into categories. This is practical as well as intuitive, since in information environments things often number in the thousands or millions. Taxonomy is the branch of information science dealing with the naming, description and organisation of categories – which can include products, content or virtually anything else.

Taxonomies are hierarchical structures of terms used to organise information. In the abstract, best practices for taxonomy construction (and storage and display) are outlined by accepted standards. In practice, taxonomists must balance these guidelines with project- and user-specific requirements.

Taxonomies are commonly found in web navigation, online product organisation and information retrieval contexts. The taxonomies used for these tasks vary in size, scope and organisation. Anyone using the web almost certainly, and perhaps unknowingly, encounters taxonomies on a daily basis.

Taxonomy intersects with (at minimum) linguistics, information architecture, library science, ethics and whatever domain(s) the vocabulary describes. Although the basic tenets of taxonomy are described in the abstract by widely accepted standards, some flexibility and creative thinking are required when designing taxonomies for real-life use cases.

# 6 User Testing and Validation

*Tom Alexander*

*Editor's note*: Tom's passion for helping users shines through in this exploration of the ways you can ensure your taxonomy will work in the real world. Sometimes this means disregarding what seems like the 'correct' way and doing something that better matches users' mental models. Through examples such as mushrooms and marathons, and a case study from one of the UK's largest charities, Tom explains not just the 'why' of taxonomy validation, but also the 'how'.

## Introduction

It's an oft-used phrase that knowledge is knowing that a tomato is a fruit, but that wisdom is knowing not to put it in a fruit salad. Something similar applies when developing a taxonomy: terms should be organised in a way that makes sense in real life. In this chapter, we'll investigate ignoring your taxonomic impulse to create the perfect classification and instead focusing on classifying in a way that makes sense to your user. That could mean arranging your taxonomy in a different way to how you first imagined.

There is a cultural hump you may need to get over when making your taxonomy work in the real world. If your user research has given you evidence that your 'tomato' content should live under 'vegetable', the purist in you may wrestle with that idea if you have always considered it a 'fruit'.

Go and listen to your users. Implement a taxonomy structure based on what they tell you. You are not your user.

What follows are examples of where I have taken a user-centred approach in my work at two well known organisations: Getty Images and Cancer Research UK.

## Pizza in a search for 'fungus'?

Getty Images' collection of rights-managed and royalty-free photography, creative and editorial content, video and music content, numbers well into the tens of millions. When I started, I was in a team of image data experts that was split three ways: image classification (things like the orientation of the image, whether it was colour or black and white, etc.); a search data team (that applied the taxonomy tags to images); and the search vocabulary team (that managed the vocabulary tree – and the team I was part of).

I went from taxonomy rookie to classification expert in the fascinating world of controlled vocabularies. Terms like 'Boolean', 'nested search query', 'keyword', 'synonym', 'exact' (a user-generated tag) and 'parent-and-child hierarchy' became the bread and butter of my professional vernacular.

This first example is where I understood that pure classification may not always work in the real world. Pop along to your local supermarket and look for the mushrooms. The first place you will think to go is the fruit and veg section. You wouldn't think to look for mushrooms in the 'fungus' section of the supermarket. You do not need to even think about this.

Finding images in Getty Images' system relied on the strength of the keywords associated with them. These keywords were arranged in a classical parent-and-child format. So, if we were to look at the part of our vocabulary tree where we had placed the word 'mushroom', it looked like this:

- Fungus
-- Mushroom

The system enforces referential integrity between these terms. That is, because 'mushroom' was placed under 'fungus', searching for 'fungus' returns images of mushrooms amongst all the images of fungi. From a classification standpoint, that would appear to make sense. After all, a mushroom is a type of fungus. It is the natural 'home' for the term 'mushroom' to exist as a subset of 'fungus'.

Why, then, did a search for fungus return images of pizza every so often? Because 'mushroom' is placed beneath 'fungus', a search on 'fungus' includes all the 'mushroom'-tagged images in the results. Within the collection, some images of pizzas – detailed, close-up shots that featured slices of mushroom nestling unctuously on a tomato sauce base – were significant enough to warrant tagging the pizza image with 'mushroom'.

Now, 'mushroom' searches would feature the odd pizza shot. And so, 'fungus' keyword searches, returning 'mushroom' images due to referential integrity between 'fungus' and 'mushroom', are therefore peppered with the occasional pizza image. A picture researcher needing a close-up of a death cap protruding ominously from the earth returned images of men with a can of lager in one hand and a slice of Fiorentina in the other.

So, we changed the 'home' of the 'mushroom' keyword and moved it to 'vegetable'. The 'fungus' keyword search now no longer featured rather out-of-place pizza images.

Now, our mushrooms were in the same category as they have them in the local supermarket, which gives this classification a reassuring sense of real-world-ness.

## Controlled vocabularies and webpages

Cancer Research UK is a very different organisation to Getty Images, as you can imagine. Apart from the obvious differences between a private media library and a third sector organisation that funds life-saving cancer research, their content and the repositories in which content is used are quite different. These differences have a knock-on effect on my professional life.

Cancer Research UK has far fewer individual items of content than Getty Images, and the content itself is very different. Most of the content consists of webpages. Webpages are a difficult entity for a taxonomy professional to work with after years honing a world-class taxonomy for digital assets. Why? Because images don't contain words themselves. Webpages do.

With so many digital assets, Getty Images invests a lot of money in classification professionals to ensure the user experience is sharp. To find an image, the system relies on the tags that are associated with them. The advantage for a taxonomy professional is that you have complete control over the data that the system uses to return search results with. It is a controlled vocabulary.

Webpages usually have words on them, which changes things. Those words are often used as part of the search index. That doesn't happen with images, since there are no words on the image. So, when your webpage contains searchable words within the content, the content (the webpage) becomes its own metadata. You search on the words on the page. You could do away with tags altogether, to a point, because the prose of the page provides tags, of a sort.

However, it can also make the searches less accurate, because **all** the text on your webpage is searchable. There are sophisticated things a search word parser can do to overcome this – stop lists that remove conjunctions and prepositions, for example – but the fact remains that, as a taxonomy professional, all your hard-won glories around perfecting a fabulous search experience using only a controlled vocabulary could be shot to pieces by moving over to webpages. Because the controlled vocabulary becomes uncontrolled.

In an image library, a concept like 'tobacco' can be split into distinct terms with different meanings. 'Smoking' could mean images of a cigarette or the act of smoking. The results will reflect this easy-to-understand distinction. This disambiguation is easy because the different terms are applied only to the relevant images.

At Cancer Research UK, we have 'smoking' as a cancer risk term and as a different word for our Tobacco Control team. However, the words 'smoking' or 'tobacco' may appear in the text of a webpage in either context. This makes disambiguation more difficult. It is where not having a controlled vocabulary becomes a problem.

However, using the best practice from my time at Getty Images, I created separate terms for 'smoking'-related content at Cancer Research UK. This allows some disambiguation, even if indexing webpages' prose can cause some results to look wrong.

## When is a marathon not running?

The word 'marathon' is one we use to describe a long-distance running race of 26.2 miles (about 42km). The word comes from the town Marathon, which lies northeast of Athens in Greece. During the Battle of Marathon in 490BC, Pheidippides, a messenger, is said to have run the distance between Marathon and Athens to deliver the news of victory during the battle.

If somebody were to ask me where the word 'marathon' should live in a taxonomy, I would answer 'under a broader term such as running'. If you visit the Wikipedia page for 'Running', there is a sub-section further down the page of 'Distances', at which point there is inserted a link to another page, 'Long-distance running'. On the Wikipedia page entitled 'Long-distance running' (https://en.wikipedia.org/wiki/Long-distance_running), there are nearly 50 separate mentions of the word 'marathon'. If you visit the 'Marathon' page, there are about 70 mentions of the word 'running'.

So, there is a clear relation, in people's minds, between the two terms.

## User testing the options for the Find an Event dropdown

We were re-factoring our Find an Event page at Cancer Research UK, where potential participants can select an event to take part in from a dropdown list. They are then taken to the event page, where they can sign up to their challenge and raise money for the charity.

But what happens if the events in that dropdown list are arranged in a confusing way? What could we discover by doing user testing, validation and testing assumptions?

We discovered that the Find an Event page suffered a 51% drop-off rate for sports events. Further analysis showed that users did not expect to have to look under 'running' to find marathons. Many participants of our online validation exercises expected to go straight through to a 'marathon' term rather than to 'running' (see Figure 6.1).

| | | 📁 Marathons | 24 times |
| Bath Half Marathon | 2 different categories | | |
| | | 📁 Running events | 6 times |
| | | 📁 Marathons | 25 times |
| Brighton Marathon | 3 different categories | 📁 Running events | 4 times |
| | | 📁 Give It Up | 1 time |

**Figure 6.1**  *Screengrab of results from card sorting exercise in Optimal Workshop, showing number of clicks participants placed on event type categories*

Reviewing this data, I had to suspend my disbelief. It was hard to get my head around the fact that users expected to find 'marathon' on the top level, rather than below 'running events'.

So, what did we do? We tested how well our participants responded when we placed our 'marathon' content under the homepage in another online test. The results were illuminating (Figure 6.2).

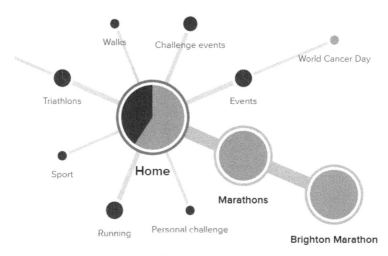

**Figure 6.2**  *Screengrab from Optimal Workshop showing participants' preferred route to finding the Brighton Marathon page*

Figure 6.2 shows that 95% of the 44 participants in this study expected to find 'marathon' under the homepage. From this, we understood that attempting to shoehorn 'running' in between the starting point and accessing the content they were looking for would be a hindrance. Only three participants went looking for their desired content via 'running'.

By reviewing how website content needs to be structured, we were forced to abandon preconceived ideas of how things are structured. Once we got past these ideas, we were able to offer a dropdown selection that makes sense to our users (Figure 6.3).

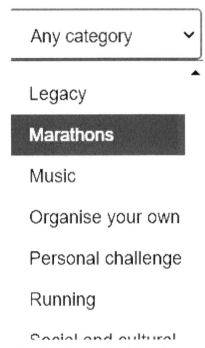

**Figure 6.3** *Screengrab of the dropdown on the Find an Event page – the revised structure places 'Marathons' and 'Running' on the same level*

Sometimes, something that makes perfect sense on paper – or on screen – doesn't fit in real life. This proved the need to test assumptions. If you test assumptions that prove to be wrong via evidence, change what you're offering to users – even if that breaks the taxonomic structure you had in your mind. Do this even if the hierarchical – even etymological – positioning of 'marathon' has always been as a child term of 'running'.

I'm sure Pheidippides himself would have seen the value of making it easier to get information to someone important.

## Sometimes, we still need a top-down approach
Despite needing to create terms that live in the real world, we should remember that there are areas of taxonomy that need to be a bit more 'top-

down' and not user-generated. Consider the following parent and child formulation we have in Cancer Research UK's taxonomy:

- Kidney cancer
-- Wilms tumour

The decisions to place 'Wilms tumour' under 'Kidney cancer' and to exclude an apostrophe after the 's' of 'Wilms' come from Cancer Research UK's Health Information team. Terms like cancer types introduce reputational risk that we must keep as low as possible. Even if we had data from user behaviour that suggested the nominated term for 'Wilms tumour' should be 'Wilms' cancer', for example, we would have to think long and hard about making a change to the spelling. We could otherwise appear to be out of synchronisation with medical classification best practice and, despite what we have seen about satisfying user need, we must also ensure we have a classification system that keeps reputational risk low.

## Information architecture and taxonomy: sharing data to create the right terms

In this final section, we will look at how sharing insights gathered from user testing both information architecture and taxonomies can help create a taxonomy that works better for users. Taking account of what's in an information architecture (IA) when developing a taxonomy pays dividends in ensuring both structures work well.

Why have a taxonomy when you already have an IA? It pays to review what a taxonomy offers that an IA is unable to.

A team had done some user research into pain points users had finding things in files and folders. I got involved when we used those pain points - issues like how to communicate between team members, what to do if someone leaves - to drive work into structuring and managing our knowledge. We used SharePoint, which has some useful taxonomy features.

After some user testing, card sorting and more user research, we had some solid foundations for an IA. They are the six categories, which are discussed below. Our research also told us that users were interested in having a document library - a place where all the content that was divided into the above areas was available in a single location.

As the taxonomy lead on this project, I asked myself: since we've done lots of testing for the IA, why not use some of that for the taxonomy? Why do we need to reinvent the wheel?

The question of how an IA relates to a taxonomy in a digital product has always intrigued me. What intrigued me more was developing an IA and a taxonomy from scratch at the same time in the same product. So I thought: why not reuse some of the categories in the IA to test in a taxonomy?

## Information architecture for a playbook

We did some initial user research around managing best practice documents, which we referred to as 'plays'. These lived in an area we called the 'playbook' - a hub for how we do things in a fast-moving technology department in the largest third sector organisation in the UK.

We gathered pain points such as:

WHEN I first land on the playbook with the intention of using it for my work
I WANT TO know what the playbook is
SO THAT I can tell immediately whether it's suitable for me and my project

Some KFC work - what we want users to Know, Feel and Commit to on a page - yielded some initial categories we wanted to develop for our Playbook:

Homepage
Theme section
Individual play page

The interesting section here was the Theme section, since this was going to have to be broken down again into smaller sub-categories:

Ways of working
Starting a project
Understanding your users
Designing and building content
Testing and improving content
Essentials for live content

This would provide a backbone for some areas of taxonomy development.

## Meanwhile, a taxonomy for a playbook

I began to build a taxonomy. After the classic bottom-up development (reviewing the cache of content that was scheduled to go into the playbook), I had produced a strawman taxonomy structure. I then refined this further by some top-down taxonomy development: asking for key terms from the subject matter experts in the respective technology fields we wanted to represent in our playbook. Things like user experience (UX), content design, project management and Search Engine Optimisation (SEO) and more.

The top-level categories from this work numbered 28. This seemed a lot. It would force users to scroll through long lists of words to find what they were looking for.

Using some of the categories from the information architecture, I began grouping terms under broader categories. The original 28-strong list became 13. I tested this structure using the Treejack function in Optimal Workshop – an online validation tool that gives data on how successful pathways to content are for your participants.

This slimmed-down structure gave a rather disappointing 26% success rate in Treejack. I went ahead and began to fold more of the top-level terms into other higher-level terms, so that we had a structure of eight top terms:

Content type
Designing and building content
Role
Software
Starting a project and setting a strategy
Testing and improving your content
Understanding your work
Ways of working

I ran a further Treejack test with this reconfigured taxonomy structure. With a less convoluted pathway for getting to content, our participants found it much easier to find what they were looking for. The success rate of reaching the page they wanted to reach improved from 26% in the earlier test to 61% in the new test. And what was interesting was that borrowing top-level categories from the information architecture didn't confuse matters – it seemed to help.

It felt efficient to re-use existing user testing data to feed into a linked – if separate – process.

We received good feedback on the project overall and it has begun to form the basis of a drive to improve our knowledge management yet further.

## Methods of user research

We have described some methods to understand how to make a taxonomy fit for the real world. This has included using online tools for card sorting and term structure validation. There are other ways in which we can gain useful information like labelling and the behaviour of the system used to access content. Some of these things are 'offline', which I think makes for an interesting and varied suite of tools and techniques that you can use to extract data on users' experiences.

### Guerrilla testing

Back in 2018/19, I was working on a categorisation structure for key terms being used in ServiceNow, the software that manages IT helpdesk workflows. You may have used it if you have an issue with your laptop or you need some new software. Given that the user base trying to find information in ServiceNow is often a stressed human being who has other work to do, it's important to get people to the page they need without stressing them further.

We had created a taxonomy of terms to help locate the right area of ServiceNow and completed two rounds of online validation. The term structure was in a good state. But we felt that one or two nominated term selections were not quite as clear as they could be. We decided to iron out these creases through guerrilla testing.

Guerrilla testing is a quick and effective way to gain valuable user insights. An early design or prototype of a digital product is taken to users to gain 'on the spot' feedback. For example, you could have a prototype donation page on a laptop or device that you take out into a café or other public space and ask people in there how easy they find it to make a donation.

For this project, we wanted to know what the most popular syntax was for three of our categories. So, we walked up to people and asked them their preference.

The categories were as on the following page (Figure 6.4):

We asked random people around our office which of the options under the headers of 'Faults', 'Requests' and 'Knowledge' was the one that made the most sense to them. We gave them a pen to write their favoured option in the columns underneath and added everything up. We then chose the option that had been written the greatest number of times against each header.

And that was it. That allowed us to understand people's preferences. Simple, easy and effective.

Faults

1. Report an Issue
2. Log an Issue

3. Report a problem
4. Get Help

Requests

1. Orders and Requests
2. Shopping centre

3. Get stuff

Knowledge

1. FAQs, guides, and information
2. Guides, Info and FAQs

3. Knowledge base

| Faults | Requests | Knowledge |
| --- | --- | --- |
|  |  |  |

**Figure 6.4** *Template used for guerrilla testing on preferred names for categories in a helpdesk application*

## Roadshows

In 2016, I worked on a project to refactor our intranet at Cancer Research UK. We had an initiative called 'DigiTechFest' – a kind of interactive roadshow to showcase and improve our digital experiences. In the spirit of a roadshow, we chose a 'pirate' theme to help gather feedback on our new intranet's IA. Though it seems a little fanciful, it turned out that having a novelty theme for user testing garnered a lot of useful data from colleagues.

We printed out themed A4 pages and placed them on a whiteboard that could be flipped. We placed a sheet of A4 with a wooden ship in the centre, representing the homepage. We then handed four further sheets to participants, each with themed references to areas of an intranet. We gave instructions on the type of content the users were looking for and asked them to place the location they expected to find them on the flipboard.

We then told them: 'Please point to the place where you can learn about pay, salary and allowances.' The participants would sift through the following pages:

'Pieces of Eight' (pay, salary and allowances)
'Find Your Cap'n and Crew' (org chart)
'Afar from Ship' (working from home)
'Treasure Chest' (rewards package)

On the board were some category terms to place the content A4 sheets on. These consisted of 'Essentials', 'Our Teams' and 'Our Services' as intermediate levels between the homepage and the content page.

At the end of the roadshow, we added the totals of content pages for a particular intermediate page, to know where to place the content page. So, if 'Pieces of Eight ' (i.e. pay, salary and allowances) was placed, say, six times under 'Essentials' and three times under any other intermediate level, we decided to place the pay, salary and allowances content page under the 'Essentials' intermediate level.

From a roadshow with a 'pirate' conceit, we now had an information architecture that went:

- Homepage
-- Essentials
--- Pay, salary and allowances

And we trust that our participants had fun in deciding that for us!

### Meetings with picture researchers

A little more prosaic, if no less effective, than Jack Sparrow-themed roadshows was the user research we did at Getty Images. It took the form of a meeting. However, this straightforwardness was what made this process work, since we had a direct line into the needs of our customers. Face-to-face chats meant we didn't have to sift through endless data pumped out of Google Analytics (GA) or card sorting software. We got the information direct from human beings.

At Getty Images, there was a team called the Picture Research team. A client would phone through to the picture researchers and give their brief. The researcher would take a note of the brief, search in our internal image library, and get back to the client with the requested imagery.

This brought up a good 'from the horse's mouth' set of data about specific client needs. The client would ask for something esoteric like 'businessmen looking a bit nervous in front of a large skyscraper with a grey car - it has to be grey or maybe blueish - in the middle distance'. The researchers were well versed in the ways of how the search tool worked, so if they passed feedback onto us on the search team, it meant using existing keywords to find those images didn't work.

Neologisms such as 'metrosexual' would make their way to us, from the client, via the picture researcher. This filtering meant we had a handle on terminology that was business critical. That was great for us – we didn't have to research the words from a list in Google Analytics – the researcher had done the work for us, explained the type of images that should be associated with the keyword, and we could just go ahead and create the term.

It always felt like an efficient way of gaining user feedback with low latency and high accuracy. Once the term was created and relevant imagery associated with the word, the researchers would then feed back to us how well the search results worked. They'd suggest images the term could be further added to, and others it could be removed from, to improve the quality of the results. Tight search-building that came from a reliable and well-informed source – it's one of the best ways of managing user feedback I've seen.

## Conclusion

At the beginning of this chapter, I suggested that we should listen to users when formulating a taxonomy. What we've learned is that this could change the words that comprise your taxonomy. It can change the way in which you approach managing your taxonomy altogether.

One of the most difficult things to learn from making your taxonomy work in the real world is knowing you may have to put aside some of the taxonomy best practices you have learned. I still pinch myself sometimes when I remember moving the term 'marathon' from under 'running'.

What drove this was a desire to make our site more user centric. It's important to remember that users of Cancer Research UK's website may be concerned about their health (or that of a loved one), or interested in how to support us, how to work with or for us, or curious to understand more about the work we're doing. In all cases, we must make our world class content accessible to all these user groups. Using the language they use is therefore paramount.

Other times, taxonomy best practice should still play a part in formulating a taxonomy. In the case of our 'cancer type' terms, we ensure that the terms adhere to recognised standards. Whether using evidence from normal users or from more specialised places, we want our content to be findable.

Reviewing all the work I've done across various organisations, the bottom line is to use evidence. That can be from Google Analytics, cancer specialists, content editors, picture researchers or just people in an office.

In all these cases, common sense is your friend and challenging norms and assumptions is key. That way, you are always stress testing your vocabulary to ensure it fits the needs of the most important people: those who want to find something.

# 7 Taxonomy and Vocabulary Interoperability

*Yonah Levenson*

*Editor's note*: In my experience, organisations often talk about reaching the holy grail of data interoperability but may not know how to achieve this. Luckily, Yonah has loads of experience of working with complex, rich data and vocabularies, and making systems talk to each other, so she was ideal to cover this topic. It is not just a matter of setting up the systems or of mapping individual data fields or taxonomy terms. She also discusses the invaluable business skills needed to make everything run as smoothly as possible.

## Introduction
Welcome to my chapter! Throughout my career, I've implemented change. The changes range from process updates and improvements to system updates and new system implementations. No matter what the changes were, data was involved. This chapter focuses on what to consider when developing approaches and solutions in taxonomical work, especially where vocabularies and systems need to talk to each other.

## Thoughts as you read this chapter
- What's the best approach to facilitate the sharing of metadata between multiple systems?
- What are the data sources for each system?
- What are the data targets?
- What metadata needs to be shared? All of it? Some of it?
- What systems should be integrated with each other? How?

Your organisation has a database that is the central source of assets and their data, which traverse in and out, typically from multiple sources and going to multiple targets. How do those assets go in and out of the system?

What kind of information is exchanged for each transaction? It all comes down to metadata and workflows and ensuring that there are systems in your organisation to hold and manage this data.

Each system in an organisation is its own database of information and assets. In an ideal world, each system has the same metadata fields and controlled vocabulary values as other systems in the organisation, as well as externally.

The reality is that the metadata fields in each system differ, sometimes with just a few nuances here and there, while the names of other metadata fields vary widely. When the metadata field names differ, interoperability issues will exist.

## Why is interoperability between systems important?

In today's world, system users typically work on more than one application. When the metadata terms differ between systems, extra work is required to make sure any data that is imported from one system to another ends up in the proper metadata field. If there is exported data, that data also needs to end up in the right target fields.

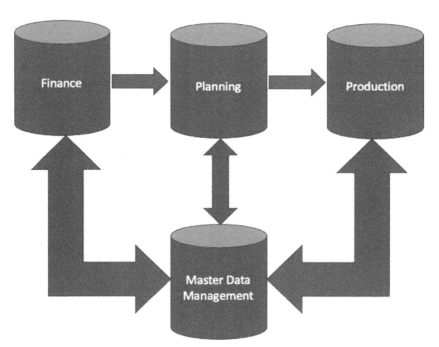

**Figure 7.1** *How metadata payloads are transferred between Master Data Management (MDM) and other systems*

In this use case, the organisation sells audio and video content (physical and streaming) throughout the country. There are multiple systems/databases that hold different data and assets, including:

- Marketing and advertising
  - Digital asset management (DAM)
    - Photography
    - Descriptions
    - Finished marketing and advertising pieces
- Media asset management (MAM)
  - Used for holding large media files such as video
  - Production work, including editing, is often performed in a MAM
- Product information management (PIM)
  - Production/inventory
  - Technical data including size, weight, etc.
  - Metadata needed for electronic data interchange (EDI)
- Sales/Points of Contact
  - Consumers/clients
  - Suppliers
- Financial
  - General ledger
  - Payroll.

Each of these systems will have its own metadata models or schemas. The systems need to interact with each other. The way to tie the systems together from a metadata standpoint is to have common metadata implemented throughout all of them.

## Metadata examples
There are seven typical classes of metadata, as well as Dublin Core's initial 15 metadata fields. These metadata standards are a good framework when considering interoperability.

### Seven classes of metadata
Here is a list of the seven classes of metadata. (Note: I am of the opinion that there may be an additional class of metadata specifically for analytics or measurement. Research is underway. See also Casey Schmidt's 'The subtle 6: Types of metadata you need to know' (2021), www.canto.com/blog/types-of-metadata.) It's important to keep these seven classes in mind

as you work on your implementation project, as systems in the organisation may have specific audiences and the data stored in each system is often specific to each audience.

1  Descriptive: the 'aboutness' of the asset.
2  Technical: information about the asset's file type, size, etc.
3  Administrative: when was the asset created? Who created it and last edited it?
4  Usage: where was the asset used?
5  Structural: what does it take to re-create this asset? If it's part of a group (like a book), what is the order of placement for this asset?
6  Preservation/provenance: metadata needed from an archival or preservation perspective.
7  Rights: can this asset be used? What context?

Below are examples of the seven classes of metadata as applied to the Dublin Core standard set of metadata.

## Dublin Core examples

**Table 7.1**  *Populated Dublin Core examples and metadata classes*

| Dublin Core | Metadata class | Example 1 | Example 2 |
|---|---|---|---|
| Contributor | Descriptive | Chadwick Boseman, actor | Charles Hart and Eliot Shaw, performers |
| Coverage | Usage | US limited release | New York |
| Creator | Descriptive | August Wilson, playwright | George Benoit, Robert Levenson, Alfred Doyle, lyricists. Ted Garton, composer |
| Date | Administrative | 2020 (release year) 2020-11-25 (theatrical release) | 1918 |
| Description | Descriptive | Ma Rainey and her band at a 1927 recording session in Chicago | 'My Belgian Rose' depicts the American military effort in Europe, particularly focused on the viewpoint of the soldiers. The soldiers describe an appreciation for the beauty that has been destroyed in the war and they express the hope of restoring that beauty once again.* |

\* Gier, C. (2008) Gender, Politics, and the Fighting Soldier's Song in America during World War I, *Music & Politics*, II (1), doi:10.3998/mp.9460447.0002.104.

*Continued*

| Dublin Core | Metadata class | Example 1 | Example 2 |
|---|---|---|---|
| **Table 7.1** *Continued* | | | |
| Format | Technical | HDR (streaming) | Notated Music |
| Identifier | Descriptive, Preservation | 10.5240/F845-2E38-C447-3888-9E41-Q (EIDR) Tt10514222 (IMDB) | Library of Congress Control Number 2013566353 |
| Language | Descriptive | en (English) | en (English) |
| Publisher | Usage, Rights | Sony Pictures Entertainment | Leo Feist, Inc. |
| Relation | Usage, Structural | Based on the play of the same name by August Wilson | World War I Sheet Music (13,976) The Library of Congress Celebrates the Songs of America (98,551) Performing Arts Encyclopedia (135,235) Library of Congress Online Catalog (1,164,959) |
| Rights | Rights | Sony Pictures Entertainment | Public Domain |
| Source | Administrative | Netflix | Library of Congress |
| Subject | Descriptive | Drama, Music | Songs and Music, World War |
| Title | Descriptive | Ma Rainey's Black Bottom | My Belgian Rose |
| Type | Technical | Movie | Sheet Music |

## The concept of minimum viable metadata (MVM)

An organisation may have a few or many thousands of employees. No matter what the size of the organisation, there will be multiple systems/applications. Metadata will need to be transferred from one system to another and/or be shared between systems.

How does one decide which metadata should be shared and/or transferred between systems? The best practice approach is to figure out what metadata each system needs. Then, create a mapping table or cross-map of all the metadata fields to find out which fields the systems have in common, and then further analyse the common metadata fields to determine which of those common fields are required (versus optional) for each system. Once the analysis is complete, those remaining fields are the MVM or minimum viable metadata.

Here is an example of the fewest number of metadata fields, or minimum viable metadata (MVM) (www.copyright.com/blog/let-minimum-viable-metadata-maximize-your-content-roi), that an organisation might need in each system in order to confirm that the asset returned via a search is in fact the desired asset:

- Title
- Language
- Quantity
- Customer ID
- Part # (Part ID)
- Format
- Date last edited.

Common metadata is the key to interoperability. MVM is the set of bare minimum information applied to each asset in order to facilitate interoperability between systems.

The terms listed in Table 7.1 may be enough metadata so that the searcher can confirm that the right asset has been found no matter what system someone is in/using.

## Inventory of existing metadata fields

An inventory of the metadata fields from each system is needed in order to determine:

- minimum viable metadata
- additional system specific metadata fields
- whatever other metadata fields 'shake out'.

The best way to conduct a metadata inventory is by cross-mapping all the metadata fields from each system in a workbook (see Appendix C), such as Excel or Google Sheets.

### Approach

What follows are the steps that one typically has to go through in order to get the list(s) of existing metadata fields:

- Request lists of metadata fields and their controlled vocabularies from the technology point of contact for each system
  - Ideally, the list(s) are in XML and/or worksheet
  - If not, take what you can get, as long as the information provided can be interpreted
- Ask for a data dictionary or a glossary of terms for each system
  - Is there a 'quick start' guide or instructional aid that is available?

- - Sometimes these types of documents have information about how to populate the fields in a specific system and therefore can be useful when researching metadata field definitions, etc.
- Populate the cross-map workbook
  - Overview tab: first tab of every workbook
    - Describe the purpose of the cross-map
    - Data sources
    - Links if they exist
  - Tab 2: Cross-map of the metadata fields
  - Tabs 3+: Create a tab for the master list of metadata fields for each system
    - Label the tab with the system name
    - Include as much detail as possible by capturing the following in separate columns:
      - Metadata field name
      - Definition
      - Source(s)
      - Cardinality
      - Type of field: free text? Controlled vocabulary?
      - Any other available details
    - The field name column from each system tab will be copied to Tab 2 so that the cross-mapping can be done
  - Last tab: Controlled vocabulary values
    - Create a column for each metadata field that has a controlled vocabulary value
      - Row 1: name of the metadata field
      - Subsequent rows: controlled vocabulary values for that metadata field.

**Table 7.2** *Metadata field name system, cross-map example*

| Inventory | Marketing | Accounts Payable | Preferred term |
|---|---|---|---|
| Title | TTL | Name | Title |
| Language | Lang | Lng | Language |
| Quantity | Number | Count | Count |
| Customer ID | Customer Number | Cust # | Customer ID |
| Part # | Pt Nmbr | Part ID | Part SKU |
| Format | Type | Digital | Type |
| Date Last Edited | Date Last Edited | [n/a] | Date Last Edited |

| Table 7.3 *Controlled vocabulary, cross-map example* | | | | |
|---|---|---|---|---|
| Language (system a) | Language (system b) | Language (system c) | Preferred controlled vocabulary | Notes |
| Eng | En | English | en | ISO 639 and IETF-BCP-47 |
| SPA | Sp | Spanish | es | ISO 639 and IETF-BCP-47 |
| Ger | Gm | German | de | ISO 639 and IETF-BCP-47 |
| Ital | it | Italian | it | ISO 639 and IETF-BCP-47 |
| Fr | Fr | French | fr | ISO 639 and IETF-BCP-47 |

Note: It may be necessary to also do a cross-mapping of the controlled vocabulary terms because they, like the metadata fields they're associated with, may have different values applied in each system. If that's the case, then either create a new workbook just for the controlled vocabulary values OR create a tab just for each system's controlled vocabulary values, and then do a cross-map of those controlled vocabulary values, just like for Tab 2.

## Metadata analysis

Once the cross-mapping of metadata fields and controlled vocabularies is complete, then the analysis phase can begin. To a large extent, this analysis process adheres closely to governance best practices (see Chapter 14 on governance for details on processes and approaches) and includes the same type of resources:

- stewards
    - subject matter experts
    - technology representatives, including data architects
- governors, who give the final approval
- technology/data architects.

### Analysis goals

The purpose of the analysis is to make sure the correct metadata fields and their controlled vocabularies are the ones that should be included in an integration of two or more systems.

Often, those in technology are focused on integrating systems, typically with the existing metadata. However, when updating existing systems as well as implementing new systems, it's best to look at what's available today, which is done through the cross-map exercises, and also to prepare for what's needed going forward and even future state.

Set up meetings with the stewards where open, frank conversations are held. Ask questions including:

- What are the preferred terms for each metadata field that should be used throughout the organisation?
- What metadata fields and controlled vocabularies are missing today?
- What's going on in the industry and/or the organisation and therefore what is the impact on the metadata field names?
- Are there new or upcoming departments in the organisation, such as analytics? What type of metadata do they need? Are those metadata fields and controlled vocabularies available today?

In other words, the scope of the analysis effort should be quite broad and the master list of metadata fields and controlled vocabularies should be included in the master list of metadata terms.

Once the extended lists of metadata fields and controlled vocabularies (CVs) have been collated, it's time to confirm which ones to include in each system and identify the overlapping metadata fields, including the MVM fields and controlled vocabularies.

## Workflows

Workflow knowledge and documentation are critical when planning to integrate systems. Often a metadata field will be populated initially in one system at the start of a process, and then the metadata gets updated as it traverses through various workflows.

In the content creation space, the Title or Name of the content or asset is a good example of a piece of metadata that tends to get updated periodically as it wends its way through the workflow. For example, the Title may start as 'Yonah's Working Title'. Then, as the creation process progresses, the Title may change to: 'A Day in the Life'. Further down the workflow, the final title may be: 'Yonah's Fantastical Day'.

When and where these Title updates occur is typically driven by a workflow. Additionally, the workflow has touchpoints on multiple systems.

## Sample workflow

The following is a typical high-level workflow for a movie being made by a studio (Figure 7.2 on the next page). All along the way, metadata is added and/or updated.

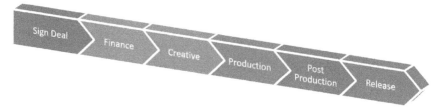

**Figure 7.2** *Typical high-level workflow for a media studio deal; metadata is added or updated at every stage*

## Workflow details

This section contains some details as to some of the metadata that's needed at each point in the workflow. Examples of metadata fields that may be updated as part of the workflow are included.

- Finance: Contract for a movie signed based on conceptual pitch
  - Minimum Viable Metadata captured
    - Ex: Title = 'Yonah's Working Title'
  - Master Project ID assigned
- Creative
  - Script editing occurs
  - Cast and crew is scouted and contracts are signed
    - Administrative: e.g., names and roles
    - Legal: rights
  - Metadata is captured in an editorial system
  - Title is updated to 'A Day in the Life'
- Production
  - Scenes are shot
  - Each original camera file (OCF) is uploaded into the MAM
    - Technical and administrative metadata is extracted from the OCF
    - Descriptive metadata is auto-applied based on dialogue and imagery
- Post Production
  - Usage: what OCFs or parts of OCFs were selected for inclusion?
  - Rights and legal: for music and images, product placement, etc.
- Release
  - Licensing
  - Sales
  - Finance.

The cross-mapping workbook should include columns for each system for which one is capturing the existing metadata fields. It should also indicate if the metadata field is initiated in that system and/or whether the field is updated in that system or further along in the workflow.

## Analysis!

Once the cross-map workbook is complete, it's time to analyse the data and figure out the patterns and how to move forward.

The following table includes representative examples of the types of data that has been gathered.

**Table 7.4** *Sample analysis of data, such as lists of metadata fields, in order to inform a system integration*

| Data needed | Analysis results | Notes |
|---|---|---|
| List of systems that share and/or require data transfers | The systems are: Finance<br>– Creative, including a database for scripts<br>– Production, including data on cast and crew, location info, dailies, etc.<br>– Post Production, including MAM for camera files, editing, etc.<br>– Marketing, including descriptive metadata<br>– Distribution, including scheduling, sales<br>– And back to Finance | Understanding the landscape is crucial for successful integration |
| Cross-map of metadata fields | MVM identified | In addition to the MVM, each system has other metadata fields unique to the system's purpose |
| System-specific lists of metadata fields | Rich, descriptive metadata is needed in the Creative, Marketing and Distribution/Scheduling systems, whereas Finance needs many identifiers for a wide variety of resources such as the content ID, cast and crew, caterers, locations, artisans, etc., to make sure invoicing and payments are correct | There are other metadata fields besides the MVM that exist in more than one system |

*Continued*

| Table 7.4 *Continued* | | |
|---|---|---|
| **Data needed** | **Analysis results** | **Notes** |
| Workflow(s) of when data will be added and/or transferred between systems | Some types of identifiers are needed from the very beginning of the project through to completion/distribution and so are very important to get right at the start – otherwise reconciliation is challenging | Knowledge of when and where the data is created, updated and exists is crucial for success |
| Metadata to be included in the Master Data Management (MDM) system | The identification of the specific metadata that is to be included in the MDM – the 'master source of truth' at any moment in time | MDMs hold the 'golden record' for metadata. Not all organisations have MDMs |

Knowledge of the data sources, the identification of where the metadata originates and which metadata fields make up the MVM, plus knowing where in the workflow the metadata may be updated, provides the foundation for system integrations.

## Mapping tables

It is a luxury to be able to create new systems simultaneously. Typically, systems are updated periodically and not all metadata fields can be renamed and/or completely synched up between systems.

When metadata fields in existing systems cannot be renamed for a variety of reasons - such as lack of budget to code those updates, document the changes, metadata payloads being sent to other systems that are not included in the update plan, etc. - there becomes a need to maintain mapping tables.

Mapping tables are literally just what they sound like: a table of metadata fields that capture the name of each metadata field in the source system and the name of the metadata field in the target system (Table 7.5).

| Table 7.5 *Mapping table example, with source and target metadata field names* | |
|---|---|
| **System A: Source** | **System B: Target** |
| Field Name | Title |
| Cust ID | Customer ID |

## Taxonomy systems

Throughout this chapter, the focus has been on using workbooks/ worksheets to capture and map metadata field names, definitions and system sources, etc.

Workbooks/worksheets are great for getting started and for presenting information in a 'flat' way that can allow one to see patterns. However, they can be problematic, as people tend to download shared workbooks to their local drives in order to do what they need to do. Thus, when updates are made to a shared workbook, the changes don't trickle down to the local instance or instances. This is when metadata terms start to get out of sync and problems are introduced.

In addition, architects and developers may end up re-keying the metadata terms, which often introduces typos and other errors. To give an example: the Title name was being transferred from system A to system B. In system B, the Title name was periodically truncated by a few letters. Upon exhaustive research, system A's field length was 103 characters and system B's field length was 98. Long titles with 99 or more characters lost the last five characters due to the inconsistent implementation of the field length names. Such errors can be time-consuming and expensive to resolve.

The next step for developing and maintaining taxonomies is to have a taxonomy tool where one can capture the same information. A huge benefit of having a taxonomy tool is to be able to capture information about each metadata term and how term(s) relate to each other.

Additionally, taxonomy tools can be integrated into an organisation's architecture and feed the metadata terms and their controlled vocabularies into specific systems. The specifics of the workflow for when new and/or updated metadata terms and controlled vocabularies are released are unique to each organisation and will need to be architected carefully to ensure that all systems are in sync.

## Master Data Management and taxonomy systems

Master Data Management (MDM) is defined as the system of record that holds the 'golden record', which is the most accurate and true metadata for an asset. An MDM system may contain other metadata as well. An MDM system's primary function is to instantly provide the best metadata of record to the requestor, whether it's a report or a metadata payload transfer.

A taxonomy system is similar to an MDM system, but instead of being a database of actual data, it holds the metadata terms for the organisation. One can identify the preferred or 'golden' terms an organisation implements. Maintaining metadata terms in a centralised taxonomy tool ensures that the best term is (a) available and (b) can be implemented, instead of hoping that the terms in spreadsheets are up to date and that no typos are inadvertently introduced.

There are many taxonomy systems out there to look into. Costs vary depending on the number of users and feature sets. They can end up paying for themselves through inferred or soft savings by avoiding rework due to incorrect metadata fields in workbooks and additional quality assurance checks.

A good set-up for taxonomy systems is to have three instances:

- Dev: development or working environment
- Production: live production environment that feeds metadata fields and controlled vocabularies to the organisation's systems
- Beta: duplicate of the Production environment that is used for testing, including integration.

## Building partnerships

Integration between systems requires effective communications between teams and departments across organisations. Sometimes, depending on the size of the organisation, some resources may be in the same department, and even the same team. Even so, it's important that there is written communications that describe the overarching project as well as specific integration goals.

Typical resources and roles needed for successful integration include:

- taxonomist(s)/ontologist(s) responsible for the master metadata field lists and cross-mapping results
- technology
  - data architects: ensure the payloads between systems are mapped correctly
  - developers: write the code to transfer data between systems
  - quality assurance for technical testing
- customer representation who performs final testing and approvals of:
  - metadata fields
  - integration between systems.

Together, these resources in their specific roles ensure that the metadata is available where it needs to be, as well as the ability to modify/update the metadata as appropriate.

Building partnerships between resources isn't always easy. When a taxonomist enters the picture, data architects and developers sometimes feel as though their territory is being encroached upon. The data architects and developers have typically been the ones who met with the customers to determine field names and definitions, with the decisions made in silos.

Adding taxonomists into the system development process, which includes determining metadata field names, definitions and examples, can be an adjustment. Some in tech welcome taxonomists to their fold as they are happy to have the burden of deciding metadata field names, documenting the definitions, cardinality, approvals, etc., no longer fall on them.

Creating partnerships between departments often means reaching out at a personal level in order to let the individual and/or team members know who you are, while you and others on your team get to know who they are. Understanding each other's perspectives makes for stronger working relationships. Here are some tips:

- Set up introductory meetings with key points of contact. Include managers so that those who have a broader view of the development landscape can learn about how they and their teams may be impacted.
- Brown bag lunch and learn sessions: After meeting with managers and key points of contact, set up time to present on how metadata management, cross-mapping and metadata standards apply to the organisation. Ask questions about their metadata pain points in order to determine positive solutions through partnerships and possibly modifying workflows.

It's always good to remind others in the organisation that success – whether it is for taxonomy terms and/or system implementations – requires team co-operation. Fostering relationships is a good way to begin.

## Integration benefits
There are many benefits that come out of applying the same metadata field names across multiple systems. Consistency provides a better experience for all who have to 'touch' the systems in any way.

Think about it. Those who interact with systems on a regular basis don't have to 'mentally' cross-map field names between Systems A and B. Data architects work with a unified data dictionary that they apply across and between systems and don't have to spend time figuring out what the metadata fields should be. The developers can often reuse existing code because the metadata field names don't change between systems, thus saving time and effort and providing typically cleaner data. The Quality Assurance or Quality Control teams also don't have to schedule as many resources and spend as much time developing new tests, as well as conducting tests, because there are few changes across systems.

Each time a consistent metadata field name is implemented in an existing system or in a new system, the organisation ultimately saves time and money because it's not necessary to reinvent the wheel.

If a new metadata field name is needed, that's fine - just be sure to adhere to best practices by performing due diligence. Conduct research and ask the following questions:

- Where did the request originate? Why?
- Does the metadata field already exist in another system? If so, will it work for this request? If not, why?
- What other systems will also need this new metadata field?
- If it's a new field, be sure to document it in all the right places.
- What are the resource requirements for adding a new metadata field? Approvers? Data architects? Developers? Quality assurance? Documentation and training?

## Conclusion

Successful integration of metadata terms and controlled vocabulary values can be straightforward when the right processes and systems are in place and when those who are responsible for the integration recognise the benefits and are on board for adhering to established processes, procedures, tools and systems.

Be sure to document agreed upon decisions so that when questions come up - and there will be questions - there is provenance to back up why a term was or was not used.

Prepare for the future. New metadata terms and controlled vocabularies are always going to be needed, so allow for expansion and facilitate implementation by using the right tools and systems. Systems knowledge and awareness provides perspective on integration approaches.

Build partnerships across the organisation, with peers as well as their management. Be a resource for all things metadata, including integration approaches, tools and best practices. Keep up with metadata standards appropriate for the organisation's industry and inform key contacts when there are terminology changes pending that will impact systems. These approaches facilitate planning, including budgeting, and resource requirements.

# 8 Everything that will go Wrong in your Taxonomy Project

*Ed Vald*

*Editor's note*: If you have been reading the book from the beginning, this chapter is a bit of an intermission. It is less about doing, and more about reflecting on, your taxonomy project. Once you have finished developing a taxonomy, it might be tempting to put your feet up and let the taxonomy's users and systems take over. But do not do that until you have read this chapter. Here, Ed shares some of the knottiest problems and misunderstandings that can arise from how the taxonomy is built and how it is being implemented. You may not need this chapter today, but one day you may find yourself thanking it for saving you a world of pain.

## Introduction

Whether at conferences or during sales pitches, we hear a lot about the benefits of taxonomy implementation and its untroubled project process. But what if you are not working for a company with a large budget, engaged workforce and mature digital ecosystem? Most taxonomy projects will struggle and face numerous hurdles to successfully complete, let alone succeed. Your real-world scenario may look something like this . . .

Your company has decided to take the leap and invest in a new taxonomy and you have been selected to be the new Taxonomy/ Metadata/Search/Knowledge Manager. Maybe you've been doing this for years or maybe your job has absolutely nothing to do with metadata; you just happened to be born unlucky and draw the short straw. How are you going to make this a success? Or, more importantly, how are you going to make sure as little as possible goes wrong?

Hopefully, you're knee-deep in documentation from the business and consultants (otherwise you are going to have to get busy creating it) detailing the taxonomy, the software, the integrations and the vital importance and cruciality of your mission to the digital transformation of the business. But if I were a betting man, I'd say you're working with nothing.

So, where to start?

A good place to start is to think about:

1   The taxonomy itself. Is it fit for purpose?
2   Where the taxonomy exists. The taxonomy won't live in isolation. It will be hosted in software, which is likely part of a larger digital ecosystem.
3   Who is going to use it? Let's not forget your users. Both customers and staff/cataloguers, who have to use your taxonomy and software, or . . . the dreaded C-suite/senior leadership team.

Worried? Scared? You should be.

Here's the less short and sweet version of the list above . . .

## Taxonomy build issues

Regardless of whether you built the taxonomy and have a familial and overzealous connection with its terms and relationships, or you have inherited a ready-built one and the romance is still blossoming, there's a good chance that the taxonomy is not perfect. (What does perfect even mean? Perfect for who? The taxonomist? The cataloguer? The end-user?)

As you set about implementing your taxonomy, here are some common build issues to keep an eye out for:

### Infinite loops

Have you checked your taxonomy for infinite loops? These are the occurrence by which a term is a Broader/Narrower Term of itself. Don't fool yourself into thinking this can't or hasn't happened, as it may be out of immediate sight, with two or more levels of relationships and distance between the reused term. This is more likely to happen with conceptually termed (that is, less literal and more thematic or topic based) Preferred Terms, or where relationships may be more ontological than hierarchical, but don't assume it can't happen to you. Some software may prevent you from creating infinite loops, but if your taxonomy allows polyhierarchies (the ability for a term to have multiple Broader Terms), the opportunity for an infinite loop increases as the rules for term creation are less likely to restrict where a term can live and its relationships. So, look out for the occasional hiccup, an example of which might look like:

- outdoor clothing
-- overcoat
--- coat
---- overcoat

Regardless of how an infinite loop was created, it can stay undiscovered until the terms are exploited, for example, through search, at which point you may find your scripts/search/functions fail to complete. Cue much head scratching from your developers. Be kind to your developers, and your users, by checking for the issue on a spreadsheet before implementing your taxonomy.

## Polyhierarchies

While we are mentioning polyhierarchies, consider during the taxonomy development phase if you really need them and, if you do, have strategies to maintain them. Good polyhierarchical relationships need clear rules, clear scope notes and user documentation, detailing how they will be created, applied and quality controlled.

For example, creating the term 'White House' as a Narrower Term of both separate 'buildings' and 'locations' branches of your taxonomy seems sensible enough:

- buildings
-- government buildings
--- White House

and

- location
-- Washington D.C.
--- White House

However, when you add the term '10 Downing Street' at a later date, how will you make sure that it also has relationships with both the Broader Terms of 'building' type and 'location' type, from the discrete branches? Will you remember? And what if you need to add 'tourist attractions' as a new Broader Term and branch at a still later date? How will you know to find all the current (and future!) 'tourist attractions' in your taxonomy?

It's worth considering using a monohierarchy (and faceted classification) and encouraging double-tagging, or triple-tagging, assets with the relevant secondary and tertiary classifications from the relevant branches, for example, create 'White House' under the Broader Term 'Washington D.C.' only:

- location
-- Washington D.C.
--- White House

Your cataloguer can then additionally tag the content with 'government buildings'. This may not seem an ideal solution, but it is one worth considering while you start building up your taxonomy – simply because it can be easier to maintain and grow a taxonomy with uncomplicated and clear rules. In this case, the rule would be, a named location lives under its geographic location and is additionally tagged with its building type and any other meaningful descriptor (geographic information, tourist attraction, landmark, etc.). Remember, just because you built it, it doesn't mean you'll be the person maintaining it. If the rules aren't clear now, they're likely to remain unclear. You can always set up a routine Boolean search string to look for 'government buildings NOT geographic locations' when you want to tidy up the catalogue and look for incomplete tagging.

## Taxonomy size

In addition to taxonomy structure, consider your taxonomy size. Bigger is not always better.

If your assets contain meaningful descriptive granular titles, does your taxonomy also need to be so granular? Consider the purpose of your taxonomy. If your taxonomy is cataloguing highly technical industrial products for a specialist audience using a 'create once publish everywhere' model, you may need a highly detailed and granular taxonomy. If you're planning on using the taxonomy for website filters, or browse navigation, a simpler, smaller choice of terms may be a better solution for your users. Making your taxonomy only as granular as the user requires will also improve cataloguing accuracy and simplify the user experience. Good things do come in small packages.

Try considering what would happen if you replaced your taxonomy with a simple flat file, controlled list, with roughly 10–50 discrete products/concepts. What would that be like for the cataloguer and front-end-users? What would your users lose and gain in terms of accurate tagging and search retrieval? Consider what functionality the taxonomy is driving and thus how complex your taxonomy really needs to be. Why should you be asking yourself this? Read on . . .

## Purpose

What's the purpose of your taxonomy? Ask this early and often. Your taxonomy structure, form and size, should only be as complex as its purpose requires. How many, and which, terms do your users require? Choice overload is very real, and users will always seek simplicity. In addition to giving the users the best, and simplest, experience, remember that every term and relationship will require maintenance, so don't give yourself (and future taxonomists) an unnecessary headache. Of course, you may be creating a complex company-wide knowledge graph, complete with multi-layered facets and ontologically confusing relationships. In which case, I pray to the taxonomic gods that you have adequate resourcing and a good mindfulness practice to keep you mentally well. Otherwise, keep it simple, Stupid. You can thank me later.

## Software and the digital ecosystem
### Bulk edits

Your taxonomy does not exist in isolation. Why do you have a taxonomy? Probably to create a list of terms to tag assets with. Have you considered how those assets will be tagged?

Even with the best user interface (UI) in the world, a system that only allows one asset to be tagged at a time will be slow for your tagger. If your content numbers thousands or millions of assets, how will you get them all catalogued? The key to good quality and useful metadata is accuracy and consistency. To help you achieve consistency you will need the ability to bulk edit your assets (adding metadata *en masse*). And not just at the time of creation, but any time a new term is created in your taxonomy and needs to be retrospectively applied to your collection.

If you have a bulk edit function, be careful. 'With great power', etc., etc. Make sure you know if you are 'overwriting' (replacing the metadata) or 'adding' (adding new metadata to the existing values) before it's too late. I won't bother frightening you by asking if you have a rollback function or strategy.

### Export to CSV

How can you audit your assets, and the consistent application of your taxonomy terms, without the ability to export a comma separated values

(CSV) file of your assets? 'Export to CSV' should be your mantra for every software supplier and/or developer you meet. Do not assume the content will live in an SQL readable database or that taxonomy terms (let alone their Narrower/Broader Terms) will be easy to review or audit. It can still be surprisingly common for software to not have the ability to export metadata to CSV. The ability to audit your catalogue, and see the metadata applied, is crucial.

## Search

Consider search configuration in parallel with your taxonomy. If your taxonomy is (in part or in full) designed to help the search experience by exploiting Non-Preferred Terms and Broader Terms, make sure you have spent effort on your search strategy. Do you even need a taxonomy strategy? Maybe you just need a search strategy?

What do you want to index in the search? Preferred Terms? Non-Preferred Terms? Broader Terms? The Non-Preferred Terms of your Broader Terms? Have you explained this to your developers/digital agency?

What about indexing the title or description or some other content descriptors of value? How about author name, topic and rights information? And which content and metadata fields do you *not* want to index to make the results as relevant as possible? Beware of indexing fields that the end-user has no interest in or that confuse the user. Online image libraries and galleries will often detail both the location depicted in an artwork and the location of the artwork, for example, Claude Monet's 'Le Grand Canal' depicts Venice, but the artwork (more accurately, one of the series) is currently located in the Museum of Fine Arts, Boston, USA. Which search term – Venice, Boston or both – would your user expect to find the image associated with?

How do you want to index the content? Are you using Boolean search and, if so, do you want a default AND or OR Boolean? Your developers will probably suggest you have a default OR Boolean. That's the default for SQL after all. But you'll want to ask for a default AND. Why? Because with an AND Boolean, even though you will get fewer results (all the search terms will need to be matched), they will likely be more relevant results. Top tip: if you're looking at the search on a website, try searching one term, then add an additional term to your first one and see if the number of results is increasing. If it is, it's likely an OR Boolean. Bear this in mind if your users are struggling with too many search results.

If you are using only Boolean operators in your search, you could consider a default AND search, but with a change to using an OR search if no results are found, though clearly marking this to the user ('these results contain any of the terms you searched for'). A developer/smart friend suggested this to me once. I still think fondly of this beautiful search solution.

Of course, if you are using search engine software such as Elasticsearch or Solr, you'll have even more choice. Maybe instead of considering your Boolean logic, you can use a 'minimum match' criteria. But what percentage of matched terms are you going to select? 100% is probably too high. 50% is definitely too low. Maybe set it at 60% (three terms in every five) and do some user testing.

Once you've decided what you want to index, and how you want to index, you'll need to give some thought to how you want your results ordered. If the desired search results don't turn up until page two, you'll need to do some more tweaking. To make the results as relevant to the search as possible, consider a 'title' match boost and/or most recent date boost. Of course, this is all very dependent on your content, your purpose and your users. So, speak to the stakeholders and especially the searchers.

But be wary of requests to make the search more 'relevant' (yes, I have used the term above . . .). Relevancy isn't a thing. It's whatever you, or your stakeholders, decide. Do you mean 'term frequency'? Or 'most up to date'? Or priority/ranking boost for a specific field? Or do you mean personalised content? Or recommended content? Or related content? You'll probably be asked to implement all of these (sometimes contradictory) results and rankings. Each stakeholder will have different opinions and concerns about this, so make sure you disappoint them all slightly rather than make just one happy.

Remember, if you hear cries of 'we need a taxonomy because the search isn't working', the problem is not necessarily a taxonomical or metadata issue. The problem is your search configuration. Fix it.

## Integrations

If you are lucky, your taxonomy will be hosted in the same software as is being used to tag and host your assets. Chances are you will not be lucky and you will need to integrate taxonomy software with your content management system (CMS), digital asset management (DAM) system, learning management system (LMS) or e-commerce platform (etc.), in addition to also plugging in search engine software to index your content.

Maybe you will need to integrate your taxonomy with more than one piece of software/platform. If that makes you feel nervous, you are right to start worrying. Repeat after me, 'every integration is a point of failure'.

Has the integration been made before? If it's not a well-used API (application programming interface) and if your developers are having to make something bespoke for you, there's an increased risk of failure. Assume it will break at some point and consider what will happen when it does. Does it prevent people from doing their job or the website from functioning? Will there be an irretrievable loss of data? (You were keeping backups with your 'export to CSV' function, right?)

Unless your software has native taxonomy functionalities, there may be no way around an integration (unless you have already decided to ditch your taxonomy in favour of that flat file list). So, tread lightly. Make sure you have a plan for when it breaks and have a good relationship with your developers. A great relationship with your developers would be even better.

### Artificial intelligence

At some point, someone higher up in the business will suggest using artificial intelligence (AI). It is at this point that you must immediately produce your AI swear jar (£5, or equivalent in the currency of your choice, is a suitable amount to fine for every instance of the term). Politely explain how you will need a massive corpus of content, preferably with existing accurate metadata associated, to train the AI (or more correctly, machine learning). You will also need to request a large sack of cash to purchase the overpriced software and overpaid consultants. If the cash arrives, you may want to add it to the other sack of cash you requested when you were asked to 'make the search like Google' or 'make the shop like Amazon'.

### Who are the users?

We've mentioned developer support and this is worth reiterating. Even with a relatively straightforward digital ecosystem or single piece of software, you'll need developer support. Are they in-house or an external agency? How much time will they have to support you and make any fixes or changes you require? Do they understand what you are doing? It's not enough to show people a fancy PowerPoint presentation – building understanding and relationships are more important in the long run.

If you don't have dedicated support, plan on making your systems and integrations as simple as possible for when they inevitably break.

In all likelihood, you've designed the taxonomy for the front-end-user, the seekers of content or information, and maybe your overly complex taxonomy has been shelved for a nice, small and clean taxonomy with a sensibly configured search, giving your front-end-user a great user experience. But what about your back-end taxonomy users? Your cataloguers, uploaders and content producers? They have to use the taxonomy on a daily basis. Have you built a taxonomy that is easy to understand without reams of documentation? Are taxonomy terms easy to find and apply? Are scope notes accessible and understandable? Consider staff turnover and the need to train and engage with new colleagues who may have little interest in taxonomy, metadata and search (yes, these people walk among us). There's plenty of information and advice online about how to work with senior business stakeholders and customers, but don't forget about your back-end system users, the cataloguers, indexers, taggers and content uploaders. If you aren't going to be tagging content yourself, speak to the people who will be and try to make their lives easier. Can they navigate the taxonomy and software interface easily? I've come across instructions longer than a page detailing how to use an autocomplete function for a taxonomy term selection tool! More than a page! To explain how to use an autocomplete. Why? Because the UI was badly designed (and the taxonomy too large). If you don't have an easy to use and understandable back-end and UI, you won't get quality metadata. Garbage in, garbage out.

Make your taxonomy, and its interfaces usable, not perfect.

## Conclusion

Hopefully the abovementioned cautions and recommendations may help you avoid some of the more common issues you might come across in your taxonomy project. Or at least help you mentally prepare for some of the areas that will inevitably not go to plan. Bear in mind, taxonomies don't live in isolation. They require not only taxonomic considerations in their build and maintenance, but also holistic considerations of (breakable) integrated systems, (uninterested) users and (ridiculous) business requirements.

Be realistic, keep it simple, (stupid).

Oh, and assume everything will break, because it probably will.

# Part 3
# Applications

# 9 Enterprise Search

*Michele Jenkins*

*Editor's note*: I was so glad that Michele agreed to write this chapter. Not only is she fun to work with, she is also a proper taxonomy and search geek. We've both had the experience of being asked to make an enterprise or e-commerce search work *just like Google* (spoiler: this is near-impossible if you don't have the money and developers that Google does). This chapter packs in a lot of detail about, among other things, search engines, facet design and synonyms.

## Introduction

As a taxonomy and information architecture consultant over the past 20 years, I have worked with dozens of organisations in industries ranging from public health education to snowmobile manufacturing. The domain, asset types, users and business goals are always different but the struggle with how to best connect people with information remains a constant.

Whether you are managing content, products or digital assets, such as images and video, taxonomy can play a critical role in supporting search from both a back-end and front-end perspective. When search is supporting several systems, either through a federated or pure enterprise search engine, having a unified organising system becomes even more important in order to provide users with intuitive, relevant and consistent results.

In the case of content, taxonomy and other metadata elements enhance the out-of-the-box text indexing and help make the link between natural/free text and your structured and controlled information architecture. While search engines are constantly refining and advancing the algorithms used to parse and extract meaning from text, they can still benefit greatly from the addition of taxonomy driven metadata. In the case of products and digital asset management (DAM), search is totally reliant on the metadata associated with the object (excepting cases of advanced artificial intelligence (AI), which can, in some cases, derive an understanding of a digital object – but even then, dig down and you will find taxonomy supporting the underlying ontology!).

Understanding the different ways in which search can leverage taxonomy will help you understand the impacts on taxonomy design including:

- considerations for term selection and form
- the importance of having a semantic hierarchy
- how extensive and rich your synonyms need to be (and which kinds)
- other term metadata that may be needed (e.g., associative relationships).

## A little bit about how search engines work

While we will not get into the deep technical details of search engines (much of which is very platform specific), it is useful to have an understanding of the high-level process behind the scenes (Figure 9.1).

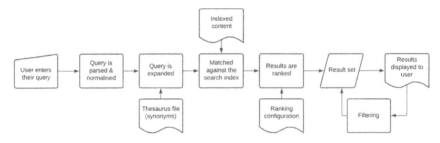

**Figure 9.1**  *High-level diagram of search engine mechanics*

The key points at which a taxonomy can impact site search optimisation are:

- The **thesaurus file** (sometimes called a 'dictionary') allows the search engine to add more to the query to increase the likelihood of a match. E.g., a user might search an e-commerce website for a 'night table' but the actual search would include 'night table', 'nightstand' and 'bedside table'.
- **Ranking** determines how fields, including taxonomy-driven metadata, should be prioritised. E.g., displaying a match on a subject term above a match in the body of the content.
- **Faceted filtering** allows the user to reduce the result set to only items that match terms selected from one or more facets.

'Why can't it just work like Google?' is a common refrain from users and stakeholders. Google will parse your query and then review billions of pages to determine which is the most relevant, authoritative and recent. It is important to understand that Google and other open search engines are able to leverage massive amounts of data based on links between content items –and the behaviour (and personal profiles) of millions of users entering millions of queries (both within a site and across the entire web). There's also the simple fact that there is an entire industry built around optimising sites specifically for Google's search indexer. Your site search will never have that sort of power behind it but you do have the advantage of having a finite set of assets and (hopefully) a clear understanding of your users' goals.

## Types of search

Search engines can manage many different kinds of digital resources in different contexts, each with different implications for taxonomy design:

- **Text searches** – On the surface, searching for words in a text, which is solely composed of words, would seem to be the easiest scenario to support. But human language is tricky: we can use one word to refer to multiple, distinct concepts and we can also use many words to refer to a single concept. Often, we can talk *around* a subject without ever actually referring to it in words. An article on reducing household trash may never say 'environmental sustainability', while a long, involved recipe blog post about grandma's spaghetti sauce might never include the words 'Italian food'. Taxonomy provides semantic hooks into natural language, offloading the work of understanding the meaning behind the words.
- **Digital asset search** – Unlike textual content assets, digital assets, such as images, videos and data visualisations, do not have a rich body of machine-readable information built in. While algorithms for autoclassification of images are becoming increasingly powerful, computers still have a very hard time telling the difference between two brands of shoes or styles of humour.
- **Product search** – Products may have extensive metadata associated with them, including technical specifications, financial details, marketing information and legal attributes. Some of those facets will be useful to internal users during product development, marketing or ongoing management, while only a subset may be useful for customers.

- **Enterprise search** – Enterprise search can return result items that span across multiple systems owned by different business units each with their own terminology and mental models. A granular taxonomy, well supported by synonyms and alternative labels, can allow different user groups to cut across silos.

## Development considerations

Taxonomies need to be designed and developed to support their specific use cases, the needs of the end-users and the goals of the organisation. In the context of site search, this impacts the selection of terms, the form of preferred terms, the types of synonyms and the structure of relationships.

### Term selection and form

A key decision point in defining your term selection and form criteria is whether or not the terms will be exposed to end-users, for example as search filters, and who those users are. If terms are going to be displayed, for example, in clickable links or filters, there may be limits on the number of terms that can be displayed at each level of a hierarchy or the overall length of a term.

A basic principle of taxonomy design is that each concept should be represented by one term only, but in practice we often rely on compounds and pre-coordination to support usability, increase precision or because of technical limitations (e.g., if it is not possible to combine multiple filters with a Boolean AND).

Compounds should be used sparingly and be made up of clear, individual concepts that are always discussed together or very closely aligned but not synonymous terms. For example:

- metrics and analytics
- machine learning and artificial intelligence
- food allergies and intolerances
- acne and oily skin.

A drawback of compounds is that they limit the ability to be more specific, for example, if you include a term such as 'Cholesterol, diabetes and hypertension screening', there is no way for a user to filter down to just 'diabetes screening' if it is not a child term. Additionally, compounds make it challenging to manage synonyms or mappings to other taxonomies.

Pre-coordinated terms combine multiple concepts, sometimes from different facets, to create a single, more specific concept. Creating pre-coordinated terms provides a shortcut to support a regular need to access content with that precise combination of terms, but overuse of pre-coordination will result in a bloated, unmanageable taxonomy.

## Examples of pre- vs post-coordination

**Table 9.1** *Comparison of pre- and post-coordinated terms*

| Pre-coordinated | Post-coordinated |
|---|---|
| Small red skirts | Colours: |
| Small blue skirts |   Red |
| Small red pants |   Blue |
| Small blue pants | Clothing category: |
| Medium red skirts |   Pants |
| Medium blue skirts |   Skirts |
| Medium red pants | Size: |
| Medium blue pants |   Small |
| Large red skirts |   Medium |
| Large blue skirts |   Large |
| Large red pants | |
| Large blue pants | |

Judicious use of pre-coordination can increase the precision of searches because there is a direct association between all the concepts and the target item. For example, if we define 'California university libraries' as a term and then tag several articles with the term, it is sure to appear at the very top of any searches for 'California university libraries'. This will perform better than if the content were tagged 'California', 'Universities' and 'Libraries'.

## Precision and recall

Precision and recall are two ways to measure the success of an information retrieval request.

High precision means that a large percentage of the total relevant documents were returned. For example, if there are 100 documents in a collection relevant to the search 'leadership skills' and 99 of them were returned by the search, then there was a high level of precision. But this does not take into consideration how many other, less relevant items were also returned. By this measure, returning every single document would have 100% precision (even if it's not very useful to the user!).

The level of recall, on the other hand, is concerned with the percentage of results that are actually relevant to the query. So, in our example from above, returning all the documents would have a recall level of zero but returning only 1 of the 100 useful documents would have a recall of 100%. Again, not very useful for an end-user.

Perfect recall and precision would mean returning *all and only* the desired documents. In the real world, this is difficult to achieve – but it is possible to tune the search for a specific subset of high-priority queries to get pretty close.

It is also important to consider the types of search that users are conducting. If they are mostly looking for an example or sample, such as any photo of a cat, then a high level of recall is fine. It is not a problem that they did not get every single photo of a cat. But if they are conducting a background search on a legal matter, then getting every single precedent is crucial, even if they have to disregard a number of irrelevant items.

## Structure

Facets should be mutually exclusive and homogeneous, that is, each facet should describe only one aspect of the asset and everything in the list should be the same 'kind' of thing.

When a taxonomy is only used for browsing or simple display, you can get away with having loose criteria for hierarchical relationships. However, when using taxonomy for search – specifically in search expansion and faceted filtering – it is important to keep the structure semantically correct. Ideally, a parent-child relationship should fall into one of the following categories (source: ANSI/NISO Z39.19-1993, 'Guidelines for the Construction, Format, and Management of Monolingual Thesauri'):

1  Child term is a **more specific kind** of parent term.
2  Child term is a **part of** parent term.
3  Child term is a **major and direct sub-topic** of parent term.

The third category is the most subjective and therefore most challenging. In many cases, it is easy to make a series of seemingly logical connections between concepts in the taxonomy that result in problematic hierarchies. Understanding where to use a hierarchical relationship versus an associative (related term) relationship often requires stepping back and viewing the taxonomy as a whole.

For example, you may start with Gardening, add the more specific subtype of Vegetable Gardening, then delve into Tomatoes, which are used in Spaghetti Sauce. But now your search engine thinks that Spaghetti Sauce is a subtopic of Gardening . . . Instead, clearly defined branches should separate the activity from the sauces.

If the taxonomy is used for hierarchical faceted filtering, the top levels must be useful and meaningful entry points for users to find lower-level terms. Tree testing is a useful tool for assessing the intuitiveness of your hierarchy. You can easily see where users' mental models differ from your assumptions. For example, if you ask users how they would navigate to the term to filter on the subject 'Accounting Standards' you may find that they first click on 'Finance' (because it is about money) instead of where subject matter experts placed it under 'Corporate Governance'. The deeper the hierarchy, the more choices users have to make.

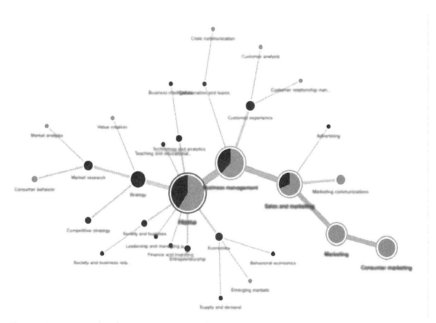

**Figure 9.2** *Example of a tree test output showing the correct route through a hierarchy (highlighted by the thicker line) and all the other places users went. (The text has been deliberately obscured for client anonymity; the diagram is provided in order to illustrate the complexities of building a hierarchy that can work even though users have many different mental models.)*

In cases where there is a deep split between different perspectives, you may need to resort to polyhierarchy – allowing more than one parent for a term. Note that not all search engines can handle polyhierarchy appropriately, so be sure to understand the technical implications before making any design changes. An alternative approach is to pick one parent and use an associative relationship to link to the less directly related broader concept.

Related terms can also be used to make shortcuts across the hierarchy to support getting the user from one term to another in cases where they do not satisfy the criteria for a hierarchical relationship (or a hierarchy would lead you down the garden path to spaghetti). When to create an associative relationship really comes down to whether it would be useful for an end-user. Search results derived from these relationships are best presented distinct from more direct results, often in a 'You may also be interested in . . .' context. Not all content management systems and search engines can make use of associative relationships.

## Synonyms

Human language is varied and messy. Explicitly defining terms as equivalent by adding synonyms to the taxonomy (which technically would then be considered a thesaurus) goes a long way to making the connection between users' needs and the search engine's code.

Selecting the correct approach to synonym development requires understanding how your specific search technology handles spelling correction and normalisation. Ideally, you should not need to create synonyms for regular variations such as verb tenses, plurals or common misspellings. But frequent review of search logs may reveal site-specific variations that are not properly captured by the search engine. If you are not able to make modifications to these functionalities, adding a limited number of targeted synonyms may be helpful to users.

While it is possible to use standard lists of equivalent terms (e.g., lists of British vs American English are widely available, https://en.wikipedia.org/wiki/Wikipedia:List_of_spelling_variants), much of the nuance will always be domain specific, that is, what may be considered 'close enough' in one context could be a crucial difference in another. In a general knowledge corpus, it may be enough to say a search for 'kittens' should return content about 'cats', but in a pet food store search or veterinary journal, this would lead to user frustration.

Table 9.2 opposite demonstrates flavours of synonyms.

**Stemming and lemmatisation**
- **Stemming** involves removing recognisable suffixes from words in order to get to their root, for example, 'caring', 'cared' and 'carer' would all result in the stem 'car'. This root may or may not be a valid word on its own. There are a number of different algorithms for stemming different languages with minor differences in their approach and output.

- **Lemmatisation** is a similar process that attempts to normalise a term to a basic word. Using the previous example, lemmatisation would be a much more complex algorithm that attempts to take into account the context of the word as well as basic rules about the target language's morphological rules.

**Table 9.2** *Different types of synonyms, with usage guidance and examples*

| Type | Used for | Example |
|---|---|---|
| *True equivalencies* | Multiple labels that mean specifically the same thing, i.e., address the same concept. Generally, true equivalencies should be truly synonymous in all contexts | Lift / elevator |
| *Acronyms and abbreviations* | Common shortenings of terms | CDC / Center for Disease Control |
| *Updated terms* | When the terminology has changed (but still refers to the same underlying concept) | Dotcoms / Start-ups |
| *Irregular stems* | When the search engine is not accurately accounting for different plural forms | Diagnosis / Diagnoses |
| *Alternate spellings* | When there is more than one accepted spelling | Flautist/ Flutist |
| *Common misspellings* | In cases where the search engine does not support spellcheck or it is not catching common misspellings | Knoweldge / Knowledge |
| *Domain-specific / unusual spellings* | When the content contains specialised or non-English words, e.g., recipe ingredients | Urfa biber / Isot pepper |
| **Near-synonyms** | Multiple labels that are *close enough* that users will expect them to be treated as synonyms in most cases | |
| Trade names | When a trade name is commonly used as a generic term (i.e., not all cotton swabs are Q-tips brand) | Q-tips / Cotton swabs |
| Vernacular | When there is a non-technical / layperson's term that may not match the technical definition | Vagina / Vulva |
| Jargon and slang | When users may have a shorthand for a more formal concept. Often useful when dealing with policy documents | Flex time / Flexible hours scheduling |
| **Expansion keywords** | Not true synonyms but can be used to broaden a search or support natural language processing (NLP) processes. | Singapore / Asia |

**Case study: taxonomy-driven search improvements**

A large, international content publisher was having multiple issues with user satisfaction around search, an essential part of their overall user experience (UX). A relevancy analysis showed that the key content was not appearing in the crucial first page of search results. A review of search logs revealed that users were encountering an unhealthy amount of zero results and even internal users, including staff and content contributors, were having difficulty finding things. Site analytics indicated that some users were giving up and leaving the site after looking at results and not finding what they expected.

Search relevancy

The first area we investigated was the overall search relevancy. One pattern that quickly became apparent was that less academic content meant for the general consumer audience was performing much worse in search relevancy. Content was not showing up in the first page of results even for very straightforward searches on a simple subject (which we knew there was content for).

We dove deeper into the search engine configuration and found that the out-of-the-box set up was prioritising matches found within the content's Title and Abstract field. This had worked fine for the other academic content collection where the Abstract field was a concise summary of the content, written for the express purpose of findability. The less formal content, on the other hand, often had creative titles and 'teasers' – captured in the Abstract field – to encourage users to click through. Unfortunately, many of these were useless for search retrieval: either lacking substantive concepts or using words that could easily mislead the search engine. For example:

Title: '10 Ways to Bring the Party'
Abstract: 'A least 6 of these will change how you do company onsites forever!'

Title: 'Don't Sweat It'
Abstract: 'Quick calorie burns you can fit in between meetings'

Title: 'Investment Banking's Me Too Moment'
Abstract: 'How quickly can change happen?'

Search engines come with a default ranking of standard fields such as Title, Body, Publish Date, etc. In most cases, you are able to add custom fields, such as taxonomy facets, and adjust the order to prioritise specific fields. Changes should be done with careful consideration and, ideally, tested thoroughly in a development environment before deploying into production. Note that not all search engines allow fine-grained control of ranking per collection or content type.

In the case study, the search relevancy ranking was adjusted (Figure 9.3) to boost the taxonomy-driven metadata fields – including Subject, Geography, Industry and Audience – above Title and Abstract for this specific content type. This way, the content authors were able to clearly indicate what the content was about while retaining their editorial freedom to have pithy titles and teasers.

| 1 = most important / 5 = least important | | | | | | |
|---|---|---|---|---|---|---|
| Query is topic term | ◉ 1 | ○ 2 | ○ 3 | ○ 4 | ○ 5 | ○ ignore |
| Query in title | ○ 1 | ○ 2 | ○ 3 | ◉ 4 | ○ 5 | ○ ignore |
| Query in abstract | ○ 1 | ◉ 2 | ○ 3 | ○ 4 | ○ 5 | ○ ignore |
| Query in body text | ○ 1 | ○ 2 | ◉ 3 | ○ 4 | ○ 5 | ○ ignore |
| Query in teaser | ○ 1 | ○ 2 | ○ 3 | ○ 4 | ○ 5 | ◉ ignore |

**Figure 9.3** *Example of search engine ranking configuration UI*

This same approach was applied to another collection of content in which the majority of content was PDFs hosted within a system that could not index the PDF body. In that case, the search relevancy was reliant entirely on the metadata.

For other content types, we took a more balanced approach but still kept the taxonomy-driven metadata fields high in 'the mix'. If a search query matched a term in *both* the abstract and a taxonomy term, that should rank quite high – well above a match in the body or title alone.

Search expansion
Going back to the search logs, we classified a sample of searches and how successful they were. We then identified key patterns in less successful searches (i.e., ones where the most relevant content did not appear on the first page of results). We found that users were having trouble when they:

- used different terminology than was found in the content
- used broader or narrower search terms
- searched on a closely related topic (for which there was no specific content).

This suggested there were issues with the search engine's thesaurus. The taxonomy being used by this system had very few synonyms, meaning that users had to search on the exact same term in order to benefit from the tagging and the search engine was also missing potential matches within the body content (Table 9.3).

| Table 9.3 *Examples of user search terms that did not match terms in the taxonomy* | |
|---|---|
| **User's search term** | **Taxonomy term(s)** |
| White-collar crime | Business crime |
| New York Times | Publishing Industry |
| Scandinavia | Denmark, Norway, Sweden |
| Cilantro | Coriander |

We evaluated the need for using synonyms, as well as expansion keywords in the thesaurus file. Within the thesaurus, there are two ways terms can be mapped:

1 **One-way mappings** support including more granular terms or specific instances of a kind of thing, e.g., searching for 'California' would include a search for any mention of 'San Francisco' and 'Los Angeles' (but a search for 'San Francisco' would *not* search for 'California' or 'Los Angeles').
2 **Two-way** (sometimes called all-to-all) mapping is used for true synonyms/equivalencies. Searching for any of the terms 'night table', 'nightstand' or 'bedside table' searches for all terms. (Actual implementation of thesaurus mappings is very platform specific, e.g., https://docs.oracle.com/cd/E80490_01/Cloud.16-6/ExtendingCC/html/s2213understandthesaurusentries01.html and https://docs.microsoft.com/en-us/azure/search/search-synonyms.

More advanced approaches to search expansion can include 'backfilling' by offering up potentially useful results based on taxonomy term relationships. For example, if a user searches for 'Scandinavia' and there are no results, they may be interested in results associated with 'Sweden' or 'Denmark', which are related terms. (You may have noticed how Netflix's streaming service makes extensive use of backfilling to ensure there is always a result for any search.)

Faceted filtering

Facet filtering allows users to narrow their search using taxonomy terms from different facets. Part of the initial taxonomy framework development is understanding which facets are useful to users, in what context and applied to which content types. User research included asking actual users about how they look for things and what they usually know as a starting point.

For example:

- 'I usually have a general idea of the topic but I don't always know what words they are going to use, so I drop in some likely keywords and then use the filters to get more exact results.'
- 'I like to stay up to date on whatever is trending in my industry, so being able to zoom in on anything related to Aerospace would be really helpful.'
- 'For me, I get a lot more out of watching a video than reading text so the first thing I do when I get search results is filter on format.'

It is also helpful to review search logs and map the searches to broad categories, for example, are they looking for subjects, people's names, places, product categories, etc.

Once you have selected the useful facets, they should be displayed according to priority/usefulness (with the most useful/ frequently used at the top). User testing with clickable wireframes or mock-ups can help ensure you have things in the right place and that the facet labels are intuitive. You may not want to use the internal names as facet labels, for example, 'Content type' or 'Asset format' may be confusing to end-users.

After faceted search is launched, keep an eye on analytics to see if people are actually using them. If not, go ahead and remove/simplify.

Search result pages

Our research suggested that a significant percentage of users were not necessarily looking for a specific document but were engaged in 'berrypicking' (sometimes called an 'evolving search') where they perform a search and learn from the results how to better refine their search or explore related material. Through this process they collect 'berries' of information.

Berrypicking behaviour can be supported by providing a rich – but not overwhelming – search results page. When designing the overall page, taxonomy can be used to highlight related content to explore, even from separate systems, such as training available in a learning management system (LMS) or people that have expertise in a topic. It is also possible to use the taxonomy associated with a set of items to control the page layout, for example, creating a sidebar of videos ('content type' = 'video'), highlighting a specific subject or creating expandable groupings by other common elements.

# Conclusion

Search engine technology is a rapidly evolving domain. While many organisations still struggle with the fundamentals of customising and optimising site search, others are experimenting with innovations in natural language processing, interactive chatbots and voice-based systems.

Artificial intelligence and machine learning can seem like a magical solution that can do away with the need for content models, taxonomies or fiddling with search ranking. But these approaches derive their intelligence and learning *from* explicitly defined underlying structures and relationships, that is, taxonomies, ontologies and semantically structured content. If anything, they make solid, usable taxonomy even more critical because it will be used to make thousands of decisions about meaning and relevancy without the direct oversight of humans. Taxonomists and other information architects are critical to understanding the needs of users and translating machine intelligence into good user experiences. Regardless of which of these technologies become mainstream, for the near future at least there will remain a need for humans and their deep, intuitive understanding of content, context and intent.

# 10 Taxonomy and Digital Asset Management

*Sara James and Jeremy Bright*

*Editor's note*: When I was searching for someone to write about taxonomies and digital asset management (DAM), Sara and Jeremy came highly recommended from friends in the industry. Their chapter is adapted from a wide-ranging conversation between them and covers all the bases for anyone who needs to plan and manage DAM taxonomies. Unlike taxonomies for predominantly text-based content, DAM taxonomies also have to account for the attributes of images, videos and other multimedia assets, which may be part of a complex lifecycle from commissioning through to rights management, usage and potentially reuse too.

## When you think about strategy for taxonomy and DAM, what stakeholders do you have in mind?

**Jeremy Bright**: Well, I think there's general users, business users, platform owners, administrators, etc. So, thinking of end-users, the people who actually need to access the content, business users, the people providing the content, and then platform owners and even dev. I think that each of them has a role in what this all looks like. And they're different pieces of the story.

## Where is the right place to start?

**Sara James**: Let's start with the ecosystem. I think, when we're talking about the DAM itself, there's always a question of where it sits within the ecosystem and whether or not it can be standalone technology or whether or not it has to connect and share its data, share its metadata and share its taxonomy. Plus, whether it has to play nicely with other pieces of technology and data or whether or not it can go solo. There are many things to consider, including what you are trying to accomplish and what success looks like. For example, are you doing e-commerce, in-store, packaging, etc.? Are you doing something that involves a lot of other moving pieces? Usually, it's better to think about DAM and its taxonomy and metadata as it sits within the full ecosystem. If you're doing a lot of FMCPG (fast-moving consumer product goods) work or pharma work, where else does this fit within your ecosystem? DAM is rarely able to stand alone; it usually has to be a part of something else – your content management system (CMS), your product information management (PIM) system. Once you start thinking about the other places your metadata has to exist and interact, then master data has to be a consideration. When you do it piecemeal, you run the risk of creating metadata and taxonomy schema that don't align with the rest of the business and has to be redone over time.

**Jeremy:** I think a piece that I've seen lots of folks struggle with is the idea of a technical integration versus taxonomy as the integration. It takes a lot of dev time and it's expensive to integrate systems that are not built to be integrated. If you think of your taxonomy in a way that is easily cross-mapped/cross-walked, or whether it uses similar terminology across multiple systems, then you're creating a situation and a context where you never have a standalone system – you never have siloed data in any way. It's integrating across multiple systems, even if it's not a technical integration. It's thinking about taxonomy broadly, about how it applies to all of your business needs, not just DAM specifically. Because, like you said, DAM is almost never a standalone platform. You have to think about how your taxonomy can be used for multiple purposes in language that's understandable for everyone who needs to use it; it creates a less expensive version of 'integration'.

**Sara:** I think that's a great point. There's the whole idea of everything being user-friendly. Thinking way back to the beginning of my career, which was very heavily CMS- and web-focused, there was a focus on all of your content vocabulary being for the end-user. It had to be consumable by a web audience. And so when you built your back-end metadata schema for CMS, it was 'how do you map that to your front end-user experience?' Expanding upon what you're saying, that vocabulary set should be able to be extrapolated across the entire ecosystem and from the back-end to the front-end. In the old days, we used to do that with a thesaurus. It was A LOT of thesaurus mapping – that's a lot of work. If you're thinking strategically and holistically about your data set, you're thinking about 'what is the common vocabulary/this common language, and how can I extrapolate it across the system so that I'm not at cross purposes?' Does your DAM have to use such siloed language or can you have shared vocabulary, the same vocabulary that you're using in your CMS, in your PIM, in all your e-commerce systems, and so forth? If you can create that common vocabulary set, everything else is easy. It's the vocabulary that's hard. And understanding your content creators and your content consumers, making sure that they all have shared vocabulary as well. Often, your content creators use jargon that your content consumers don't understand at all.

**Jeremy:** EXACTLY. The taxonomy is the bridge between content creators and content consumers. Think about language that suits both of them. Even if it feels too simple for one and slightly too advanced for the other, you'd rather end up in the middle ground where anyone can come in and know what you're talking about immediately, just based on the taxonomy that exists. When most people think about strategy, they focus on planning forward, but they never think planning forward also means legacy. What can I leave behind that someone else can easily pick up and start working with without having to dig through mountains of documentation to understand why decisions were made? Clear decisions up front about creating controlled vocabulary - it being clear, even instinctively, why it's controlled rather than free text - can make such a big difference, even if it changes and modifies over time. Think about what happens the day that you're not there, because that is when it really comes into its own, capturing all the decisions and work you have put into it.

**Sara:** I totally agree. When I lead a lot of taxonomy workshops, I like to say, 'It's so important to think about this in terms of your new users - the new person who is starting today. That person has never seen our product list; they have never seen our assets before. As they sit down at the DAM, can they find where to upload their assets? Can they understand how to tag them correctly with metadata?' If you have created overly complicated schema, the answer is no. If you have created fields that are illogical in how one is free text and another is a dropdown, and they don't understand what is permissible free text, then you have this new person who is going to struggle to learn the system and learn best practices. Whereas, if you make it clean and intuitive - I know intuitive gets thrown around a lot - but when you make it as intuitive as possible, then someone sits down and goes, 'Oh this isn't that hard'. That's the experience you want people to have.

**Speaking of system integrations, including technical integrations between multiple platforms, is there really a lot of overlap between PIM and DAM that would necessitate a shared vocabulary?**

**Jeremy:** You have to think of the shared taxonomy between them and how it makes sense. PIM is a good example. Lots of corporate DAMS are connected to PIMS in order to provide the right visuals with the product information, so that you can get that data out. If there is even one mistake in there, it becomes much more complicated to manage. Some people who are using one system or another may not have the foresight to think, 'How far ahead should I be thinking about what I'm doing now?' This is especially true if you're a very large organisation. Flexibility is not always a strong suit, because you have to think about so much information and so many stakeholders. It just necessarily takes more planning and resources.

**Sara:** Sometimes, people say, 'I'm the platform owner for DAM. I'm the platform owner for PIM. So all I'm worried about is my platform, my users, my data. What you do with your platform is your problem.' And they build their platform in a silo, and then they just want to plug and play. They just want to plug it in and have it work. 'If your stuff doesn't talk to my stuff, that's not my problem.' That is very small thinking and it is very typical of large organisations because people have their little fiefdoms. Which is why we tend to advocate for a master data team to own the data. If they own the data and the data tables, the data pushes from the master data set into the various platforms and there isn't that idea that 'I've created all my PIM data and all you DAM people just have to live with it.' There should be data standards and everyone has to play by these shared rules. Common language and vocabulary are at the heart of those rules. You might have a subset that is unique to your platform so there's master data that's true for all. That's the 80/20 rules. There might be 20% just for DAM, 20% just for PIM, but they don't need to talk to each other ever, for whatever reason. But that master data is key to making everything in the ecosystem work together. It's probably not exactly 80/20, it's probably closer to 90/10. But there's still that ability to have that governed table that everyone doesn't get to mess with.

**How do you get away from the silos and towards consensus?**

**Jeremy:** One of the biggest pitfalls that I see is the way that some conversations are had and not having all the right people in the room at the same time. Instead, you come up with the plan, then you bring it to someone and they're like, 'Wait, wait - now I have to think about what I'm doing and how it fits into this.' Instead, bring everyone together at once, talk about what the goal is and collectively decide how to get there. That's where success is. Success is in collaboration. There is inevitably some need that you don't know about that someone has for your system and that need should be reflected in what you're doing.

**Sara:** 100%. Totally agree.

**Jeremy:** If there's any kind of syndication platform attached to either your DAM or your PIM, and there are assets flowing between them, understanding the difference between a value and a label and how taxonomy can work between systems can help anyone you're syndicating content to. I can guarantee you that the retailer you're working with who is a giant national chain is not going to use the same language that you are. Always remember that content doesn't just live in a DAM – taxonomy creates the methods of distribution. Otherwise, what's the point of putting it there?

**Sara:** Yes. It's a really good callout about how it gets distributed as well. Your DAM should set you up. The whole ecosystem and how you create your taxonomy should set you up for that distribution. You're not just creating assets because they're pretty and you want to store them somewhere, you want to reuse them. You want to use them as a part of campaigns, you want to reuse them as a part of your business. Your ability to use them is your ability to distribute them. You might be using a distributor or an aggregator for distribution to push to those different retailers, but all those different retailers have different requirements. You have to understand that your language is transferable to each of those. That means that whatever technology you're using as the interim technology between your DAM and that retailer's site also has to have language that's a good pass through.

**Jeremy:** Inevitably, we're all going to run into a situation where we have to think about cleaning up data. It happens to all of us all the time. In a situation like that, the first thing I'm going to do is ask, 'What's the most important thing you need to get out? What's the second most? The third most? Tell me the least important thing, so I don't even have to think about it right now.' That thing may either be one whole set of assets or one field for all assets in the system. It doesn't really matter, but understanding the importance of the restructure, the change, the end-user, is how you can actually create a realistic plan that allows you to transform things quickly and clean up the way you need to. And the key to that is having consistent data and a consistent taxonomy. When you have that, it allows you to very quickly pull out what you need, look at the commonalities between them, make changes, ingest and update, and repeat until your assets or your data are in the place that you need them to be. The moment you break away from consistency, you make the problem much harder to resolve. And planning for it – any plan will have snags that you haven't thought about.

The less consistent your data is, the more snags you will encounter, particularly unanticipated snags that slow down the process.

**Sara:** I think you're absolutely right. That makes me think about migrations and new platforms. When you're migrating to a new platform (which you invariably will be) or you're installing a new piece of technology that you haven't previously used, having that modular vocabulary enables you to onboard new technology really easily. And it allows you to be technology agnostic, so it's really important from a perspective of 'Should I use this DAM or that DAM?' or 'We used this DAM for the last five years, but it's time to switch to a new DAM because this old DAM doesn't have the three things that we need and this new DAM does.' If you have that clarity of your data, you can plug and play your technology. Your new technology plugs in, your data ports over – it's not a problem.

Same thing if you put something new into the ecosystem – you just put in a new piece of technology and the data works. But if you have any garbage in your data set, then trying to move and migrate from old DAM to new DAM becomes a huge mapping exercise that is time-consuming, nauseating and it makes your eyes cross. It's a huge loss of time and productivity. I've seen so many migrations fail, because they have a massive data set – 50k, 500k assets – and some of the mapping went wrong. Because the vocabulary set didn't match because of data set A and data set B. Because the new DAM is structured *this* way and the old DAM was structured *that* way, and the platform owner who got control of their platform vocabulary said, 'Well, we think there's a better way to structure the taxonomy. And I own the platform, so I'm going to redo it.' Well, great – you've now just created this massive headache and thing to untangle. And now this mapping exercise has failed. I saw this with a client years ago where they were moving from platform A to platform B. They had a terabyte of assets. I don't know how many rows it was – I think they had close to a million rows in a spreadsheet and each one of them errored out.

**Jeremy:** I would die.

**You both work at ICP, which advocates for being platform agnostic. But when is the time to change platforms? When is the grass greener?**

**Sara:** There's a lot of things to take into consideration. The step that people always skip, which is where they call us in, is where they haven't done due diligence on what their requirements are. What is working well today? And what is not working for us? People always do the 'Nothing's working today. Please make it better.' But they don't do the 'Well, there are a series of things that if you took away today would shut everything down.'

**Jeremy:** Yup.

**Sara:** We need this functionality and we're used to doing our jobs in a certain way that works for us. There's also the functionality that we don't have today that is impacting our ability to do our jobs. Look at your existing platform and ask yourself, 'Can the platform do everything we need?' Have you configured the functionality within the platform in a way that is causing problems or a sub-par user experience? Or does the platform not have key functionality to create the optimum user experience? If it does not have those things and you need it to do them, it's time to start looking at other platforms. There's also some older platforms and some nice platforms that don't have storage capabilities. If you're getting to a point where you have 5, 10, 15 terabytes of data, you've ruled out a whole subsection of DAMs.

**Jeremy:** Circling back just a little, requirements gathering is one of the most important pieces and therefore the thing you should do first. Don't first aim for a platform and THEN do requirements gathering because then you've already biased yourselves. First talk about what is working and what isn't working. Then open up to any of the other platforms that exist out there. For some platforms, it can be a lot easier to have flexibility around taxonomy than it would be to not have flexibility. Some are so tightly controlled that you have what you have and you have to make it work. Others are not as tightly controlled and are very flexible but require a lot of dev time to build in needed flexibility. Others require no dev time because they're built in with the flexibility that's needed. Think about that because it is a cost in one way or another. Super stringent? Probably fine for a smaller organisation with fewer needs. Not as stringent or requires dev time? Great – you need to have budget to support it. The most flexible system probably requires a lot more maintenance to ensure that it's continuing to evolve and meet the needs of your organisation without becoming stagnant.

**Sara:** And understanding all of the needs that you have, back to requirements – there's requirements for upload, download, workflows, metadata, storage – so many different areas. Understand the robust depth of your need in each of those areas. Taking metadata as an example, if I look at some of the older platforms, there was one that was notorious for logging and inflating the data table every time you did anything with your metadata. Whether you changed a value on your asset, whether you deleted a value in your metadata, any change that you made to the metadata on that asset, it did a log back to the master log. Slowed down performance.

You created this massive audit log that was a huge bloat. It was a call to the log every time for any change to metadata. If you were never going to touch your assets and it was just for storage – you were going to upload your asset once and be done, treating it like an archive – great. But if you were going to actively use the assets day in and day out, it was horrible for performance. You'll get five users in the system and the thing would grind to a halt. I'm not going to name names . . .

**Jeremy:** That's not doable!

**Sara:** You want to know what your metadata needs are. Are you actually touching your metadata frequently? Are you uploading assets and tagging them with a whole bunch of metadata once? Are you treating this like an archive? Is this just a storage box? That's a different need all together. Remember to ask the people creating content or a platform owner. Do we have people who are in the system day in and day out? Do we have to have top performance? My guess is yes; you always need good performance. Do you need an audit log? I always lean toward yes.

**Jeremy:** Unless you're the only one using the system, you NEED an audit log. If there's anyone else touching it, you do actually need the log because you need to know how assets have changed. Particularly when it comes to migration – you need to understand what *was* before you can understand what you *want to be.* Because there will always be a point where data has changed three times – you have an asset that's older and you want to figure out why does this metadata look the way it does? It doesn't match anything else, or there's a mysterious value, or I don't understand why it's titled this way – let me look at the legacy metadata or the audit log. Was it actually a system problem? Did something in the system cause a change I didn't action?

**Sara:** Exactly – that was going to be my next point. When do you need to roll back? An admin will come in and say, 'I was told to come in and make this change.' And they just do what they were told because it's all just this system stuff, no big whoop. And they go in and make this change and they don't realise that they've just edited thousands of assets – and that impacts the ability of users to find and utilise those assets. But they don't know – they were just following orders. And now they've just decimated an entire collection of assets. The audit log is crucial. Some DAMs don't have an audit log. It's important to know what the limitations are but also what your needs are. When you talk about 'Should we re-platform?', I think that executives come from a place where new technology solves problems and they always want to find a shiny object and play with a new toy. First, start from: what works today? What doesn't work today? What are you unsuccessful in accomplishing? What does success look like for you? If you can define success, you can define your requirements. If you can do that, you can determine whether or not you move to a new platform. And if so, which is the new platform for you.

**Jeremy:** Exactly.

**Sara:** But I don't just say, 'Oh yeah, there's a new platform on the market. You should totally try it. It's cool.' That's never the right way to go. It's funny, years ago, when Google was relatively new you could implement them as your internal search engine. The company I worked for at the time said, 'We want to buy this.' And I said, 'Don't do it. The experience you have on the web is not going to be the same as your internal experience because of the way the algorithm depends upon the number of people searching AND what they do with the search results. On the web, Google gets millions of people searching and selecting results every minute. That helps the engine refine the result set. Internally, at our little company, it would take a dozen years to get enough data to refine the algorithm. We cannot provide enough data to the machine to get the intelligence we are used to on google.com.'

Sure enough they bought it and sure enough everybody was like, 'Why does it suck? You did it wrong.' The team said, 'We did exactly what Google told us to do.' And we went and reverted back to our old search engine. You have to know what this thing can actually do and did we do it right as well. In that instance, we had none of our internal content tagged with appropriate metadata. That's when I had to learn all about metadata. And then, you know, you have to tag everything correctly so it's findable. Whether it's findable by search engine or findable by your DAM. Or whatever it is. You've got to know that you've got the infrastructure for that technology to be successful. And then it is the right technology and not just the coolest new toy.

**Circling back to user stories, what is the value of creating them and why do you need to create them?**

**Jeremy:** The two most important user stories to consider are content creators and content consumers. For your creators, you *want* them to be super users of the system. You want them to understand exactly how to use it to get what they want so they can get content in. Your content consumers? Never expect that they'll be super users. You may have folks who can come in and figure it out, but they may never understand the depth of the platform in the same way as a content creator. Especially if it's a creator who's ingesting content. Make them evangelisers of both the platform and the taxonomy, because it's really people with that knowledge who can help explain why something is. In asking their input and creating the user story of why they need a platform and a taxonomy to work a particular way, that's when you get the most buy-in. And when you're actually creating something for users rather than product owners.

**Sara**: When you look at consumer user stories, you have to think about it almost from a novice perspective. This is someone who's going to be coming in randomly, from time to time - this is not the job that they do all day long, day in and day out. It's something that they are coming into as part of what they're trying to accomplish, they're just dipping in, grabbing what they need and getting right out. Therefore, you want this to be as easy to use and as intuitive as possible, so that they can come in and grab what they need without interrupting the rest of their workflow. It should not interrupt the rest of what they're trying to accomplish. You have to think of it from the perspective of when was the last time you did something completely unfamiliar to you? How easily could you pick that task up and do it in two minutes flat?

**Jeremy:** It's really important to make sure that when someone is accessing any assets, they're seeing the right metadata for them. I think one of the most important pieces for protected intellectual property is rights management. Making your rights statements clear, making sure that this field is clearly labelled as *'this is how this can be used'* creates less risk for the organisation, but also informs users who may just be looking for something that has no rights on it. It can be used in any way so that they can transform it, or if they want to localise it for their market or want to recreate it in a different way. Give them the information that they need in order to do whatever job they're doing, whether that's in the public sector where they're taking publicly available, accessible and usable information and transforming it and using it in a different way; or the private sector, where they're taking information that may need to stay protected in one way or another and using it within whatever rights there are.

**Sara:** If I'm a user who comes in once a month, the system, from my experience, looks the same in January, in February, in March, in April - my ability to interact with it, get in and get out, is the same. The metadata schema isn't radically changing. If new metadata is introduced, if a new taxonomy is introduced, it follows the same logic that it has always followed. I'm not relearning the system all the time. It also benefits the content creators - if you're thinking in terms of how to make it simple for the content consumers, that makes it simple for the content creators as well. As long as the vocabulary is a shared vocabulary. That's back to where we started this journey – a lot of times, consumer and creators don't have the same vocabulary. If you can get their vocabulary aligned, then when you're creating that experience for the consumer, you're creating an easy experience for the creator as well.

**Jeremy**: I think that's where governance really comes in. The only way to accurately reflect in a taxonomy what actual needs are for all of your user groups is through governance. Even within a single platform, needs will change over time. Know that it will happen. Unless it's a pure archive, never to be touched again, never added to, never changed, rarely accessed or accessed from a read-only standpoint, it will change. It will grow. You will have new needs. You will have new user groups. Governance is where that really becomes an easier process. You establish the right people who always should be in the room to make changes, you ensure that you have a regular cadence, if the cadence is 'no updates, everything is fine', which is probably not going to happen, especially if you're part of a larger organisation. Your user groups are necessary for input. You'll learn more from having all those people in the room and having the right conversation – even if you're just a facilitator, rather than a decision-maker. Understanding what needs exist can help inform how your taxonomy needs to change over time. Having a governance group leads to more cohesion, rather than less. It seems like people might fight when they want something, but if they have to make a case to a room, rather than a person, they're more likely to bring a stronger case. They're more likely to say, 'Here's why this is important, here's the outcome I'm looking for.' And even if their plan or their preference isn't something that can be met, understanding the outcome means that the whole group can decide on how to move forward in a collective mindset about the importance of the DAM, the importance of the taxonomy and the importance of end-users.

## Conclusion

At the end of the day, building taxonomy and metadata for your DAM is about the legacy you are leaving after you are gone. Will this system be intuitive to a new user? Will this system be adaptable and scalable? When someone else is maintaining this system, will they know what decisions were made about your naming conventions, your overall governance and rules, and can they successfully add new values seamlessly? If your taxonomy is so complex that the people that come after you cannot manage it, it will never stand the test of time. The planning you do up front to ensure you taxonomy is sustainable and scalable, can cross-walk across platforms and can be understood by new and infrequent users, is the key to creating a taxonomy legacy that any admin would be thrilled to inherit.

# 11 Powering Structured Content with Taxonomies

*Rahel Anne Bailie*

*Editor's note*: Structured content is an exciting evolution of digital publishing that promises both efficiency and opportunity for organisations that are willing to upend their traditional content production processes. Tagging and taxonomies are key components – otherwise, how does the system know what something is and where it should go? Rahel has evangelised the structured content approach for years and we have worked together on projects for clients who are interested in reaping the benefits.

## Introduction

When it comes to content, the statement by Greek philosopher, Heraclitus, is the most appropriate: the only constant in life is change.

Content goes back beyond even hieroglyphics to scratchings on cave walls. During the course of my own career, content went from analogue and output to print, to digital and output to interfaces; from book-based content to topic-based content to molecular content (for an elaboration of the rise of molecular content and its place in product content, see https://storyneedle. com/molecular-content-and-the-separation-of-concerns); from keywords to metadata back to keywords as metadata; from information architecture to taxonomies and now information architecture *and* taxonomies; and from taxonomies to knowledge graphs. Every few years would see a change in how content needed to be formed and structured.

In the early days, this meant a change in writing style to enforce consistency across a corpus of mix-and-match content. Then, it became a change in form in addition to writing style, going from chapters and sections to topic-based content that was used for in-software help or aggregated into a longer form, such as a manual. The next change was to add topic keywords and, shortly after that, breaking content into smaller units that could be modelled. With many of the changes came new processes and new production software – and often collaboration with new professions.

The pace at which content production processes change is increasing and we may soon be on the cusp of not having to structure content for it to be *reliably* understood by search technologies – note the emphasis on reliably. It may feel like structured content has been around for a long time, but industry has a long time to go yet until we reach the threshold where structured content is more common than not. Meanwhile, the need for structure has evolved even more, as organisations struggle to dynamically populate interfaces, such as mobile apps, with snippets of content as short as a phrase or a word. What we do know is how things work at this point in time and that technologies understand structured content with way more reliability than unstructured content.

The focus has shifted from code-based tagging, where all of the heavy lifting is done programmatically at the delivery end, to a semantic-based approach that combines content structure and the structure of a taxonomy, which culminates in a whole that is greater than its parts. This, in large part, is due to the collaboration between two groups: those who used to be called 'back end' content strategists – the shift has started to a designation of content operations strategists – and taxonomists. This chapter discusses the nature of structured content and the benefits, and how taxonomies, and the professionals who develop taxonomies, work together to increase the power of content.

## What we mean by structured content

Structured content has several definitions that overlap somewhat like a Venn diagram. For the purposes of this chapter, we define structured content as information organised in a predictable way and classified using metadata. The structure may be organised in one of two ways.

First, the content may follow a recognised schema. A schema is a representation – a schematic drawing, in the literal sense – of a structured framework. A content schema is not as much of a drawing as it is an outline of sorts. The outline is made up of a series of elements that we generally represent in a hierarchical way – for example:

H1   **Section heading**
>        Body text related to the section heading.
H2   **Subsection heading**
>        Body text related to the subsection heading.

The purpose of using a schema is to create a reliable content structure for the use of software applications. The outline needs to be a strict structure for applications to be able to process content with a high degree of certainty. Virtually all applications use some sort of structure to process content. If you use 'Styles' in Microsoft Word, the application can generate an 'Outline View' with a hierarchical representation of the content in your document. When an external application wants to process your Word document, it will read and interpret the structure to determine what the elements are and what to do with each element. The schemas for a news release or an event, for example, have very prescribed elements that make it easy to share that content with both internal and external applications: news aggregators such as Associated Press for news releases and event listings sites such as TicketMaster.

Second, structures may be bespoke - this is often the case with marketing material, where the layout of a webpage meant to persuade does not conform to a rigid set of rules. Outside of marketing, content is often constructed around a recognised schema.

Also, when we discuss content structure, we are also talking about semantics. Semantics apply to the structure and to the metadata added to content to provide more meaning.

- Structural richness means building semantics right into the structure naming convention to help applications understand how to process content. Building on the earlier example, <H1>Cats</H1> has very basic semantics - a heading about cats. A structurally rich heading would be written as:

```
<div itemscope="" itemtype="
https://schema.org/TheaterEvent">
<span itemprop="name">Cats</span>
```

- The added semantics clearly tell an application, such as a search engine, that this is not a generic heading, but the name of a theatre production of *Cats*. The semantics also tell a content management system (CMS) to display the name of the production in the correct position, equivalent to how all the other event names are displayed.
- Semantic categorisation means adding more metadata that help applications find other ways to categorise the information. In the *Cats* example, the theatre production could be categorised with keywords such as 'Andrew Lloyd Webber', 'TS Eliot', 'family entertainment', 'musical', and so on. This is helpful to applications such as search engines, which are continually creating links between search terms to help users discover the most useful information.

## Standards vs conventions

One of the potentially confusing ideas used when describing structured content is the distinction between the technical and editorial aspects of content.

Standards are codified, are formally recognised and allow applications to process content. An easy way to explain a standard is to look at electrical equipment. The standards to which equipment must be manufactured allows us to buy an electrical device with confidence, knowing that the plug will fit into the wall socket and that the device will not short-circuit when connected to a power source. Content standards help computers process content with a high degree of reliability. Artificial intelligence aside, computers are still quite rigid about what they understand. Standards make it possible for applications to do things such as let content interoperate with other content from multiple sources and do bulk processing of content. The rules are strictly enforced for the sake of automation.

Conversely, what is often called editorial standards are actually editorial conventions. The terminology choices, sentence structures, tone and other editorial decisions are guidelines that can be broken. This is because editorial conventions are what people use to understand content and, more importantly, context. There can be exceptions made when we know those exceptions will help people to better understand our content. For example, in the previous sentence, I deliberately used a split infinitive verb to make the sentence flow more smoothly. Breaking the grammatical 'rule' against using split infinitives did not stop the processing dead in its tracks.

The distinction between standards and conventions is an important one, as it keeps us aware of the use of structured content standards and the benefits it can bring.

## Benefits of structured content

The benefits that structured content can bring falls into two basic areas: business benefits and operational benefits. It may seem obvious to state that the business is far more likely to be interested in the business benefits than the operational benefits. The irony of that line of thinking is that the business side of the benefits are far less likely to be achieved until the operational side of the benefits are realised. In the discussion that follows, the connection between the two sides becomes clear.

## Business benefits

Structured content, combined with the power of semantics, has the potential to exponentially increase the potential of content. Content is not inconsequential to develop, so getting the most benefit from your content assets is a sound investment.

There is no universal set of benefits, because each organisation has a different strategy and different goals. Having said that, we can look at some common objectives across the business landscape. Organisations want their content to support their delivery initiatives, for example, in areas such as multichannel - pushing content out to multiple channels - or omnichannel deliveries - pushing out content specific to a stage in the customer journey. They want content to support personalisation, thereby increasing engagement.

Thinking of content as a value stream is helpful here because it progresses in lockstep with the operational or development value streams already in play. A value stream is a series of steps used toward implementing a solution that provides a flow of value to a customer. If software development is a value stream, and design is a value stream, they cannot deliver their value without a value stream for content. And content without semantics provides less value when that content has a rich metadata strategy applied to it.

The concept of 'intelligent content' (a term coined by Ann Rockley and explained in *Intelligent Content: A Primer* by Rockley, Cooper and Abel, 2015) is worth mentioning here because of the potential that structural and descriptive metadata unleashes. The combined efforts of the content strategists who develop the content model - which informs the structural metadata - and taxonomists who develop the taxonomy model - which informs the descriptive metadata - work in tandem to ensure that content can be automatically discoverable, adaptable, reusable and reconfigurable. The first two attributes are discussed here, while the latter two are discussed in the context of operational benefits.

- **Automatically discoverable**. The metadata helps content be found through search - both internal search and search engines - and can expand the various ways that the content can be surfaced. Descriptive metadata extends the scope of findability; e.g., using synonyms will increase the chances of finding a particular piece of content. Structural metadata helps with intent; e.g., the search results for 'wine bar' is a list of venues while 'buy wine bar' shows products that use the Product schema. This same principle applies to delivering content to specific outputs, such as websites, tablets, mobile phones, game consoles, augmented reality apps, printed material, and so on. The metadata also allows for filtering based on pre-configured criteria, such as personas, stages in a customer journey, product types or a status such as in-warranty or out-of-warranty.

- **Adaptable**. Adaptive content goes hand-in-hand with responsive design. 'Adaptive content is designed to adapt to the needs of the customer, not just cosmetically, but also in substance and in capability. Adaptive content automatically responds to the screen size and orientation of any device, but goes further by displaying relevant content that takes full advantage of the specific capabilities of the device being used' (Charles Cooper, The Rockley Group). An example would be the humble boarding pass. You get the required information from the same source, but adapted to different formats, depending on how you request it: as a PDF document attached to an email, a QR code on your mobile phone, a thermal paper printout with a bar code at the airport, or a flimsy cardboard rectangle given to you by the desk clerk.

## Operational benefits

The operational benefits that arise from structured content and metadata can be understood as all the ways that content can be manipulated during the production process to build in efficiencies. The Wikipedia definition of an operating model is 'both an abstract or visual representation (model) of how an organisation delivers value to its customers or beneficiaries as well as how an organisation actually runs itself' (https://en.wikipedia.org/wiki/Operating_model).

The earlier assertion that management is more interested in business benefits than operational benefits is evident in the general lack of investment in robust content ecosystems. However, when operational inefficiencies get in the way of realising business benefits, there is more interest in eliminating waste from the content production processes (see Imran Aseed Tariq's 2018 article on LinkedIn, https://www.linkedin.com/pulse/what-8-wastes-service-hindering-lean-transformation-cssbb-). A lack of a metadata strategy is one of those opportunity costs that can be prevented through the collaboration of a content strategist with a taxonomist to develop a set of terminology that can be applied as metadata to content that needs to be delivered in flexible ways.

Looking back to the benefits of intelligent content, we come to appreciate the operational benefits that arise from developing content that is reusable and reconfigurable.

- **Reusable**. Content components are created once and then, rather than copy-and-pasted, re-used through a technique called 'transclusion' across the body of content. Transclusion means 'inclusion by reference' in which an author can view what seem to be copies of a piece of content, but that actually exist as a single source, with a hologram effect projecting virtual copies in many places. A common example of re-using content at a word level is company, product or programme names – anything that tends to be volatile and would need to be changed wholesale. Another example is compliance statements that get re-used across a body of content in multiple places. Transcluding the compliance statements means that when a change is needed, the content developer updates the source and all of the virtual copies are automatically updated. Metadata plays an important role as it determines where content gets systematically reused. Systematic reuse relies on a content management system and dynamic content delivery (see Rockley and Manning, The Architecture of Content Reuse, *ASIS&T*, **39** (1), 471–2, https://asistdl.onlinelibrary. wiley.com/doi/full/10.1002/meet.1450390165). As content revisions can balloon the cost of content maintenance, containing the number of original content components is a strong part of an efficient operational model.
- **Reconfigurable**. Writing and tagging modular content allows content to be mixed and matched to create new contexts. This allows organisations to rapidly respond to changing user needs. Content components can be combined and recombined into a multitude of configurations as needed. Furthermore, when these modules have the right metadata associated with them, they can be auto-assembled and delivered to multiple channels and in multiple formats to meet the needs of multiple audiences.

These operational benefits feed into the business benefits as they contribute to automating continuous delivery pipelines. As more and more organisations move to an Agile development model, the need to deliver content on a sprint basis becomes a critical component of improving the value stream in order to deliver more benefit to users. In other words, the more efficiency that can be built into the content production processes, the more business benefits can be delivered. Using metadata in the context of intelligent content is a significant aspect of this efficiency.

## Taxonomies

Metadata plays a significant role in structured content in the many ways described in this chapter. If metadata is an important player, then the taxonomy is the coach. A good taxonomist, working with the content strategist, can map out ways to structure the taxonomy so that content developers can readily apply the terminology during the writing and editing process.

### Applying taxonomy terms to structured content

Developing content, particularly product content, can be messy. Not only are content developers thinking about how to create content that is meaningful to the eventual reader, they are also thinking of the information architecture used to present that content, watching that the right labels are used for the CMS to transport the content to the right end points and organising their content by categories specific to their work environment.

The vocabulary of a taxonomy helps categorise content with additional terms that help authors find and use content and assemble it quickly in the content hub where they do their editing. For example, certain pages on a website may include one of a few possible disclaimer or compliance statements. The taxonomy for the website would not include a label for disclaimers because the disclaimer is simply one paragraph about whatever product or topic is being covered. In the work environment, however, it makes sense to store all the disclaimers and compliance statements together, so that a content developer can reliably locate them, choose the appropriate one and include it with the other content destined for that webpage.

Looking at a similar example, consider a content model for a company that sells some products that need a disclaimer, such as lithium batteries that are too hazardous to ship by air. Product pages get auto-populated from a content hub in a product information management (PIM) system – it would be way too costly to hand-assemble tens of thousands of product pages – so the content model needs some mechanism to associate the appropriate disclaimer with the hazardous products and include the disclaimer on only those pages. This outcome could be architected in multiple ways, all involving structural metadata and taxonomy terminology.

The consistency factor should not be underestimated in either of these examples. When the semantic labelling and taxonomic categorisation is done well, the content developers' work is made that much easier and the information architecture is fed that much more reliably. When the up-front metadata strategy is neglected, this can result in significant administrative overhead and unreliable information being presented to end-users.

## Increasing the power of content

A taxonomy creates consistency across a content corpus. As content developers work on content, they can label the various conditions that will determine how content gets routed by any downstream systems that present content to users. When taxonomy terms are offered up as part of the writing process, it becomes a powerful tool in the content developer's toolkit. The term 'personalisation' is usually associated with targeting content to a particular subset of an audience but, in the bigger picture, personalisation is simply increasing the relevance of content. A range of content labels could apply to a wide range of conditions, such as country, platform, product version or variant, language or language variant, and so on.

Organisations may already do this level of broad-brush personalisation without labelling it as such, because technologically the ability to do context switching through semantics is not available. This could apply to product content by country or health content by gender. The ability to future-proof content through a combination of chunking and tagging content is an eye-opening moment. It is the moment when an organisation discovers that the technology that smooths the process of switching broad-brush contexts can easily be extended to smooth the process for more fine-grained personalisation. Instead of simply segmenting content by country or gender, a semantic approach can segment by a number of simultaneous factors. The big factor in achieving this, of course, is setting up the semantic framework well at the start, to match up the personalised delivery needs with the content needs and the metadata needs. This requires a high level of collaboration between the taxonomist, content strategist or content engineer, technologists who produce the technical aspects - code, AI (artificial intelligence) logic, etc. - to aggregate the content into the interfaces, and the product designers who are orchestrating the overall user experience.

## Conclusion

The changes that have happened in content production over the years show no sign of slowing down. If anything, the velocity of the change is increasing. It's easy to think of content as a murmuration of starlings, swirling and diving in unison at rapid speed. Content is expected to be dynamically delivered into a multitude of interfaces on a multitude of devices, in a multitude of markets. From Google's Instant Answers to Amazon's Alexa app to IKEA's augmented reality app to IoT-connected (Internet of Things-connected) appliances to increasingly complex chatbots, content is involved. Content is expected to just 'be there' no matter where 'there' is and no matter how fast the user wants it. Albert Einstein rightly said that 'we can't solve problems by using the same kind of thinking we used when we created them'. Likewise, we can't solve content problems by using the same kind of processes we used to create content. It is imperative that content strategists and taxonomists collaborate to make the semantic approach work its magic.

# 12 Information Architecture and E-commerce

*Mags Hanley*

*Editor's note*: I've been lucky enough to work with Mags on three separate occasions. She is a superb communicator and thinker, having been one of the pioneers of information architecture (IA) and the wider user experience (UX) field. This chapter covers search, metadata and navigation design for e-commerce, an area where taxonomy practitioners can and do make a big difference to the success of websites and apps. Also included is a discussion of different kinds of mental models that customers may have and some crucial Search Engine Optimisation (SEO) basics for taxonomists.

## Introduction

Information architecture (IA) is:

> The art and science of organizing and labelling web sites, intranets, online communities and software to support usability and findability.
> (The Information Architecture Institute, What is Information Architecture?, 2012,
> http://iainstitute.org/en/learn/resources/what_is_ia.php)

IA in e-commerce uses the principles of library and information science to design navigation, search, product pages and data for customers, and perform Search Engine Optimisation (SEO) for search engines like Google, Bing and DuckDuckGo.

The definition above says 'supporting usability and findability'. To this end, the aims of information specialists in e-commerce are threefold:

1 Create metadata and controlled vocabularies that describe the products to the right level of detail based on the products' inherent properties and customers' mental models.

2  Structure the product content to make it usable for customers.
3  Design navigation and search systems that increase findability by customers and search engines.

We approach this from a top-down and bottom-up perspective (Figure 12.1).

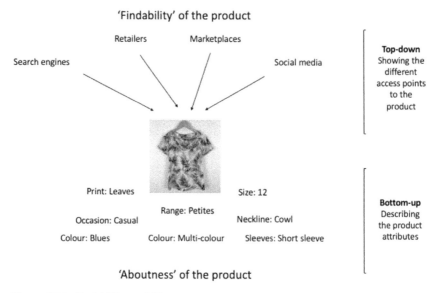

**Figure 12.1** *Findability model for e-commerce*

Top-down is focused on findability: designing as many paths as possible to get the customer to the product. Common paths include search engines such as Google, search and navigation on the website, syndicating the product content on marketplaces, editorial features and social media.

Bottom-up is focused on describing the 'aboutness' of a product to be used by these different paths, using structured metadata and controlled vocabularies.

For example, using metadata fields *Size, Colour* and *Product Category* for a top means that it can be found via a specific Google query like 'size 12 blue tops', via navigation (Tops > Blue > size 12) or via an editorial page showcasing blue as the colour of the season.

In this chapter, we will cover:

• understanding customers when designing e-commerce IA
• designing top-down paths for findability

  - navigation
  - search
  - SEO
- describing the products from the bottom-up, focusing on developing metadata schemas and controlled vocabularies.

## Understanding customers when designing e-commerce IA
### Researching our customers

As information professionals, our role in designing e-commerce is to ensure the labels and categories the product suppliers and retailers use to describe their products match the way customers think of the products; the concept of connecting literary warrant with user warrant.

The difference between traditional controlled vocabulary development and e-commerce is that user warrant takes precedence over literary warrant. Our preferred terms are the customers' language, not the industry's. The only exception is when industry terms have been taught to the customers. This tends to happen in highly specialised domains where the majority of customers are invested and have learned the terminology, such as Gaming.

To match the customers' language, we need to understand their mental models of the domain. For example, suppliers may think of high-performance cameras as 'interchangeable lens cameras', but customers think of them as 'DSLRs' or 'Mirrorless cameras'.

### Exploratory research vs usability testing

There are two types of research we perform on e-commerce sites:

1 Exploratory research
2 Usability testing.

**Exploratory research** is less focused on the outcome and more focused on how the customer got there and their mental models of the site and brand. This research is task-based but is not outcome driven.

**Usability testing** is focused on understanding whether the designs we've created are usable. We determine whether customers can find the right products and services to match the task. The methods we use are:

- card sorting
- tree testing

- interactive prototypes
- content usability testing.

If you want to know more about this, read Donna Spencer's *Card Sorting: Designing Usable Categories* (2009, Rosenfeld Media) and articles by Ginny Redish and Caroline Jarrett on how to test content for understanding (see How to Test the Usability of Documents, *UX Matters*, 2020, https://www.uxmatters.com/mt/archives/2020/05/how-to-test-the-usability-of-documents.php).

## Navigation

Navigation in e-commerce is the combination of two things:

1 The navigation model – the interface elements that support the user to find content and product on the site.
2 The labels linking to product category and description pages, and editorial and brand pages.

Before we discuss these two elements in detail, there are two things to note:

1 Navigation is not the same as browsing.
2 Navigation and categories do not have to reflect each other.

### Navigation ≠ browsing

Marica Bates, in her 'Modes of information seeking' model, describes 'browsing' as the *active* and *undirected* way of searching for information, meaning the user 'sort of knows' what they want, but needs help in finding the content. 'Search' on the other hand is *active* and *directed*, the user knows what they want and goes directly to it.

Navigation can support both modes of information seeking: a woman looking for a dress knows exactly what she is looking for and she has an established domain of knowledge about dresses. On an e-commerce site, she can either use navigation (Women > Clothing > Dresses) and filter for her size, favourite colours and type and then scan the results, or she can search for 'cocktail dresses' and narrow her results down via the filters.

Browsing is also supported by search and navigation. For example, when the user is unknowledgeable about the domain, such as buying a new mattress (a once in every 5-10 years' experience), navigation shows the user the categories of products, thereby educating them about the domain.

Search can also do this: a search for 'mattress' will show all the important properties of mattresses, combining educating and narrowing in the same activity.

## Navigation labels and product categories can be different

E-commerce navigation is the shop window into a retailer's offerings, therefore it is not always mapped to the primary product categories' controlled vocabulary. It is the place where the retailer's, product suppliers' and user's needs blend together to showcase what's in style, on promotion, in season and the product categories. For example, navigation for selling computers at 'back to school' time could include buying guides for parents and links to the promoted brands, as well as product categories like laptops, desktops and tablets.

## Navigation models

A navigation model shows all the navigation types together in an interface. There are many styles used in displaying navigation within a site including Mega-navigation, Inverted L-shape and Hamburger menus. The decision on the types to use in a site depends on:

- the number of products or items being sold
- the levels in the product hierarchy
- the types of other information, such as editorial pages and guides to be linked.

The designer then matches that data to the navigation types available. The art is getting them to work together in the interface, meeting the needs of the users seeking the information and not making the interface look busy or cluttered.

### *Types of navigation*

There are nine types of navigation:

1 **Global navigation** is the primary way of finding the products, showing customers what's on the site. It is not always mapped to the primary product categories; it needs to show the depth and breadth of the products on sale, as well as promoting the goods.

2 **Local navigation** shows all of the categories within the section to the customer. In comparison to global navigation, it is complete and usually maps to the product categories, as well as displaying additional relevant content like buying guides and brand pages.

3 **Contextual navigation** gives the customer a way to move between products without having to go back up to the global navigation. The product shown in contextual navigation is based on the metadata attached to the original product. For example, showing products that are usually sold with the product, like a monitor with a computer (buying patterns data), other products sold by the same brand or other products from the same product category.

4 **Supplementary navigation** provides alternative ways to access products. In e-commerce, the main supplementary navigation is a brand index – a list of all the brands stocked by the retailer. Other types of supplementary navigation include guides to products (how to buy a fridge), or quizzes like a perfume finder where the customer answers questions based on facets to narrow the list of perfumes. The questions are based on the attributes attached to the products in the category.

5 **Breadcrumbs** provide the customer with a sense of place for the product. It shows the primary category for the product and allows the customer to go directly to the full set of products assigned to that category.

6 **Page and social navigation** allow the customer to interact with the page including printing, saving, emailing to another or sharing on social media.

7 **Account navigation** allows the customer to log in and see order, account and wish lists.

8 **Utility navigation** provides the customer with access to Help and Support, Contact Us, About Us and Store Locators, if the retailer has a physical presence.

9 **Footer navigation** shows the customers organisation-wide information such as Jobs, Help and Support, and delivery options.

Figure 12.2 opposite shows how these types of navigation are reflected on a site.

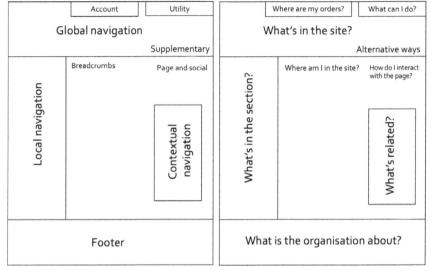

**Figure 12.2** *The navigation model, showing the type of navigation and its purpose on the site*

## Rules for designing and choosing the right navigation model

There are four rules for designing the right navigation model for an e-commerce site:

1 Know the amount of content or products your customers or users need access to. This will change the style of navigation you use. A site that sells only three types of products can use a simple top navigation, while one with 15 main categories and hundreds of sub-categories will need an inverted L-shape.
2 Design the model completely across the site. It's not just the top and bottom of a page. Navigation cannot be plopped on top of a template. It supports customers moving back, forth and between products, and therefore needs to be designed as a whole system tightly connected to each template. Ask whether the customer can:
a Move between sections of the site?
b See where they are in the site?
c Access social, their account or store locations?
3 Mobile navigation is so important as mobile traffic is increasingly the dominant form of access. Both desktop and mobile navigation should be designed together. To learn about how customers navigate on mobile:
a Use click and event tracking.

b Use a heatmap of products to see what they click on.

c Watch them use the mobile site in usability testing.

4 Create HTML prototypes and test them on mobile and desktop. Using prototyping tools doesn't provide the fidelity of mobile testing needed for whole scale redesign. Use HTML, the real product categories and content to identify the right navigation model by viewing how the navigation works on at least three break points. Watch how the customers use hamburgers for product categories, scroll on mobile screens, and use filters and sort orders when viewing product lists.

## Labels for navigation

Labels are the names given to each link in the navigation. They should be the same as the page title they are linking to.

The cardinal rule for labels in navigation is that they must reflect user warrant - the words the customers use when thinking and searching for this product. In academia, a blend of user and literary warrant is used when creating controlled vocabularies. In e-commerce, the aim is to reflect the language of the customers; there should be no guessing games on what a product is called by using industry specific terms.

### *Global navigation labels*

Global navigation labels are usually a combination of product categories, supplementary organisational schemes, promotions and brands. To decide on the blend, the designer needs to understand the way the customers think about the product category identifying the primary organisational scheme.

Most primary organisational schemes in e-commerce are based on product categories, but there are two other organisational schemes that are commonly used - Brand and Room.

For example, in Women's clothing and footwear, the primary organisation scheme is Product category. Supplementary access could include Fit (Petite, Maternity and Plus sizes) and Brand.

Brand works particularly well for products like mobile phones, beauty products and computers, where the brand is a major decision in purchasing. Many customers in beauty are repurchasing so know the brand and product that works for them or are making decisions based on recommendations from social media. Mobile phones and computers are often being purchased based on brand reputation.

Room is used in Homewares, organising products by Kitchen, Bathroom or Living Room. The only problem with Room is that many products could live in multiple places, therefore the best organisational scheme for Homewares is usually a combination of product and room.

## Mixing granularity

When we normally create controlled vocabularies, we are careful about ensuring the granularity of the terms are consistent at each level. When we display product categories in global navigation, our focus is access to products and promotions, not ensuring consistency. Therefore, you may find small products in 'Cameras' navigation like 'SD cards' being promoted in the navigation as if they were the same weight as 'All cameras'.

## Local navigation labels

Local navigation labels are the product categories for that section.

For primary schemes based on product categories, the local navigation labels are the subcategories in the controlled vocabulary for product. For example, in 'Women's clothing > Dresses' the subcategories could be 'Smart dresses', 'Casual dresses', 'Maxi-dresses' and 'Cocktail dresses'.

For Brand and Room schemes, the product categories are based on the combination of the brand and the main global navigation group. For example, in 'Beauty > Fenty', the next levels would be 'Make-up' and 'Skincare' – the two top-level product subcategories that are found in the combination of Beauty and Fenty. For 'Homewares > Bedroom', the categories would be 'Beds', 'Mattresses', 'Bedroom furniture' and 'Lighting'.

## Contextual navigation

Contextual navigation allows the customer to navigate to other products that are similar to the product they are viewing or to see other products from the product categories. The labels used in contextual navigation are the names of the products or the editorial pages. It is important to give customers context about why these links are being provided. For example, by labelling a group 'Other products from this brand' or 'Recommendations based on your previous purchases'.

## Supplementary navigation

Supplementary navigation is usually based on exact organisational schemes like Brand or Product name, therefore the labels are usually organised alphabetically by name.

## Site search

In a seminal post from 2001, Peter Morville talked about the components of search – thinking of search as a system (Figure 12.3) where every part can be designed and changed by knowing how it works.

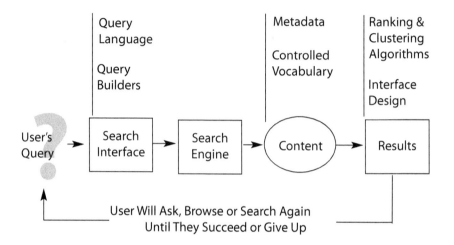

**Figure 12.3** *The components of search – from Peter Morville's 'In Defence of Search' (https://semanticstudios.com/in_defense_of_search)*

In e-commerce, we can adjust and tune four areas:

1 The search interface – leveraging metadata to support good query formation.
2 The search results – helping the customers to quickly filter their results to see a manageable number of results.
3 Controlled vocabularies used within the search engine to improve retrieval.
4 Results – where we can rank and boost results that are important to both the customers and the business.

## Search interface

When I was a library student in the 1990s, we were taught to construct our queries using Boolean logic, refining the search and getting it checked over by a reference librarian, before being allowed to log in to expensive online databases and run the query. We thought very carefully about our searches because every additional minute dialled into the database cost the university money.

Now, searching online has no cost. We expect our interfaces to give us hints on the validity of our query with auto-complete, error messages that show us when we've misspelt a word, and refinement options so we can search broadly and then quickly refine the results. Search interfaces in e-commerce work hard, so customers don't have to.

There are two aspects of search interfaces that are valuable to understand in detail: auto-complete and search results.

## Auto-complete

Auto-complete is predictive text on the search interface: a dropdown that appears showing the customer potential words that match what they are typing in. It is a pattern that is incredibly useful as it reduces misspellings and helps the user correctly format their queries.

In e-commerce, these suggestions could come from two places:

1 The popular words that customers themselves put into the search box.
2 Common words from the corpus – the set of words that make up the index.

My recommendation for this feature is to do a combination of both if possible; show popular words from the customers within the lens of the available product data. We only want customers to search on words that will produce results.

An example of when this doesn't work is when a customer searches for a brand that is not stocked by a retailer. For example, if a customer searched for 'Reebok sneakers' on the Nike website, there may be many searches for it but there are no products. There should be no auto-complete for the term; an error message instead should be displayed that tells the customer the product is not stocked.

## Search results

E-commerce search results should be designed for two different types of customers:

1 People who know what they are looking for (Searchers).
2 People who are new to a product category and need guidance in making a purchase (Browsers).

Searchers know what they are looking for; they know the product set, they can quickly refine the search and scan the results to see which products meet their needs.

Browsers, on the other hand, have a general idea of what they are looking for; they don't purchase these products frequently so look carefully at the results and try different filters to see the difference between the products.

Searchers need:

- filters with clear facet values to narrow down
- large or adjustable result lists for them to scan through
- multiple sort orders
- good pictures and product descriptions in the results to identify the properties they care about.

Browsers need:

- filters with clear facet values that educate about the properties of the product
- results ordered by bestselling or best rated to give guidance
- visual sub-category navigation that shows (not tells) the differences of each type of product
- good pictures and product descriptions in the results to identify the properties they care about.

An example is a woman looking for a dress for a summer garden wedding. She knows from attending weddings that a garden wedding is informal. Therefore, a lighter-weight fabric would work for the season and knee or tea-length dresses would be most appropriate. She can quickly scan a list of dresses and see which ones would work.

On the other hand, when she needs to buy a new coffee machine – a once in every five years' purchase – she doesn't know enough about coffee machines to quickly look at the results and make a decision. She needs explanations on the differences between each type of machine in the search results. She receives that information with visual sub-category navigation – pictures of each type of coffee machine – and clear facet values explaining the difference between machines, for example: facet – coffee type, values – pods, ground coffee or beans.

## Ranking of results

The fundamentals of search are ensuring we return the relevant search results (meet the intent and needs of the customers) while returning all the possible results for the customer (recall).

In e-commerce, we balance only showing relevant results with all possible results by focusing on ranking results that both match the search needs of the customer and make the retailer money. The first rule of ranking in e-commerce is 'don't show irrelevant results to the customer', even if it showcases popular content. But the aim of boosting results is to order relevant results in a way that will make money for the retailer.

Boosting means giving each relevant result a score based on its properties to move it higher up the list. Boosting is divided into two parts:

1  To increase relevant products appearing at the top of the list.
2  To put those relevant results in an order that will make more money for the retailer.

To show relevant results, we boost our results by giving extra weight to three parts of the product information: title, tags and product description. Tags are most relevant, then title, and lastly product description.

An example of boosting for relevancy is for dresses. A search query for 'size 12 blue smart dresses' would find dresses that match all three facets 'size', 'colour' and 'product category' then expand out to find dresses that may match only one or two of the facets, or have the information only within the title or description.

The results would then firstly rank by dresses with the product category of 'smart dresses', available in size 12 and blue, then list the rest by the words found in the title, and lastly in the product description.

We then re-order those results by aspects that help the retailer to sell more product. We boost the results by giving scores to aspects that help sell or save money.

Common aspects that are used to boost results, reordering the relevancy order, are:

1  Popularity – a combination of sales and clicks.
2  Profitability – products the retailer makes more money from.
3  Customer ratings – the most highly rated products, therefore with a lower chance of the item being returned.

In the case of the size 12, blue, smart dresses, the retailer would add a score to each product and re-order the products from highest to lowest score.

For Popularity, each dress would be given a number from 100 to 1, with 100 for the most popular and 1 for the least popular.

For Profitability, each dress would be assigned a number based on gross profit to the retailer. A dress that made £100 profit would be assigned a number higher than one that made £50.

For Customer ratings, each dress would be given a score based on the customer ratings, a dress with five stars would be given a score of 25, over a dress with one star out of five.

For five dresses that all met the customer's search criteria, the maths would be:

**Table 12.1** *Comparison of scores for different boost factors determining the order of search results*

| Dress name | Popularity | Profitability | Customer rating | Total score |
|---|---|---|---|---|
| Navy blue dress with polka dots | 90 | 30 | 20 | 140 |
| Sky blue floral dress | 10 | 10 | 0 | 20 |
| Royal blue colour-block dress | 60 | 20 | 15 | 95 |
| Navy print smart dress | 40 | 30 | 15 | 85 |
| Peacock blue shift dress | 95 | 60 | 25 | 180 |

The new order would be:

**Table 12.2** *Comparison of alphabetical and boosted search results*

| Alphabetical order | Boosted results |
|---|---|
| 1 Navy blue dress with polka dots | 1 Peacock blue shift dress |
| 2 Navy print smart dress | 2 Navy blue dress with polka dots |
| 3 Peacock blue shift dress | 3 Royal blue colour-block dress |
| 4 Royal blue colour-block dress | 4 Navy print smart dress |
| 5 Sky blue floral dress | 5 Sky blue floral dress |

## Search Engine Optimisation

Search Engine Optimisation (SEO) is the process of optimising a website's titles, URLs, descriptions and copy to increase the site's search results ranking in search engines such as Google and Bing.

### The importance of SEO

Retailers want to sell more product and the biggest percentage of customer traffic comes via search engines. For retailers 42% of traffic comes via a search engine. This is by far the source of the highest percentage of traffic, with the next largest being customers going directly to the site at 20% (*KPI Report 2019*, Wolfgang Digital, https://www.wolfgangdigital.com/kpi-2019).

Therefore, it is imperative a retailer's products come up at the top of the search results every time a customer puts in a query. To do this, we focus on increasing the authority of the page, carefully crafting content and reusing categories.

There are four IA-based aspects we focus on:

1  Product categories
2  Titles and descriptions
3  URLs
4  Good content.

### Product categories

To increase the likelihood of customers finding products, we ensure that product categories match the terms customers are putting into search engines. As well as using any data from the internal search engines, retailers should extract words from search engines to see what people are looking for and match their words with the product category names. As searches change by season and fashion, retailers should continue to monitor terms and integrate within the site.

Each product needs to be assigned a primary category. This primary category will be used in the URL and titles to enhance the aboutness of the product to search engines, as well as in breadcrumbs.

### Titles and descriptions

The page title of each product category and description page must be well formulated and ideally created automatically. Only a small number of pages will have handcrafted titles and descriptions because it requires time and is unmanageable with thousands of products.

Optimised product page titles are created from the product name, category and site name. The format is [Product name] – [category] – [site name]. For example: Peacock blue cotton shift dress – Work dresses – Dresses R Us.

Product category titles are created from the product category and site name. The format is [Product category] – [site name]. For example: Work dresses – Dresses R Us.

Descriptions help search engines by putting more context around the page. For example, a description for the peacock blue cotton shift dress could be: *This blue shift dress combines the breathability of cotton with a touch of stretch elastane to make it a comfortable dress for work or play.*

In this description, we are re-enforcing the colour (blue), its material (cotton), the shape of the dress (shift) and the category (work dress). The aim is to give the page more authority on the important words for the customer.

## URLs

URLs also help increase the authority for a page. They should be limited to 70 characters, so the focus is using the descriptive page title and the primary category to give context. Examples are:

Peacock blue cotton shift dress
https://www.dressesrus.com/work-dresses/peacock-blue-cotton-shift-dress

Work dresses at Dresses R Us
https://www.dressesrus.com/work-dresses/

## Good content

Product pages will have more authority and relevancy if the content created for each product page is 'good' content – text that if well written, gives context to the customer about the product and contains specific information about the product matching customer search terms. If text reads well for a person, it will provide additional authority for a search engine, increasing the likelihood of being found by a search.

## Conclusion

As information professionals, we can use our professional skills to increase the findability, usability and effectiveness of e-commerce. There are five aspects where we can design, specify and influence e-commerce to make the sites better for retailers and customers:

1 Understanding customers and the ways they seek information about products, bringing that knowledge into the language and features used on the site.
2 Designing navigation using the principles of categorisation and classification to ensure user language is the basis of the organisation schemes used on the site.
3 Designing search systems that take away the burden of customers crafting search queries to helping them narrow and refine their searches.
4 Designing search results to support the customer's information seeking modes and make the retailer money.
5 Structuring and describing products to enhance SEO by improving the authority of product category and description pages, and reinforcing 'aboutness' of a page in URLs, titles and descriptions.

# Part 4
# Business Adoption

# 13 Implementing Taxonomies and Metadata: Lessons from a Busy Newsroom

*Annette Feldman*

*Editor's note*: It seems a little counter-intuitive that one of the top insights from Annette's chapter is that taxonomies are not interesting to many people you work with. But this need not be a problem; it just means that the taxonomy has to be implemented properly in order to make people's lives easier or products more attractive to customers. Annette is a seasoned pro working in a global news organisation and her insights are useful, no matter what kind of taxonomy work you are doing or where you are doing it.

## Introduction

As a part of the Metadata Technology group at The Associated Press (AP), I work with a handful of taxonomy, metadata and data science specialists. Across our group on any given day, someone might be: managing our taxonomies or schemas; diving into news content to build a natural language processing (NLP) training set; diving into content metadata to inform updates to our classification rules; troubleshooting a classification tool problem; or designing metadata for a new editorial workflow. We juggle many projects at the same time and there is always something new to learn. My colleagues and I agree that we enjoy the fast pace and the wide variety of our jobs. What brings us together as a group, within the AP's larger technology department, is that everything we work on is related to news metadata.

In this chapter, we will look into some aspects of news metadata at AP, including what kinds of metadata and taxonomies we care about, where that metadata comes from, and how it is added to the content that we license and distribute. We will look at which practices lead to successful implementations that let AP's metadata keep pace with the demands of a

24/7 news cycle. Using examples from some recent system implementations, my goal here is to identify some broader tactics and principles
that are important for any successful metadata programme.

## Who is The Associated Press and what do we do?

The Associated Press is an independent global news organisation dedicated
to factual reporting, that supplies news in all media formats to our
members and customers around the world. It was started in 1846 as a way
for five New York City newspapers to share the cost of bringing home news
of the Mexican-American war. Today, the AP is in 250 locations in 100
countries, telling the world's stories. More than half the world's population
sees AP journalism every day.

News is a fast moving, always-on business. Our mission is to inform the
world and we do it by reporting the news quickly, accurately and honestly.
The work of AP journalists reflects one of our oldest sayings, 'Get it first,
but first, get it right'. AP staffers are often working on deadline and
sometimes in difficult conditions. They worry about things like fact
checking their information, getting the best camera angle, keeping ahead
of competing news agencies and staying out of harm's way while still
getting the story. In the most inaccessible and hostile places on earth, they
definitely do not worry about metadata.

But metadata is what lets us deliver the right news to the right people
in the right format at the right time – it is what drives our business. As a
former AP CIO put it, 'Metadata is the center of our universe'.

So, how does AP meet the challenge to get the roughly 200,000 stories,
photos, videos and other items that we publish daily tagged with the right
metadata so that each one can be found, licensed and delivered, without
slowing down the news?

## What does 'metadata implementation' mean?

It depends who you are . . . For AP, implementing metadata is more than
creating taxonomies, though that is certainly part of the story.
Implementation includes the end-to-end functionality that captures
editorial intent and provides customers with access to content that the
Product teams define and that the Sales teams sell. It also includes
supplying the back office business processes with what they need to
correctly pay for and charge for content, as per our agreements with our
many content suppliers and customers.

AP's Metadata Technology team is concerned with defining taxonomy terms for use in AP's automated classification systems as well as the other tools and systems where those terms are used. We are involved in the overall flow of content metadata, from content creation or acquisition, through classification and other internal enrichment processes and on to distribution, accounting and analysis. Nothing about metadata exists in a vacuum - defining schema and taxonomy values, as well as collecting and using content metadata, requires collaboration with our colleagues in Editorial, Products and Sales, Operations and, of course, with the rest of our Technology team. Even though metadata is not the primary concern of anyone outside of the Metadata Technology team, every group at AP that touches news content in some way has requirements for what they need metadata to do for them and for how they will interact with our taxonomies.

AP journalists, including those who gather and edit the news, need taxonomies to:

- support search within the tools they use daily - to be able to find text stories, photos or video, singly or in groups, based on topic, date, story type, creator or any number of other dimensions
- create content that carries all of the above noted metadata without having to stop and think about doing it - the process of applying metadata needs to be as integrated with content production workflow as possible. Metadata application cannot get in the way of publishing the news as quickly as possible.

For our colleagues in the Products and Sales departments, taxonomies drive some very important functions. The metadata on content allows our systems to:

- support customers' search for topics, events and names in the news, both in AP's platforms and in whatever ways our customers offer news content to *their* customers
- bundle and deliver the news quickly, based on predetermined queries against the metadata
- deliver news items correctly, to the correct customers and, equally important, keep items away from customers who are not entitled.

In our revenue focused divisions, like Sales operations and Finance, metadata supports:

- correctly identifying what each client should receive and on what terms
- billing clients correctly
- paying providers correctly.

For our groups that are concerned with markets and operating strategy, including Analytics and Business Intelligence, metadata supports the ability to:

- make data-driven decisions about resource allocation
- understand trends that let AP meet the market with products and services that are growing in demand.

For AP Technology, taxonomies need to be:

- well defined for integration in all pipeline tools and systems, from end to end across the technical platform
- performant and not add significant latency to the end-to-end process.

## How we do it

To address all these different requirements, AP's Metadata Technology team works closely with Editorial, Business and Technology colleagues to implement the application of mission critical metadata.

The tools we have are: Schemas, Rules and Templates, and Taxonomies.

## Schemas

Although our content spans many media types (text, photos, graphics, video, audio and websites), time frames (today's news and decades of archive content) and uses (breaking stories and stock images/footage), we have a single, standard structure, or schema, for metadata for all content. Not all content uses every field in our schema, but having a standard container for our internal metadata makes it possible to blend content for maximum benefit.

## Rules and templates

Because of our need for speed and accuracy, a goal of any AP metadata implementation is a workflow where we do not ask a person to input information if that information can be determined automatically. Based on journalists' workflows, we leverage actions they are already taking when they choose templates to capture editorial and product choices that trigger application of metadata.

We leverage the fact that even though news breaks quickly and unexpectedly, news reporting is almost entirely planned, even if that planning only happens minutes ahead of the information being gathered. A reporter or photographer has a good idea of the coverage they will be producing as part of an assignment before putting digital pen to digital paper or lifting up a camera.

For example, a reporter at an NBA basketball game does not know who will win or what the highlight of the game will be, but they know that they will be describing the game that is in progress and is about to finish. Rather than write the story and only then start to add metadata, that staffer's workflow begins with choosing a template for a Game Story. With that choice, many of the Administrative metadata fields are prepopulated – we know the source, the default audiences, the default subject, as well as the media type, the content type, the language, not to mention the date and time, the author's name and workgroup, the version of the story and much else. The Technical metadata will be captured based on the output of the editorial tool or by examining the produced asset itself. Most of the Descriptive metadata will come from automated classification rules that examine any text that the staffer has written and apply subject and entity terms. The only thing our staffer needs to type is the actual story and specific story related fields, like the headline. The only metadata that needs to be selected is anything unusual to add to the defaults. If the staffer wants to link photos or videos to the text, the keywords from the story are already in the authoring tool's 'search for media' screen, and media can be selected and added with a couple of clicks.

Photo and video workflows similarly make extensive use of templates prepared ahead of planned events, as well as ingest rules that are part of daily workflows to minimise choices and typing when items are ready to be filed. The goal is to make any keystrokes a journalist types as focused as possible on the news itself, not on adding metadata that can be determined by examining the story, photo or video or by agreed upon knowledge of what a newsperson does as part of their job.

There are important exceptions to all of the automated workflows described above. Where the experienced judgement of an editor brings value, it is important to make sure the workflow makes room for it. For example, editorial curation of stories and images is part of the journalistic process. Lest you think that some algorithm is determining what you see as the day's top news, AP editors select what stories and images merit inclusion in national headlines packages and other featured content sets. The important point is that everyone involved has agreed that this is a valuable use of experienced staffers' time. And, in those cases where we do ask people to manually engage with a small selection of taxonomy values, choices are presented in a way that is integrated within the journalists' tools and workflow.

## Taxonomies

Just thinking about Descriptive taxonomies for news content can be a daunting task. AP's journalists can cover stories about any event on any subject from anywhere in the world (or outer space!). So, AP has created an extensive taxonomy of subjects and events, as well as people, places, organisations and companies. These are applied via automated rules that make the richness of AP's coverage accessible for portal search, product creation and customer use.

Given the scope and scale of AP's news coverage and the realities of available resourcing, a foundational tenet of our taxonomy development is that we need taxonomies FOR doing what we need to do, not taxonomies OF every possible thing that could exist in the world. In the content set that we tag, that is a tremendously important distinction. Our taxonomies need to enable customer search and creation of our product set, not describe every aspect of the entire world.

Descriptive metadata may be the 'sexy' one, and the first that comes to mind, but there are other types of metadata that are crucial for providing responsive search results and correctly gathering content sets for display and delivery. Beyond Descriptive metadata, our products and processes depend heavily on values in the categories of Administrative, Technical and several other types of metadata.

Here is a small sample of the metadata that we capture, and some associated taxonomies and sample values:

- **Descriptive metadata** - for each entry there is a taxonomy term created as well as rules to disambiguate that term from others that it resembles ('Notre Dame' - the cathedral in Paris? The University? The football team from the University? One of many high schools or other institutions around the world?) and to identify when a term should be applied to content:
  - subjects - news topics, events
  - entities - people, places, organisations, companies

- **Administrative metadata** – these taxonomies may be less obviously essential than those in the Descriptive metadata section, but are examples of the kind of 'nuts and bolts' that are used to make sure that the right content is delivered and that the distribution permissions and restrictions that are in place are respected:
  - media type - text, photos, graphics, video, audio, websites
  - language – English, Spanish and 25 other languages
  - source and provider- the name and type of organisation that created or provided the item
  - type of content – spot news, sports scores, news analysis, obituary, advisory, headlines package, raw video, packaged story, etc.
  - usage rights – geographic restrictions, contextual restrictions, time restrictions, etc.
- **Technical metadata** – the technical characteristics of an item are important for a customer to know, or be able to specify in a search, to know how they can actually print, display or play an item.
  - word count
  - photo or video file type
  - file size, bitrate, dimensions, aspect ratio, etc.
  - orientation, colouration, etc.

Creating the taxonomies for each of these metadata areas is done in close collaboration with the Products team to make sure that we are providing the values needed to group and deliver content along the dimensions in which products are developed, and with the Editorial and Technology teams to make sure that we can capture information about each item when it is created with minimal user intervention.

## A word about collaboration

If you are a taxonomist or other information professional in any organisation, then you may already be aware that clean, complete, correct metadata is NOT the most important thing on anyone's mind except yours. But you also know that you need to do your job for everyone else to be able to do theirs.

To return to where we started, none of the taxonomy or other metadata work at AP is done in a vacuum. It is all done as part of the workflow or system development surrounding the content that we create, license and deliver. Even if no one else stops to think about it, our metadata really is 'the center of our universe'. A little-noticed but important aspect in any work that the Metadata Technology team does is building and maintaining relationships with people in all areas and at all levels of the organisation. We stay aware of trends in news coverage and new business opportunities that will require new modes of content grouping. We keep an ear out for new audiences our Sales team are pursuing who may have different requirements for how to slice and dice what they license from our news feeds. Experience has shown that developing active partnerships with our revenue generating colleagues is key to making sure that when the time comes to package and deliver a new product or swap out an editorial tool, metadata is part of the conversation and will contribute to the AP's success.

## A word about 'not yet successful' efforts

We have just said that metadata work is collaborative and we work closely with stakeholders across the organisation. Most often, those collaborations yield better results than would separate efforts by either metadata professionals or any other stakeholder acting independently. But being part of a larger organisation means that metadata considerations are not the only priorities for attention and resources. Sometimes there are choices made in projects, maybe in design, or in tool selection, or in prioritisation of effort, that don't fit our vision for metadata. This is just part of working in any organisation. But it is worth mentioning as metadata work is foundational to so much else in our technology projects.

For example, AP has a long history of providing services to our customers who have different levels of technical readiness to upgrade as technologies evolve. So, it is not surprising that the AP still supports some legacy systems, though slated for retirement, that require the use of legacy metadata and workflows that run counter to our goals of automating and streamlining metadata application.

Although progress toward metadata goals is steady, sometimes we must wait until resources and organisational priorities permit work to proceed. Through delays and constraints along the way, it is important to remain engaged and flexible, to work with the resources that are available while continuing to communicate the goals we eventually want to reach. We have found it to be productive to be opportunistic – to have work requests written down as agile 'user stories', ready to present to development teams whenever work is being scheduled.

Each successful implementation is an advertisement for the next one. A track record of being a good partner in successful projects, even when the metadata implementation is not ideal, brings more opportunities to work toward those goals.

**Case study: Working to implement a taxonomy upgrade**
Up until now, we have focused on already-built implementations and how they are meant to work. It may be useful to also take a look at an emerging set of taxonomies to see how the collaborative development process leads to their ultimate use within AP's systems.

Project goals
As an example of how all the different components of implementation are addressed, we can look at a recent project to upgrade the AP's Rights-related taxonomies. A business need was identified to improve AP's Rights metadata, and the systems that use it, to:

- make it more machine usable
- make it more consistent across media type
- provide clearer instruction about who needs to take action
- provide clearer, more precisely defined terms around certain kinds of permissions and restrictions
- require less human intervention in getting Rights from contracts applied to content, where it can be interpreted by display and delivery systems.

This is typical of the kind of iterative work that our Metadata team is asked to do – something is already in place and in use, but needs to be refined as business opportunities arise.

Tracks of work
Table 13.1 outlines some of the collaborative conversations between AP's Metadata team and others in the organisation involved in the several tracks of work associated with a request like this one:

**Table 13.1** *Different tracks of work on an upgrade project and what their goals are*

| Working with ... | To accomplish ... |
| --- | --- |
| Editorial management, who are the experts in news gathering workflow | Understanding where we can integrate tools and metadata and where we can automate the process |
| Products, Sales and Legal, who are the experts in current Rights agreements | Developing the taxonomies of Rights information that needs to be captured and conveyed |
| Editorial and Products, as a cross-media governance team | Normalising taxonomy terms and definitions across the entire organisation |
| Technology, as the experts in data architecture | Creating an expanded schema structure for capturing the agreed upon taxonomy categories and terms |

Pulling it all together

At AP, our Metadata Technology team is responsible for giving shape to the standardised collection of information by creating and implementing metadata schemas and taxonomies. But we cannot succeed in that work unless it happens in concert with those responsible for creating and delivering our revenue generating product – in our case, our news content.

Metadata design and development at scale are not quick projects. Ultimately, successful implementation comes from the collaborative process, making sure that the delivered, integrated taxonomies meet the commercial needs of the business and accommodate the constraints of necessary workflows. Without that collaboration, a perfectly beautiful and complete set of taxonomies will sit on a shelf, unused.

## Conclusion

Here are my top takeaways for any person or group charged with designing and implementing metadata standards, schemas or taxonomies in an organisation:

- Know your organisation's goals - there are a lot of things that can be described that don't help you sell or deliver your content. Don't over describe - it's just noise and more to maintain.
- Know your organisation's workflows - the goal is to add the right metadata at the right place in the workflow, whether automated or manual:
  - Respect your users' time and energy - don't ask anyone to do something twice, or even once, if it can be automated.
  - As jobs and workflows change, metadata and taxonomy need to keep up.
- Taxonomies are not interesting to most of the people you work with, but everyone wants his or her own job to be easier. Part of implementing a taxonomy should be making it seamless or at least easy to work with:
  - Automate everything you can.
  - Consider how to have the smallest impact on your users' workflow for things you can't automate.
  - Consider how integrating metadata additions in existing tools and workflows minimises or even eliminates the need for training of users. As people come and go from your organisation, how helpful would it be to not have to worry about continual retraining of staff?

- Even people who are interested in their own taxonomies are not necessarily interested in those used by OTHER departments. Your Products and Sales teams may have a deep understanding of the metadata they need, but your Production group does not necessarily use the same names for that information or group the same activities together. As a taxonomist familiar with both of their requirements and workflows, it may fall to you to make that connection across groups:
  - Find opportunities to highlight the benefits of consistent, clear, correct metadata and taxonomies to the organisation *as a whole*.
  - Work with allies in every area to cultivate a culture of information literacy and good governance.
  - Taxonomists' work is never done. As business needs change, taxonomies and related systems need to adapt.
- Be a good partner to your colleagues – too many taxonomists complain that they are not pulled into projects early enough to have a positive impact toward their organisation's goals. Make sure your colleagues consider you an asset to a project, not just a drag on progress. Successful metadata implementations include taxonomies that serve their organisation's goals:
  - Maintain relationships across your organisation. Even if you are not naturally outgoing, make the effort to connect with others in any way that you can. They can't call you if they don't know who you are.
  - Get involved in industry groups for the core business of your organisation, not only those for information professionals. The better you understand the business you are working to support, the more helpful you can be to your non-metadata engaged colleagues.
  - Ask questions, be curious and listen to understand your organisation's needs and ever-changing strategic priorities.
  - Pick your battles. There is often room for compromise and phased accomplishments.
  - Do your homework. Be prepared to show why your ideas are good ones that bring value to the organisation.
  - Deliver what you promise (if not more).

# 14 Taxonomy Governance

*Cynthia Knowles*

*Editor's note*: In-house taxonomy practitioners can often end up wearing many hats. They deal with everyday tasks and taxonomy updates, as well as strategic planning and maybe even people management. Cynthia is one of the finest exponents of handling all these different demands that I have ever met. Using analogies drawn from the world of video games, she describes how to lay the foundations for a pragmatic, sustainable taxonomy governance framework.

## Introduction

When you embark on a new taxonomy project the primary focus is often the design and rollout of the taxonomy, with little thought about how it will be managed. Governance is often an afterthought, a panicked response to a taxonomy that is out-of-date, out-of-control or failing to meet business needs and offer value to the organisation. A governance plan should be developed at the beginning of a new project, well before your taxonomy is launched.

Governance clarifies expectations about how the taxonomy will be managed, defines roles and responsibilities, establishes processes and guidelines, and defines metrics for measuring success. A governance plan helps ensure sustainable evolution in response to changes in user and business needs and reduces the likelihood of expensive taxonomy redesigns. It helps to maintain the integrity of your carefully designed taxonomy.

If you have already implemented a taxonomy and skipped this important work, introducing late-stage governance is better than no governance at all. This chapter will describe a step-by-step approach for designing a governance plan. Throughout the chapter, Electronic Arts (EA) will be used as a case study to illustrate how we developed our governance plan and what we have learned during the early stages of our rollout.

EA is a global leader in digital interactive entertainment. It develops and delivers games, content and online services to consoles, mobile devices and personal computers. EA has a portfolio of critically acclaimed, high-quality brands such as The Sims™, Madden NFL, EA SPORTS™ FIFA, Battlefield™, Need for Speed™, Dragon Age™ and Plants vs. Zombies™ and more than 450 million registered players around the world.

Let's get into the game!

## What's your game?

If your organisation is kicking off a new taxonomy project, now is an ideal time to identify the scope of your future taxonomy and clearly articulate its purpose. (See Chapter 1 for more detail on how to go about this.) If your taxonomy has already been implemented, it's invaluable to be clear about its scope before you begin to create a governance plan. What is your mission? Why do you need a taxonomy? How will the taxonomy provide value to your organisation?

A governance plan is designed to work within the context of your organisation and there is no ready-made solution that will work for every taxonomy. Being very clear about your scope and purpose will help guide the development of your governance plan. It is easy to stray offside if you don't know what game you're playing.

## Choose your game plan

Your next step will be choosing the type of governance model you will use. A taxonomy can range from a small number of terms managed in a spreadsheet to highly specialised taxonomies consisting of thousands of terms that are deployed to dozens of consuming systems. The approach you choose will depend upon the size of the taxonomy, the structure and culture of your organisation, the number of stakeholders involved in taxonomy development, the skills and resources available, and how much control is required.

Will your taxonomy governance be centralised or decentralised? There are advantages and disadvantages to each approach, so you must assess your playing field and select the model that will work best for your organisation.

### Centralised governance

In a centralised model, the taxonomist, or a team of taxonomists, is responsible for creating the governance plan and defining organisation-wide processes and policies. All taxonomies are controlled and managed by one governing body. The governing body, which may be a solo taxonomist in a small organisation, controls how taxonomies are developed, managed and used within the organisation.

This model is a good choice for highly regulated or risk-averse organisations that must tightly control changes to their taxonomies. Centralised governance also works well for small organisations with a solo taxonomist who is knowledgeable about the organisation's needs and solely responsible for maintaining the taxonomy. The main drawback of this model is that it requires a robust governance team as they will have significant responsibility and it offers less flexibility and autonomy to local teams.

## Decentralised governance

A decentralised model delegates or distributes governance to persons or teams throughout the organisation. Each team manages their own taxonomies, perhaps extracting relevant categories and terms from a central taxonomy. A decentralised approach allows local teams to be self-sufficient and they can quickly develop taxonomies that fit their unique needs.

Decentralisation works well when you have people with the right training and skills throughout your organisation. A major disadvantage of this approach is less control can impact taxonomy integrity as it is difficult to keep the local taxonomies aligned across the organisation. Inevitably, some taxonomies will be outdated or unevenly developed if they are managed by different teams with no centralised control.

It is also possible to use a hybrid approach in which certain aspects of governance are managed centrally while other responsibilities are delegated to local teams. This is the game plan EA chose.

## EA's game plan

Our Enterprise Taxonomy is a collection of dozens of taxonomies used within EA systems and platforms. These taxonomies, which may be internal or public-facing, are used for managing, controlling and finding data and content for product management, reporting and analytics, and displaying information to players via e-mail, web or in-game experiences.

When we began work on our governance plan, we were playing catch-up as the taxonomies were already in play and there were no enterprise-wide processes or policies in place to govern them. We quickly realised it was not practical for our small, newly created team to directly manage all taxonomies at EA. We also recognised that some taxonomies needed to be tightly governed and managed centrally by professional taxonomists. For example, our game rating taxonomies, which are critical to ensure EA offers legally compliant, age-appropriate games to our players.

We decided to use a hybrid governance model in which higher-level strategic oversight and tactical planning would be centralised, but day-to-day maintenance activities for specific taxonomies would be decentralised among the partner teams who were currently maintaining them.

Our taxonomies were categorised as either global or local. Global taxonomies are strategically important to EA and consumed in many different systems and platforms. The central team would be responsible for all levels of governance related to these critical taxonomies.

Local taxonomies, created for the use of a single team and with little or no impact on enterprise-wide systems, would rely upon a decentralised governance approach. These taxonomies would be managed by the teams using them, with strategic oversight and advice from the central team, following agreed upon governance guidelines.

## Build your team
### Identify the players
As a first step in building your governance team, identify the players, all the teams or individuals who will be stakeholders in your governance plan. Think about who will be responsible for developing the governance plan and setting the overall strategic direction for governance. Does your taxonomy project already have an executive sponsor to provide high-level guidance and advocacy for your governance plan? Will you need to form a governance committee with representatives from business groups, information technology and taxonomy consumers? In a small organisation, one person may function as both the owner and manager and a governance committee may not be required.

Stakeholders also include anyone involved in the ongoing management of the taxonomy. Who will maintain the taxonomy? Are you a solo taxonomist or are there other taxonomists and information architecture experts in your organisation? Will responsibility for maintaining the taxonomy be shared among teams?

Next, consider taxonomy consumers inside and outside your organisation. Which business users, customers or citizens will use the taxonomy? Taxonomy users may include content managers, content strategists, taggers and cataloguers, user experience and web designers, content creators, and others involved in site search, search engine marketing (SEM) and Search Engine Optimisation (SEO), or business intelligence.

Subject matter experts (SMEs) have an important role as they provide expert advice on business processes and subject areas described by taxonomies, and they can be excellent champions for promoting the value of the taxonomy. SMEs are usually involved in taxonomy development processes and are frequently taxonomy consumers themselves.

Finally, think about the system in which the taxonomy will be managed as well as any systems or platforms in which the taxonomy will be deployed. Who are the IT system administrators or technical staff who manage these systems?

## Player roles and responsibilities

Using your list of stakeholders, begin to create a RACI matrix. A RACI defines and documents who is Responsible for governance activities, who is ultimately Accountable, who will be Consulted and who will be Informed about changes. The letter (R, A, C, or I) assigned to each stakeholder role clarifies their level of engagement in decisions about governance.

The RACI matrix, which will be further refined as you develop your processes and have a better understanding of the stakeholders' responsibilities, will be useful for viewing gaps or inconsistencies in your process designs and developing a change management communication plan.

## EA's players

When we began to develop our governance strategy, we needed to identify the players who were already involved in taxonomy management. Our roster of key players has evolved as our governance plan matures and it currently includes:

- Taxonomy atomic team – a newly created governing body composed of taxonomy and ontology leaders. The atomic team's primary focus is to establish strategic goals and develop organisation-wide policies for taxonomy management. The team also oversees decisions on major changes, evaluating the costs and benefits of any newly suggested taxonomies, and provides peer review of new taxonomy designs.
- Taxonomists – a cross-team group of EA professionals whose primary job focus is developing controlled vocabularies and taxonomies. This group owns and manages global taxonomies. They also provide consultation and expertise to ensure local taxonomies, which are owned and managed by other teams, follow EA's best practices.

- Taxonomy collaborators – designated representatives from partner teams who work with the taxonomists to maintain local taxonomies and are responsible for adding new terms, synonyms and scope notes to the local taxonomies they govern.
- Subject matter experts – SMEs provide expertise on business processes, technical infrastructure and other subject areas described by enterprise taxonomies. They support taxonomy development and maintenance by sharing expert knowledge of their discipline or domain.
- IT system owners and technical representatives – these players represent the needs and perspective of the IT team and provide insight into the effects taxonomy decisions may have on IT systems and infrastructure.
- Taxonomy consumers – teams and individuals using taxonomy data in their day-to-day work, such as cataloguing or tagging assets, developing new consuming systems, content management or strategy, user experience, SEO, marketing and business intelligence activities.

The player roster helped us to identify which stakeholders would need to be involved in each stage of our governance planning and implementation.

## Identify the top plays

No taxonomy is static — taxonomy terms are continually added, edited, merged and deprecated. The goal of governance is to create repeatable, accountable, visible and predictable processes for managing these changes. Processes outline the activities that are performed in accordance with your policies and guidelines (covered in the next section).

Start by looking at business processes that are already in use within your organisation. The best governance plans take advantage of existing workflows and processes as this simplifies taxonomy stakeholders' adoption and compliance.

Every governance plan must clearly explain how users can request changes to the taxonomy and how change requests are approved. New terms that overlap or duplicate another term can disrupt the quality of your taxonomy: your governance plan should ensure that no new term is added to a taxonomy without a formal approval or review process. In a small organisation, the taxonomist may be both the reviewer and approver, but you will need a transparent decision-making process that stakeholders can understand.

Think about the following questions:

- How will taxonomy users submit change requests? Do they require access to the taxonomy management system?
- What is the process for reviewing suggested changes? What is considered in the review process and how frequently do reviews occur?
- How are changes evaluated? How are change requests prioritised?
- Who is involved in the decision to approve/disapprove changes? Are SMEs and taxonomy consumers consulted? Is there a vote? Who gets to vote?
- Will term suggestions be tracked and maintained for further review in the future (when they may be more suitable or relevant)? Are change decisions documented?
- How will you communicate changes to stakeholders? Will taxonomy users be notified every time a change is made or at a predetermined frequency (e.g., weekly, monthly or quarterly)?

At a minimum, you will need to develop processes for the most common activities:

- adding terms
- modifying terms, including renaming, moving, splitting, merging or demoting terms
- deleting or archiving terms
- adding categories
- modifying categories
- deleting or archiving categories.

## Change triggers

Consider the types of activities or events that are likely to trigger a change. Some common change triggers include:

- Business-driven changes – the development of new kinds of content or changes to product lines or services.
- Market changes – customer demand, new competitors, government regulations, political changes or world events.
- Organisational changes – corporate restructuring, mergers and acquisitions, or new locations.
- Technological changes – new platforms, systems or processes, or changes in search engine or content management system (CMS) requirements.

- Ongoing review and management – identification of new terms needed within existing taxonomies, periodic taxonomic review or analysis of qualitative and quantitative metrics.
- User feedback – user surveys, interviews or usability studies.

Knowing your organisation's triggers will help you to anticipate and plan for changes. You may be able to identify business priorities, cycles or cadences that will impact your process decisions.

## Leverage technology

Be sure to leverage the functionality of your taxonomy management software or content management system as you develop your processes. Many taxonomy management systems provide tools for workflow and governance enforcement. Governance processes that are built into your tool are more likely to succeed because governance does not have to be taught or enforced. It seamlessly happens as you use the system because that is how the system was designed.

For example, most taxonomy management systems have reporting features that allow you to identify orphan terms, terms with missing relationships or attribute values, or terms that are not being used regularly. Some systems have workflows that allow taxonomy users to provide suggestions directly to the taxonomy team or features to alert users when a new term is added. CMS or customer relationship management (CRM) systems may also have workflow capabilities that can be leveraged for taxonomy management.

If your taxonomy project includes the acquisition of new taxonomy software, be sure your request for proposals (RFP) includes feature requirements that will support governance processes.

## EA's top plays

After identifying our change triggers, we developed a three-tiered classification to describe the severity and disruptiveness of the changes:

- Major changes – high-risk changes that impact many taxonomy consumers, multiple consuming systems or require a significant commitment of taxonomist resources.
- Medium changes – changes to existing taxonomies, such as adding or archiving many terms or modifying a taxonomy hierarchy.

- Minor changes – low-risk changes involving a single term or a small number of terms with a minimal impact on taxonomy users and consuming systems, e.g., spelling corrections or adding individual terms or synonyms.

We looked at our existing technology and identified four systems that would be incorporated into our governance processes:

- taxonomy management system
- bug/issue tracking system
- business communication system with direct messaging and chat channels
- e-mail.

Then we identified the foundational processes that we needed to get started. We will look in more detail at one of the top plays that EA developed.

## Top play: global taxonomy change request process

We created a process for requesting global taxonomy changes, such as adding, editing, merging, archiving or deleting terms or categories. The process needed to be very simple and easy to track and we wanted to maintain the history of these requests.

Our taxonomy management system was not set up with built-in workflows for suggesting candidate terms. We decided that new requests should be created directly within our bug/issue tracking system as many EA teams were already familiar with the system. To simplify the process, we created a custom e-mail address that would automatically populate an issue ticket in the tracking system using details pulled from the e-mail.

We considered the type of information we wanted requestors to provide. Since change requests could vary in complexity, we decided to ask for minimal details including any known requirements or use cases, SMEs to be consulted and a need by date. These details are amended and expanded when our team reviews the ticket and determines whether the change is major, medium or minor.

Next, we considered how incoming change requests would be reviewed and prioritised. Minor change requests follow a fast-track approval process. More complex changes (medium and major changes) are reviewed and triaged by our team. Major changes must be approved by our taxonomy atomic team.

After we've assessed the impact, we prioritise the request. Changes that will benefit our players or support business and marketing activities are given a high priority, as are minor requests to fix issues.

## Write the rule book

In this step you write the game rules, the policies and guidelines that work in tandem with your processes. Remember to write for non-taxonomists, avoiding overly technical jargon that requires the reader to be knowledgeable about taxonomy terminology.

### Style and editorial guidelines

Every taxonomy should have an editorial style guide to ensure consistency in term labels. The guide should be relevant to your organisation and the consumers of the taxonomy. Public-facing taxonomies and internal-only taxonomies have audiences with varying levels of familiarity with your organisation's vocabulary. For example, abbreviations and acronyms that are frequently used within your company may be confusing and easily misinterpreted by public consumers.

A taxonomy style guide provides clear guidelines to follow when creating term labels. Commonly this will include rules related to:

- term label length
- term ordering
- capitalisation
- language and spelling
- multilingual terms
- special characters (e.g., ampersands, colons, hyphens)
- single word versus multi-word terms
- singular versus plural terms
- compound and pre-coordinated terms
- abbreviations and acronyms
- synonyms
- non-hierarchical and polyhierarchical relationships
- disambiguation and qualifiers
- scope notes.

The guidelines should also document any exceptions to the rules that may be relevant within your organisation.

## Taxonomy usage guidelines

Usage guidelines describe how the taxonomy should be used for indexing, tagging and categorisation. For example, indexing guidelines explain what content should be indexed and what content is not indexed. Content tagging guidelines help to ensure that content tags are applied correctly and consistently. They typically provide recommendations for the number of tags to apply, the desired depth and level of tagging, and the use of general versus specific tags.

Usage guidelines should also describe the systems in which the taxonomy is designed to be used. Systems may impose technical constraints, limitations that impact taxonomy structure and design. These constraints could include limits to hierarchy depth, number of terms, term length or the use of symbols.

## EA's rulebook

We created an editorial style guide, based on ANSI/NISO Z39.19, to document our rules for term choice and form, including relevant examples from our company and industry. For example:

- Single concepts are preferred; pre-coordinated or compound terms should be avoided.
- American English is the preferred language, with Commonwealth English included as synonyms.
- Term labels should preferably be nouns, noun phrases or gerunds (verbs ending in -ing).
- Term labels are sentence case, with exceptions for proper and trademarked names.

The guide also defines which term categories require scope notes and our preferred style for these notes.

## Communicate with your players

A good communication strategy is essential to good governance. This is your opportunity to explain the actions of the governance team and its decision-making process, demonstrate that you are responsive and proactive, and highlight the value of your governance plan.

Governance communications often explain recent changes or upcoming changes. If your organisation has a change management strategy, align with existing policies that are already familiar. Consider how you will communicate changes and progress updates to taxonomy stakeholders:

- What type of changes need to be communicated, and to whom?
- Who will be responsible for communicating the changes?
- What is the timing of the communications?
- What are the most effective communication channels to reach your audience?
- How can you create ways to connect with taxonomy users and establish two-way channels for feedback?
- How will you evaluate the effectiveness of your communications?

Once again, referring to your RACI will ensure that you are targeting and communicating with the right stakeholders.

## EA's communication plan

We were playing catch-up as our taxonomies were already in play before we began work on the governance plan. We needed to collaborate with several teams to explain why we were implementing governance and obtain buy-in for our approach as it would impact the work of their teams. The need for better governance was not a difficult sell as there was a strong desire for more control over the taxonomies.

Our communication plan is based upon our three levels of change: major, medium and minor. Using our RACI, we documented each stakeholder's information needs, identified the appropriate communicator and determined the timing of the communication and the channels that would be used.

For example, major changes such as new taxonomies or restructuring of taxonomy hierarchies require significant communication. Our taxonomists need to be consulted while we are designing major changes and they may be responsible for certain activities. Taxonomy collaborators, the designated representatives from partner teams, need to be informed about upcoming changes in the very early stages of these projects. Subject matter experts, who are likely to be consulted during the design phase of major projects, also need to be kept informed. IT system owners need to be consulted about any changes that impact technology, including timelines for implementing changes within these systems.

Major changes are communicated by the lead taxonomist as soon as they have been approved by our governing body. Minor or medium changes impact fewer stakeholders, but timely communication is critical.

Taxonomy consumers need to be informed about changes that will impact their day-to-day activities before the changes are implemented. They also need to be informed as soon as the changes have been pushed to production.

A variety of channels are used to communicate with each stakeholder group:

- taxonomy requirements documents
- project update meetings and team scrums
- taxonomy management system change logs and reports
- intranet sites
- shared Google drives
- direct messaging and chat channels
- e-mail.

The bigger the change, the more channels are required to communicate the change and create forums for collaboration and dialogue.

## Check the score
### Metrics and usage

Metrics allow you to validate the quality of the taxonomy through quantifiable, direct measurement of taxonomy performance and to assess whether you are meeting business and user needs. Think about the types of quantifiable metrics you can track to monitor how well the taxonomy is measuring up:

- Has the taxonomy improved search results?
- Has website usability been enhanced?
- Is it easier to find and share content across systems or teams?
- Has content tagging quality been upgraded?
- Has your regulatory compliance improved with better content management?
- How does the taxonomy support business capabilities or processes?

Your taxonomy software's reporting features provide a wealth of information about the effectiveness of specific taxonomy terms. Which terms are being used, which are not? Which terms are frequently being used together?

You will also want to measure the effectiveness of your governance processes:

- Are your stakeholders following the processes?
- Are you delivering changes within agreed upon timelines?
- Do any of the processes need revision?
- Do you have new or changed stakeholders?

Also consider how you will capture feedback about the taxonomy. Surveys and periodic reviews with stakeholders can help assess whether the taxonomy is hitting the mark.

## EA's scorecard

Our work to capture and analyse metrics is in its infancy. We are currently implementing a new taxonomy management system that will allow us to automate many of our laborious workflows and enhance our ability to collect quantifiable metrics. We've identified the metrics that we want to track and now we're working to implement the software that will allow us to do so.

## Conclusion: celebrate your wins

Taxonomy governance all comes down to creating and adhering to roles, responsibilities and processes that support the long-term development, management and use of taxonomies within an organisation. Do not attempt to develop the perfect governance plan before you implement it. Keep it simple to start with and refine and reiterate the plan over time as you learn what does and does not work. Take time to celebrate as you complete each step of the process.

Enjoy the game!

# 15 Taxonomy Maintenance

*Helen Challinor*

*Editor's note*: There aren't many better practitioners, in my opinion, to write a chapter about taxonomy maintenance – the sometimes neglected, often under-valued art of ensuring the taxonomy remains useful, relevant and accurate. Drawing from her experience in a government department in England, Helen covers the kinds of scenarios that could arise, from political changes to the insistent senior stakeholder who wants a term updated without the due process any other request would have to go through.

## Introduction

Today is a great day! Your taxonomy has finally launched. All of your planning and preparation has come together. Whether you had a 'big bang' or a lower key gradual implementation, today has been your 'go live' day.

You can allow yourself a moment to reflect, deal with any last-minute issues and finish writing up your lessons learned report. But what happens tomorrow? And the day after that? How do you manage, maintain and develop what you have so that it remains relevant to the work of your organisation?

This chapter provides practical examples. We will look at setting the scene for taxonomy maintenance in your organisation, maintenance programme planning and the ongoing sourcing and creation of new terms. We will cover checks and reviews of terms for you, your team and subject matter experts, coping with organisational restructures and the record keeping that you might need to consider.

This case study includes ideas that have been tested in the real world and asks questions to make you think about what might suit you in your organisation. Hopefully this will give you some pointers for how you might want to set up your maintenance processes. Not everything will work everywhere, so treat this as a 'pick and mix' menu of techniques that you can adapt for your situation.

The ideas in this chapter are drawn from my experience of managing the subject taxonomy at the Department for Education (DfE) in England.

The purpose of the taxonomy at DfE is to help the department to categorise its information, correspondence and telephone calls in a consistent way.

The coverage of the taxonomy spans all of the subject areas for which the DfE has responsibility, plus terms that cover internal administration. This means that everyone in the department and its agencies (approximately 7,000 people in January 2021), whether they be working in policy development, delivery of services or operational activities, should be able to find subject terms to meet their requirements. For much of this time I have been the only person working on the subject taxonomy, which has been in use since 2014.

## Set the scene in your organisation

There must have been senior management buy-in to create the taxonomy in the first place. So, whether you set it up or have inherited the project, there should be an acknowledgement that this work is important in your organisation.

However, the taxonomy that exists is only as good as the last term that was created. It is only as useful as the last time it was used to describe content. Now that it is live there should also be an acknowledgement that it must be maintained.

One way to spell out that your role includes the maintenance of the taxonomy is to add this to the top line of your performance objectives. I have always ensured that a phrase such as 'managing, maintaining and developing the taxonomy' is written into my job description and I treat this as my mission statement.

'Developing' is a helpful word to include, because it gives you some scope to look for opportunities to expand taxonomy use into other applications, or different areas of the business. The idea of 'developing the taxonomy' also covers stakeholder and end-user training and education, which should form part of your role. This should be an extension of the user engagement work, which ideally would already have been undertaken in setting up the taxonomy.

## Planning the maintenance programme

How you set up your maintenance regime will, to some extent, depend on your organisation and the resources that you have available to you. Maintaining a taxonomy in a singleton post will be very different to working with a team of people.

In a singleton post, you are often the judge and jury. Although you work with subject matter experts, the buck stops with you. It is your job to manage the quality and internal consistency of the terms. Ideas for the checks and reviews you will need are covered later.

Thinking about a team setting, would you need to have a formal editorial board with set review periods? Or would daily stand ups with your team provide what you need? Or maybe a combination of the two, with fast-moving updates covered at the stand ups and ratified at more formal meetings?

Whether you work alone, or in a team, you need to think about how you continue to engage with your experts and users. If you set up the taxonomy, then this will involve building on the relationships that you cultivated at the start. If you joined the project with a taxonomy already in place, then you will need to find the subject matter experts and bring them on board. Will you need to schedule regular appointments with particular groups for review meetings? Perhaps combining this with ad hoc calls for quick updates?

How will you use your taxonomy management software? Does your system allow for candidate terms to be added? Will you open this up to the user community, keep it within your team or allow a mixture?

Only you can answer these questions and make the processes that you implement work in your circumstances. Be realistic! If you have other responsibilities within your organisation (and the taxonomy is just one element of your job) then set expectations and don't be too hard on yourself if sometimes routine tasks slip.

It is important that you review your maintenance processes periodically to confirm that they are still working for you, the taxonomy and the organisation. Documenting your procedures can help with reflecting on what you do and how you do it. Set yourself a reminder to review these instructions from time to time. This will help you to refine the systems that you have in place.

Once you have your processes set up there are a number of ideas that are common to all methods of maintenance. The following section begins with a guide to sourcing and creating new terms, as well as ideas for daily, weekly and periodic checks.

## Day-to-day subject taxonomy maintenance
### Sourcing and creating new terms
Finding new terms to add to the taxonomy will be one of your most important maintenance tasks. The source of these terms will depend on your domain and other business specific attributes.

From the creation phase, you may have been used to managing expectations and working with stakeholders. The difference now is that you have a living, breathing taxonomy. This can shorten timescales and might bring extra urgency to the process. You need to balance all of these demands with maintaining the usability of the taxonomy and keeping its integrity.

Day-to-day updates are part of a taxonomist's life. However, just because something is routine does not mean that you should do it on 'autopilot'. Daily additions often highlight inconsistencies or issues that the full structure may have hidden when the taxonomy was first created.

For example, you might be constrained by the taxonomy-consuming systems only allowing a set number of levels in the hierarchy. In this scenario, you may find that the new term you need would ideally be placed at a lower level. You have to decide on the best plan of action. Do you compromise the hierarchy and add the term at a higher level? Or do you restructure its broader term to something that would work better because there is more benefit for the whole taxonomy?

The subject matter expert can offer advice, but ultimately you are best placed to understand the ramifications of the changes that you make and the wider impact they will have. This is because you will have a view of the whole. This is not just the structure and content of the complete taxonomy, but also a thorough understanding of how it is used across all the applications where it is implemented. Once you have consulted and thought through the problem, make the decision and be absolutely clear about the benefits for the organisation, especially if what you are doing will impact the users of the taxonomy more widely.

### New term requests from subject matter experts

Depending on how the taxonomy is used in your organisation, you may receive requests directly from subject matter experts.

Proactive requests often mean that you will have the opportunity to work with the person and develop the term (or terms) with them, to a realistic timescale. If the user has come to you, then it is likely that they see the benefits of the taxonomy and it will be easier to work with them.

Applying some of these ideas might help when working with users. Start by researching the term for yourself so that you can have a more informed discussion with your subject expert. Then ask them to describe the term to you to check your understanding (for successful hierarchy placement) and ask for specific instances of where and when the term might be used.

Sometimes, your users might approach you with an urgent request. Be very careful about adding new terms 'on the fly'. Agreeing terms on the spur of the moment should be avoided at all costs. This could be agreeing to something in a meeting or on a call about a term that is needed straightaway.

Resist pressure from more senior colleagues to make changes, because, unless the term is completely straightforward and unique, you will always need time to think through the implications. These implications can take a number of forms. They might be:

- overlapping terms
- concepts that do not fit into the hierarchy without a re-working of a whole section
- duplicates
- decisions about whether the new term idea should be a preferred or non-preferred (alternative label) term.

Pacing the discussion also gives the subject matter expert some 'breathing space' to think about the conversation that they have had with you. Often by asking probing questions about the concept, you spark ideas or highlight complications that the requester had not thought of and these might impact the term you have devised. If there is time, and it is possible in your release schedule, then leaving a gap of several hours between fitting the term into the hierarchy and making it live is often beneficial. This 'cooling off' period allows for reflection and usually brings a better result, with more appropriate term placement. Remember, it is much easier to create new terms than it is to move or unpick terms added hastily.

However, it is just as important to avoid deprecating terms without due care and attention. There is often a disconnect between what the end-users want when they ask for deprecations and the implications for the wider taxonomy.

Often users want to remove a term because it no longer fits their latest policy or area of responsibility. Your role is to think of the wider and longer term implications. This is especially important if the taxonomy is used to provide subject metadata for document management systems, thus helping records managers in years to come.

I once agreed to remove a term when in a high-pressure meeting and I regretted it almost immediately. As soon as I had thought through all of the applications that would be affected, I knew I had to find a way to reinstate it. The solution that I devised involved refining the term using the dates of operation for the education policy that the term was referencing. This satisfied the team concerned, because it was clear that the term related to a piece of policy that was no longer current, but which we still needed as an indexing term.

Sometimes, finding a solution to one problem can help you to solve others. The technique of adding a date refinement to terms is one that I have used subsequently and it has helped me out in a number of different situations. Policy initiatives can shift in government – this might be because of a change of administration or focus. Traceability between one administration's terms and another is important and adding dates to the terms can help with this.

### New terms initiated by the taxonomist or by the taxonomy team

Do not be afraid to request terms for which you see a need. You will know your organisation well and you will be able to spot new topics or different directions coming along. The taxonomy needs to be ready and relevant.

You might find terms that you consider of sufficient importance that they should be added to the taxonomy immediately. The source for these candidate terms might be internal briefings, externally published sources, press or media reports. You will know the best places to look within your organisation.

Once you have these terms prepared, contact the relevant subject matter expert for confirmation. Be prepared to stand your ground if you think that the term is essential for the integrity and value of the taxonomy. You might find that your broader understanding of the whole organisation gives you a different perspective and foreknowledge of what might be important.

### Publicising updates

An important element in making any changes is ensuring that the users are aware of the updates. The ways that you do this will depend upon your circumstances and your organisation. I use a variety of channels including communities of practice, newsletters to particular target audiences, meetings and e-mails to specific users or categories of user.

You may also decide to publish a list of recently updated terms or brand new terms via your intranet. This works well, especially if colleagues can set alerts on the pages so that they are notified of any updates.

## Checking and reviewing the taxonomy

### Checks and reviews undertaken by the taxonomist

It is important to set aside time to systematically review the taxonomy, although the frequency of these checks will depend upon your circumstances. Is your taxonomy fairly static or more dynamic with frequent updates? You might think that the reality is that you are reviewing the structure every time you add a new term. However, if every time you add a new term you end up perpetuating the same error over and over again, then you will be building in inconsistencies and storing up issues for the future.

Scheduling regular diary time to undertake a wholescale review is time worth spending. This is because you can nip these inconsistencies in the bud and spot problems before they turn into a massive re-working. Regular, smaller updates also mean that the users of the taxonomy see a controlled set of changes, rather than a large number all in one block.

Remember, though, that you placed a term for a reason. The taxonomy must be practical and second-guessing every decision is a time-consuming path to madness! Be reasonable and trust your judgement.

Other important checks are around consistency in non-preferred terms. Some questions to consider are:

- If you added a new term and included a non-preferred term, did you use the same format for the non-preferred terms for other instances of similar terms?
- Are your users going to get the same experience across all the terms?
- How flexible are the applications that use the taxonomy? For example, do you need to provide more non-preferred terms to improve the quality of search results in the systems that use the taxonomy?

Think particularly here about abbreviations and acronyms and how they are used within your subject area. There are always confusions and issues with abbreviations that might cross between domains and mean different things to different people. For example, in the DfE domain, ITT could mean 'Initial Teacher Training' or 'Invitation to Tender'. One is about training programmes for teachers and the other is a term used to describe one of the process steps in a procurement exercise. These are both perfectly valid and in common use in my organisation. There are a couple of ways to handle abbreviations. You could use the abbreviations as non-preferred terms, or use them within the term itself. In the DfE, 'ITT bursary' would logically refer to an 'Initial Teacher Training bursary', but in your organisation you may need to add refinements to the terms or include non-preferred terms to make the meanings clear. Whatever you decide make sure that you do this consistently and in a way that works for your taxonomy.

Use your software to help you to review the taxonomy. There are often different views and reports available that you might find useful. Try the visualisation options, if you have them, to give you another window onto the taxonomy. If it is hierarchical, use the top term reports to show you the whole structure. All of these term views help you to see the taxonomy in alternative formats, which will give you another perspective on the structure and how it fits together. Looking at it through a different lens might help you to see any inconsistencies or give you ideas for new structures.

## Checks and reviews undertaken with subject matter experts

Subject matter experts play an important part in the development and maintenance of the taxonomy. How you engage with them will depend on your organisational norms and the relationships that you have built.

I ask, or at least encourage, subject specialists to look at the terms in their area of expertise every quarter. This engagement could be formally structured or via informal requests, depending on which model of the maintenance process works best for you and them. Whatever methods you use to contact your community, be prepared for the big hit of work that could come your way. Plan carefully to ensure that you will be able to cope and respond in a timely manner. Think about how you can group your experts together. Are there similar areas that could be combined for the review process? Have these colleagues worked together before? Have they worked with you before?

If they are new to the idea of the taxonomy, it is essential to brief them fully before you start. Carry out a proper introduction to the structure and term construction principles, as well as being clear about what you are expecting in return. Use tailored presentations, highlighting terms that they will be familiar with to explain the taxonomy. Doing this will save you a lot of time in the long run and clear up any misunderstandings before they take hold. Be sure to explain anything that could be confusing. One of the most common misconceptions is that polyhierarchical terms are duplicated terms, so if your taxonomy is polyhierarchical make sure that this is explained before you begin.

Think around the topic and imagine how you could explain the taxonomy to someone who has never used subject terms before. You might find that storytelling techniques are useful for bringing ideas to life in a real-world environment. An example that I have used to explain hierarchy is to ask people to think about a retail website (pick something that works in your organisation) and show them how you can start with something broad, perhaps 'shoes', and go down through the hierarchy to specify different types of shoes, for example, 'brogues' or 'sandals'.

You must have the capacity to engage with the users, so make sure that you stagger your approaches to give you time to complete one set of updates before the next come your way. This might sound like a straightforward planning exercise, but build in time for delays. The taxonomy might not be the top priority for your stakeholders, so understand when their work peaks might be. If they have regular tasks at set times of the year, then avoid those times when planning a discussion with them. Keep a note and build up a calendar for each set of stakeholders. In this way they can make the taxonomy one of their regular tasks and factor it into their schedule.

However, it is very important to leave space for the unexpected. You cannot know what these checks will bring to light. They might reveal something as straightforward as a couple of new terms or as complicated as a root and branch reorganisation of part of the structure. Do not forget to record details of the updates you make. Record keeping and reports will be covered later in the chapter.

For now, though, another unexpected activity might be a wholescale organisational restructure. We will look at this next.

## Impact of organisational restructuring

One of the challenges that you might face from time to time is a restructuring of the organisation. This could be new areas coming in or breaking away, for example, a company merger, de-merger or acquisition, or the introduction of a new product or service.

In the public sector, this could be reassignment of policy areas or changes in responsibility between different government departments. My main experience of this was in July 2016 when the areas of higher education and skills returned to be the responsibility of the DfE. Prior to this change, these areas had been within the remit of the Department for Business, Innovation and Skills.

However, whatever the nature of the major change, it inevitably leads to updates to the taxonomy. Start by taking careful stock of what the changes are and look at the whole taxonomy structure to work through the implications.

If a new area of work is coming into your organisation, then the very first thing you need to find out is whether they have an official taxonomy or use any subject terms informally. Get hold of that list! If they have an official taxonomy then there may be an existing taxonomist, or a terms expert, with whom you will need to work closely.

Adding the new terms will require a combination of techniques. It is a mixture of everything associated with creating the taxonomy and working with a new set of stakeholders, running alongside elements of maintenance. You will need to introduce taxonomy construction principles to new colleagues, as well as explain taxonomy usage and bring in existing experts as required. Remember that this could be a challenging and uncertain time for individuals, where subject taxonomies might not be at the top of their agendas. Bear this in mind and tread a careful line between moving forward with the taxonomy at an appropriate pace, whilst being mindful of personal circumstances.

The other side of the coin is if an area of work covered by the taxonomy splits away. This could be more straightforward, especially if the taxonomy is used by specific sections of your organisation.

Isolate the section 'owned' by the colleagues who are leaving and decide whether or not to deprecate those terms from the live taxonomy. This decision will depend on the applications where the taxonomy is used. If documents that have been tagged with terms remain, then you will need to ensure that these documents can be retrieved if you deprecate the terms.

If you do decide to deprecate them, make sure that your changes do not affect live terms. This is important if there are any overlaps between the terms designated as possible deprecations and terms that you want to keep. You may need to make some structural, or term, changes to work this out.

For either set of changes, you will need to review the updates in a reasonable time frame to ensure that the terms still meet the needs of your organisation. You will also need to keep notes about the changes as part of the record of taxonomy updates.

## Record keeping and reports

What records you need to keep depends on your organisational requirements, what you need to monitor about your workload and what your taxonomy software can do for you.

There is a balance to be struck here between statistics taking over your world and making sure that you have what you need. A mixture of quantitative statistics (for your own information and to provide to your managers) should sit alongside the records that you need to help you to maintain the taxonomy.

In my experience, the most important information I maintain is the change control log for each term. It is useful (possibly essential depending on how and where you work) to show new terms with the answers to the 'Who?', 'When?' and 'Why?' questions. Make a note of who asked for it, when they did so and why. This helps to maintain the corporate memory in your organisation and the traceability of the term provenance. Doing this for changed, updated or deprecated terms too will pay dividends. When making changes to terms be sure to record the previous term and the new one so that you can see the update you made. This is especially useful if you have moved terms around in the hierarchy.

If you keep this level of detail for each term, it is easier to track your decisions. Where you keep this information, either in your taxonomy tool or as a separate spreadsheet, depends on your circumstances. It is usually possible to create extra notes fields in your taxonomy software. Think about whether you want this information to form part of the actual taxonomy record or if it is better stored in a spreadsheet, where you might be able to restrict access to a smaller number of people. Again, this depends on your circumstances.

Make your taxonomy software work for you. Learn about the reports that it can create and exploit this functionality to its fullest. You might find it useful to plot the progress of the taxonomy through statistics, but make sure that you annotate these with the corresponding events to help with interpretation. A quick note to explain a sudden increase in terms, or an upturn in the number of non-preferred terms, will serve as a reminder in later years.

However, be wary about keeping metrics for the sake of it. What you keep needs to add to the understanding of your work and sometimes this is hard to show through statistics.

I keep records of the numbers of new terms that I add to the taxonomy. However, this does not take into account that some terms can be placed into the hierarchy quickly and easily, whilst others can take much longer to ensure the right fit in the structure. It can be useful to annotate your statistics sheet with this type of information as a reminder for yourself, and your managers, that there is more to the numbers than they might think.

## Conclusions

So, there we have it. Keeping the taxonomy up-to-date and fit for purpose is just as important as the initial set up. Without effective maintenance, all the work put into creating the taxonomy in the first place will go to waste. If the terms and their application are not immediately relevant to the audience, then the users will fall away. Before you know it, all you will have is a list of words that has been an expensive academic exercise.

The techniques and ideas outlined here are based on practical experience and are intended as a guide to help you in your taxonomy maintenance journey. You will know your own taxonomy, business and users. Remember that you are contributing to the wider work of your organisation - how you work and what you do should keep that bigger picture in mind.

Build on what you know to work out the best maintenance programme for your circumstances. Refine and iterate your processes into a practical programme that will take you into the future.

Here's to tomorrow!

# 16 The Taxonomist's Role in a Development Team

*Jo Kent*

*Editor's note*: This chapter is based on Jo's experiences of working in BBC teams that use the agile methodology. But the advice it contains is applicable to taxonomists working in all sorts of teams. Jo brings her extensive experience and commitment to innovation to a chapter that has lots of tips on boosting the profile of taxonomy work, making the most of team mates' diverse perspectives and progressing your own career.

## Introduction

The natural state for a taxonomist seems to be working in a team of one. Most of us thrive on having the autonomy in our working lives and practices and the control over the quality of our taxonomies that entails. However, if you are offered a role within a team there are definite advantages if you are able to adapt.

Software development teams generally either use an agile or a waterfall approach. Waterfall development follows a linear process where a lengthy planning phase precedes the build of the software - this is the more traditional approach. Agile development is incremental, it follows a cyclical process, meaning a short scoping period before building, testing then moving on to the next incremental change.

The BBC adopted agile development in the early 2000s and it has since been implemented by all our development teams. It allows us to deliver value quickly so that we can maximise the usage of the licence fee while fostering the team in a way you would expect from a public service organisation. Having worked autonomously and in agile teams within the BBC over the last 15 years, I have some insight into how you can make working in a team work for you.

I'll take you through some of the potential pitfalls of working in an agile team and show you how you can turn these to your advantage, using examples from a recent project that took a sentence and translated it into an image for a comic strip. This project required both a health taxonomy to map from the extracted terms to the images (e.g., from the word alcohol to an image of a bottle of wine) and later an image taxonomy, to define how those images could be used in relation with the image space (e.g., where they would be positioned on the page) and how they would interact with each other (e.g., behind, in front or inside) to create a unique image for each sentence.

## What you can gain from working in a team

The issue with gaining support for adoption of your data architecture (as covered in Chapter 6) is minimised. As you will be working with a band of supporters, you will not need to convince them to integrate your ideas. It does, of course, require a compromise, in that you will have to adapt what you are doing according to other people's needs, rather than sticking to principles, which can feel uncomfortable as we all want to be creating things we can be proud of. In the BBC, there is always someone to remind you that this is all for the benefit of the audience and unless it serves them, it's not justifiable. This can actually give you a greater sense of value in your own work because while we enjoy the ability to create according to our own exacting standards with no constraints, none of us wants to be building sky-castles which are never going to be embraced even within our own companies, let alone externally. While what we create may be less beautiful, it is more useful, and there is satisfaction to be gained from that.

With the health project, I looked at the brief and thought that we could make use of one of the many existing health taxonomies and started to research what was available. As the project progressed, however, it became clear that while these taxonomies were ideal in the health realm, where accuracy was paramount, the style of language used was not the same as that used in our articles. BBC journalists aim to make articles as accessible as possible to as wide an audience as possible, and therefore try to avoid unnecessarily difficult terms and sentences. They will use common names rather than Latin ones, for example, and simplify things to bacteria or virus rather than the specific type, with coronavirus and COVID-19 and its variants being notable exceptions for obvious reasons. While I could have built an accurate and complete ontology of disease, it wouldn't actually have been much use for the specific functionality we were working on, and, even later on, would still have been largely redundant. In this case, working back the other way and starting with the terms found in the text and using these as a basis for the structure was both more efficient and more useful and easier to justify as a use of my time and the licence fee.

## The benefits of an agile approach

Globally, most software development teams have embraced some form of lean or agile methodology, so they are unlikely to have a long planning phase in which to build a taxonomy before development starts. This seems like it would be incompatible with the careful planning that goes into building a robust taxonomy, particularly the time it takes to understand the scope and begin to plan the broad shape and level of detail of your hierarchy, which is a process seldom improved by rushing. Most of us are used to having time and space to do this on our own and aren't accustomed to working with people in this cerebral stage of the project.

In practice, I find the easiest method is to turn the normal way of working on its head and rather than using a top-down approach, start with one area and work on the full structure later. The key to succeeding in this is to work with the methodology. When the initial sprint planning and backlog building are taking place, you should be part of these discussions and create your own tasks to add to the project planning board. As you work with your team and start to plan what is needed for the first iteration, it will become clear that not all of the taxonomy will be needed at first. You will only need to create enough to be able to test the functionality that you are working on. Most of the time it is easy to deliver this in time for the end of the sprint, as long as you design for expediency and only what is needed at the time. Often by doing this, the rest of the structure will suggest itself as the project progresses.

Having your tasks on the board alongside the other engineering tasks gives visibility to the work that you are doing and helps your team to understand how your work fits in with theirs. All of the team can easily see the dependencies and they will be able to let you know if there are any changes that may affect you. You can also keep up to date with any changes by attending the daily stand up meeting. This has the added bonus of making you more visible to the team and therefore more approachable. I feel more involved with what is going on by attending regularly.

In the health project, although we needed eventually to cover all of the terms you might find in a health story, at first there was a small sample of stories that we were working with and planned to use for testing. It was therefore easy to focus just on the part of the taxonomy that covered these stories and build that in time for testing. As a result, I had only created a small amount of the taxonomy at the time testing took place and therefore had less to unravel when the results of the testing revealed the inevitable tweaks that would need to be made.

## Embracing flexibility in the agile development cycle

The phrase 'perfect is the enemy of done' is apposite here. While a correct taxonomy is something we pride ourselves on, and most of us would find it hard to stand by a piece of work that we know to be incomplete, in an agile team we need to let go of the idea of perfection in order to release something that can be tested. Once it has been tested, you will be able to make adjustments to anything that you have created in a way that would be sub-optimal for the full version but has been designed for expediency of delivery. This also means that no matter how happy you are with it, you may need to adjust it later following feedback. Even where what you have delivered is absolutely what is required, if the project goals have changed as a result of testing, the product will have to change with them. As frustrating as this can be, you will be in good company with the rest of the team who will also have to rework some of their code.

During the planning phase of any project, you will be able to bounce initial ideas off your team mates. Agile teams often have sessions devoted to ideation as well as planning what will be in the sprint. As part of sprint planning, in which the tasks are broken down, you will often write user stories for the end product or parts of its functionality. When working with a diverse multidisciplinary agile team, some of the team members will be able to bring use cases that had not initially been considered as part of the original brief. These can be really useful in ensuring that what you are creating is not just for you or people like you, but will have a broader usage and appeal. This is something that is very important in a publicly funded organisation like the BBC, because we need to serve everyone. This additional consideration does, of course, run the risk of extending the scope of the project and therefore inflating your workload beyond manageable levels and so needs to be balanced with the need to finish the project.

For example, our comic strip project was initially aimed at getting health news stories to young people, and particularly young women, who are interested in health but do not read long health news articles and are more likely to consume more visual media, for example, Instagram stories. As part of the BBC's public service remit, we have a duty to try to get important health information to everyone. Whilst looking at the use cases for the stories, we realised that a visual rendering of a story would be much more accessible for people with reading difficulties and would also be much easier to translate into other languages for our language services, meaning we could get our health news out to a much wider audience than we had initially considered.

This brought in additional difficulties as the image would have to work in different languages and cultures so could not rely too heavily on British metaphors. It also meant that the meaning had to be more fully conveyed by the image, not just by providing an illustration alongside the words. This is far more difficult to pull off than simply offering up a suitable image. Changes are to be expected in any project, of course, but a diverse agile team, especially one with a public service remit, will often add layers of complexity that make it much more difficult and take up a lot more time than you may have initially budgeted for.

Agile projects are designed to adapt to change and you can expect to make revisions to the overall end goal periodically. The goal for each sprint will also be different, so rather than working towards a single end goal you need to work towards each sprint goal while still bearing the end in mind. Often this can feel demoralising as work you have done or a taxonomy you have created turns out to be redundant or at least needs to be substantially reworked. If you embrace the iterative approach to building, it can actually work in your favour though; you are able to deliver only what is needed for the goal of the sprint and, if you are not happy with things, you can adjust it for the next sprint.

I generally find that the first time I create a data structure, whether that be taxonomy, ontology or database schema, it will generally be perfectly serviceable, but tweaks will occur to me over time that could make it more flexible or more efficient. There is always time in an agile project to make these adjustments in a later sprint provided they are necessary and contribute towards the goals of that sprint. Sometimes an adjustment I have in mind would have been a waste of time when looked at from the perspective of the new sprint goals, but may later become relevant. It's always worth noting improvement ideas and adding them as a task even if they get marked as a low priority.

For example, when I had initially envisaged the health taxonomy, it was as a traditional Linnaean hierarchical structure into which new concepts could be added at the correct level. I soon realised that this would not only be more complex than necessary for the project but would have been hard for the developers to work with. In fact, all that was needed was a mapping of keywords to a concept, without those keywords necessarily being synonymous with each other, as long as they could all be represented by the same image. For example, mental health issues, anxiety and social anxiety could be placed in the same bucket and be represented by the same image, even though as concepts they would have been at different levels of the hierarchy. Although it does mean this particular taxonomy is not perhaps re-usable elsewhere, it is the most efficient in this case – and that is all that is required at the prototyping stage.

## Working with the agile development cycle

Whether in agile or waterfall, much of your work will be completed before the software is ready to ship; this is the time to revisit any of those tasks that you set aside as unnecessary for the sprint goal, but perhaps useful for the end goal. It's also worth looking closely at any feedback from end-users as this might give you an idea of what is most useful to work on first or even bring up fresh ideas that you may be able to integrate into the current release, but which may also be worth investigating with future versions or new products in mind.

In agile teams, once the initial build is complete, you shouldn't have a very long wait until the release date and you'll have the opportunity to revise what you've done in that time. If you do come up with any amendments, as you are almost bound to, at least your team is geared up for integrating change when it occurs. Because regular code releases are a fundamental part of the agile methodology, unless it's a really major change, you shouldn't need to wait too long to see your changes implemented. It's unlikely in an agile team that you'll end up in the situation of seeing the product finalised and launched with something in it you'd really like to be able to tweak, which can happen in projects following a more rigid methodology.

For example, this is the point where I set to work adding additional terms to the taxonomy that were not required for testing in the initial build. These had been extracted from a much larger sample of articles. This meant there was a much higher likelihood of these terms being matched in later sprints when we moved on from the initial test articles and started bringing in random articles that needed a greater pool of terms to match against.

One way of addressing the issue of the uneven spread of your work across the project cycle and working in a more agile way is to view yourself not as a taxonomist that works with an agile team, but as a member of an agile team who has knowledge organisation as part of their skillset. When your work with one set of skills is less in need, perhaps you could involve yourself more with user testing and add this to your portfolio of skills. In this way, you could get immediate, first-hand feedback about how your work, as part of the end product, is perceived by users. Feedback from user testing can give really useful insights as we tend to be quite separate from the end-user and, in my experience, user testing always brings up things you would never have thought of yourself. This can lead to ideas for new products or improvements to existing ones, as well as giving the immediate feedback you need about the specific functionality you are working on.

If this isn't an option, perhaps you could look at some of the broader agile skills such as scrum mastery or retro management, where you facilitate the team in discussing the way the team worked in the previous cycle and how they can take forward anything they've learned into the next one. In the BBC, there is a range of training available from face-to-face formal training to online exercises and courses that you can take when needed – many other employers offer this sort of package as well. There are also free online courses and blogs available that could help you gain or refine your skills in other areas of development. These are well worth exploring if only to be sure of which areas you are really interested in and to increase your understanding of how the other roles work together within the team.

A concept in agile development is the T-shaped person, that is, someone with deep knowledge in one area but also a breadth of understanding about the work of the rest of the team and the product area. By acquiring a broad knowledge of the work of the rest of your team, not only will you be able to even out your workload across the development cycle and feel more integrated with the team, but you'll be gaining knowledge that will be of use to you in further agile teams and when applying for contracts elsewhere. By adding these additional skills, you will signpost yourself as someone who can integrate well into a multi-disciplinary team, bringing a range of skills and experience as well as your specialist knowledge. Being conversant in all of the terminology that accompanies agile development will also aid you in communicating easily within the team. I've supplemented my skills with a certified scrum master course and with coding skills as well as coaching and mentoring, I find it gives me a sense of purpose and fulfilment even when there isn't much to work on during some weeks in a project.

Even if you're not able to get involved in user testing, you should strive to keep across any changes or feedback received. In agile projects, this may mean regular attendance of stand ups and retrospectives, which should enable you to keep a weather eye out for any major changes of direction or pace that are likely to come up. In waterfall projects, you may need to have regular catch-ups with the project manager to ensure you are kept up to date. Often, it will be up to you to ensure this happens. As the project moves along and you are not as heavily involved, a busy project manager may be focusing all of their energy on the testing team, for example.

I've known plenty of cases where the people involved in the initial planning phases of a project were barely aware when the final product launched. While this is not necessarily a problem if your work is complete, it certainly helps if any changes are needed, as you'll still be familiar with the project and will understand the issues that have led to the changes being made, which could affect your solution. Where you're embedded in a team, this is unlikely to happen, but you should still aim to attend all of the planning and retro meetings that happen during the course of the development cycle. As a member of an agile team, your ideas and suggestions are as valid as anyone else on the team. As the nature of your work differs from most of the people on the team, you will be able to bring a unique insight and perspective which helps to improve the eventual output of the product in a way no one else could have.

## Benefits of agile teamwork

Once you have got into the rhythm of working in a team, you will soon find that there are many additional benefits, including the ability to run your ideas past all or some of the members of the team as you are working with them. Sometimes an impromptu chat with your colleagues who are working on software that will integrate with your structures can bring forward fresh perspectives that you would not have considered. It's all too easy when working on our own to fall into the trap of doing things the way we've done them before because we know it works, rather than tailoring the solution for the exact situation we're dealing with. The fresh eyes of developer colleagues can help steer you back on track. One of the most simple and obvious benefits that you cannot provide on your own is diversity of perspective, ideas and experience. Often your team will be able to point out possibilities you hadn't thought of or new functionality that they would like to build in future that would require different data to be accessible or for it to be accessible in a different way. This is really useful for staying ahead of the curve in a fast-moving development environment. In the health project, discussions with developers over the course of the project led to the creation of an additional taxonomy, not of the health concepts but of the images used to portray them and how those images could be manipulated and interact with each other. In this way, the project began to develop and extend in a way that none of us on our own would have envisaged or been able to realise.

This brings me on to one of the biggest benefits about being fully embedded in a team, which is that, once you are fully integrated into the workstream and working alongside the developers to create an end product, you feel a much greater sense of ownership of the end result. Often our work remains hidden. Unless there are serious errors it often goes unnoticed by people using it. If you've delivered the taxonomy early on in the process and left, it sometimes doesn't feel like your work any longer – rather something that was created using something you made as a component. But where you are part of the team, working alongside the others to deliver the final result, you not only feel you have ownership but you also have that rare and wonderful thing in a taxonomist's world: tangible examples of things you have worked on that you can point to in the outside world and show as proof of the value of your work. This is not only good for your CV but also for your self-esteem. You can enjoy the appreciation of the valuable part you played in the delivery of a successful project and are able to take part in any launch celebration along with the other members of the team.

## Conclusion

Working in a multidisciplinary team, and especially an agile team, rather than leading to compromise as you might expect, can actually improve the quality of your work by highlighting things you would never have noticed otherwise. It can lead you to becoming a better, more rounded team member by adding to your skillset – and therefore also increasing your career prospects. Finally, and probably most importantly, it can immensely increase the appreciation you receive for your work and your own sense of satisfaction in it.

# Appendix A
## Metadata Template to Capture Taxonomy Term Diversity

*Bharat Dayal Sharma*

A metadata specification of taxonomy terms, used to create a spreadsheet template for taxonomists to capture and recognise the diversity around any individual taxonomy term. See Chapter 4 for more information about the template.

| Column name | Description |
| --- | --- |
| ID | A unique number that could be used in future to provide a short unique permanent link to the term |
| Parent ID | The unique number that belongs to the parent name |
| Parent name | A lookup that defines words or phrases already in the taxonomy that represent a parent type, category, part or ownership that is separated by semicolons |
| Preferred name | A single preferred word or phrase, which should not contain any abbreviations |
| Source name | A plain English description of where this word or phrase has originated from |
| Source weblink (if available) | A web link (should begin with 'http://' or 'https://'), which could consist of where this word or phrase has originated |
| Abbreviation | The different abbreviations this word or phrase is currently known by, separated by a semicolon |
| Also known as | Free text terms separated by semicolons, used to describe what the word or phrase is also known as, such as alternative spellings or derivations of the same word |
| Example | A clear and short example of the term or phrase in use within its scope |
| Status | A dropdown of statuses, such as draft, publicly available or approved |
| Definition | The short definition of the word or phrase. If this originates from a specific place, enter this information within the author/contact originator name and link fields |

*Continued*

| Column name | Description |
| --- | --- |
| Author | The name of the primary author, organisation or contact details. If the term or metadata (for example, the definition) comes from a source such as a website, write the originator's name here |
| Useful background notes | A notes field consisting of text or links used to provide any useful background to understanding the word or phrase |
| Scope: use | Free text notes that describe where this term applies and any limitations on the context the term should be used in |
| Scope: misuse | Free text notes that describe where this term should not apply or be referred to. This can highlight if the term is offensive or outdated, for example |
| Start date | The date this started being of use |
| End date | The date this went out of use |
| Identical to | A lookup that defines words or phrases already in the glossary where this is exactly the same concept as and can be used interchangeably with confidence (not an abbreviation) |
| Term related to | Other words or phrases already in the taxonomy that represent similar areas of interest for a reader |
| Codename | A relevant codename or number (or link to one) of the word or phrase, such as an NHS Data Model and Dictionary Code |

# Appendix B
## Semantics – Some Basic Ontological Principles

*Bob Kasenchak*

## What is an ontology?

As other comprehensive volumes on this topic are widely available, the following brief explanations are offered with the caveat that this is a book about *taxonomy* and this discussion of ontologies is in that context.

### Useful but incomplete definition 1: An ontology is a taxonomy with more complex and specific relationships between terms

An ontology is a semantic structure of concepts and their relationships. Some ontologies allow only Broader Term–Narrower Term (BT–NT) and Related Term (RT) relationships and are arranged into hierarchies: we call these *taxonomies*. Therefore, all taxonomies are ontologies, but not all ontologies are taxonomies. This means, of course, that taxonomies are a valid NT of ontologies:

Ontologies
- Taxonomies

Ontologies admit more complex structures than hierarchies and more complex relationships than the now familiar BT–NT and RT thesaural types. An ontology may or may not contain one or more taxonomies.

So, one simple way to introduce ontologies (in the context of a book about taxonomies) is to imagine a taxonomy in which you may specify the *type of relationship* between terms. To return to my favourite example about 'Dogs' and 'Dog food': instead of trying to decide whether to make these two terms a BT-NT pair or use an RT to relate them, we may now use any relationship we wish to semantically connect these terms. We might, for example, say that:

Dogs        EAT          Dog food
Dog food    IS EATEN BY  Dogs

. . . wherein the second is the inverse of the first, just like BT–NT relationships. We can now reimagine any example using this logic:

Economics        HAS SUBFIELD  Microeconomics
Microeconomics   HAS TOPIC     Consumer Demand

This allows us to neatly sidestep some of the problems discussed above (such as mixing topics and subjects) by specifying any relationship we like between any two concepts.

It's important to note that the resulting structure is not a hierarchy, but rather a different and more complex graph.

## Useful but incomplete definition 2: An ontology is a bunch of taxonomies tied together

Imagine, to return to an example from publishing, that you are the publisher of some scholarly journals. You publish some number of *journals*, each of which contains *articles*. Articles are written by one or more *authors*, each of whom is affiliated with some *institution* (such as a university, hospital or research lab). Further, each article has content about some *topic* (presumably among the topic(s) that the corresponding journal is purported to cover).

In this short description, we have identified five types of objects to model:

- Articles (a bunch of content)
- Authors (a flat list)
- Institutions (a hierarchy: some universities have multiple colleges as well as labs, etc.)
- Journals (a flat list)
- Topics (a taxonomy used to index/tag the *Articles*).

Each of these is a controlled vocabulary with different structures (some are flat lists, some are hierarchies) and containing values in Attribute fields: the name and website of the author, institution and so forth.

Now, being a clever publishing executive, you have long since built a taxonomy covering the topics you publish and deployed it on your website to enhance discovery; that is, you have already associated the *Topics* and *Articles*.

Assuming clean data (which is never the case, but this is a thought experiment, not a project plan), you now want to create a database (specifically, a graph database) connecting the articles, authors, institutions, journals and topics so that you can ask questions about your content (that is, treat it like data that can be queried) like 'How many papers with more than three authors did we publish by authors from Harvard on any topic in sociology last year?'

Thinking abstractly - that is, not about any *particular* article or author or institution - we can use an ontology to say that:

| | | |
|---|---|---|
| Objects of the class *Author* | HAVE AFFILIATION | Objects of the class *Institution* |
| Objects of the class *Article* | HAVE TOPIC | Objects of the class *Topic* |
| Objects of the class *Journal* | HAVE ARTICLE | Objects of the class *Article* |

. . . and so on, specifying which types of objects can have relationships with which.

We can then plug the values of the specific objects into our abstract model to generate a large graph - an ontology - that can be queried like a database.

## Useful but incomplete definition 3: An ontology is a semantic graph describing any kinds of concepts and their relationships and specified in a machine-readable format

So, an ontology is a graph of concepts and their relationships. The astute reader will have noticed that at some point the default unit in taxonomies, the *Term*, has given way to the unit used in ontologies: the *Concept*. This subtle but important distinction is indicative of the extra magnitude of complexity (with advantages and disadvantages) offered by ontologies. In a taxonomy, the *Term* is the object, while in an ontology, the *Concept* - independent of the *Term*! - is the object, for which the *Term* is just a label. Relationships (now called *Predicates*) are customisable to express any relationship useful to model the data in question.

Ontologies, then, offer additional complexity and utility when compared to taxonomies but are correspondingly more effort to build and maintain. Ontologies have several other important properties:

- Ontologies are *extensible*: it's easy to add things to the model and extend it to include more objects.
- Ontologies are *interoperable*: ontologies are stored in (or, at least, exportable to) a data standard called RDF (Resource Description Framework), which is shareable with any other RDF-based system. (See www.bobdc.com/blog/whatisrdf for a very readable introduction to RDF by Bob DuCharme.)
- Ontologies are *shareable*: many ontologies are publicly available for download and re-use, and use of other existing ontologies is common practice.
- Ontologies are *machine-readable*: any ontology expressed in (properly defined and valid) RDF is ingestible and useable by any system, because . . .
- Ontologies use *Uniform Resource Identifiers (URIs) to name things*: every object in a (properly defined) ontology is a persistent URI web link that can be read and resolved.

Ontologies are useful for modelling product information, supply chains, workflows and anything you can represent as objects and relationships.

## SKOS

Simple Knowledge Organization System (SKOS) is an ontology for representing and storing taxonomies.

Returning to the publishing example above, the abstract model in which *Articles* HAVE *Topics* is just that: a model, which once populated with specific information will store information like *The Origin of Species* HAS TOPIC *Evolution*. This abstract model (sometimes called the 'upper ontology') defines the relationships objects are allowed to have with one another.

SKOS provides an upper ontology to store taxonomies, so it represents ideas like BT–NT relationships, RTs, non-preferred terms (NPTs) and common attribute fields like Definitions and Scope Notes. SKOS also has some useful built-in relationships like *Exact Match*, *Broad Match* and *Narrow Match* used to map (relate terms between) one taxonomy to another with various levels of specificity.

Familiarity with basic SKOS concepts should be considered required for taxonomists.

# Appendix C
## Metadata Model Template

*Yonah Levenson*

This appendix contains an example of a metadata template - populated and unpopulated. The example is a good starting point for metadata development. See Chapter 7 for full information about working with metadata, particularly for projects where interoperability between different systems is required.

Spreadsheets are the suggested best format to use in a real project, due to their flexibility. When the metadata entities are in a spreadsheet, it can facilitate loading of those metadata entities into a taxonomy application, if one is available.

The tables in this appendix may also be copied into, or created as, a text file - whatever works best for the project and its audience(s).

A typical metadata workbook has at least three tabs:

- overview of the workbook including:
  - who created it
  - what is the purpose of the workbook
  - when was it created and last edited
  - where one can find relevant links used for research, etc. (optional)
  - description of each tab
  - any other details that may be helpful to someone referencing the workbook.
- tab for the metadata entities
- tab for the controlled vocabularies.

This document contains an example of each of these tabs. Capturing metadata in a workbook also facilitates cross-map efforts.

### Metadata template: overview
Use this template as the starting point for creating metadata models.

**Workbook Overview: Tab 1**

| | |
|---|---|
| Creation date | [date here] |
| Created by | your name |
| Last edited by | whoever made the last changes |
| Date last edited | [date of last edit here] |

| Field names | Definitions |
|---|---|
| *Metadata template* | |
| **Parent entity** | Parent or op level entity |
| **Sub-entity (optional)** | Child term to a parent term.Sub-entity<br>Note: There may be sub-sub entities. IF needed, add<br>additional columns |
| **Definition** | Definition of the term |
| **Type** | Describes the format of the entity, e.g., string, numerical, etc. |
| **Min** | If a string, what are the minimum number of characters? |
| **Max** | If a string, what are the maximum number of characters? |
| **Cardinality** | How many times can this entity exist?<br>0+ = 0 or more<br>1 = one and only one<br>1+ = one or more |

# Metadata Table Examples: Tabs 2 and 3

### Tab 2: Metadata entities template – unpopulated

| Parent entity | Sub-entity (child) | Definition | Type | Min | Max | Cardinality | Example |
|---|---|---|---|---|---|---|---|
| | | | | | | | |
| | | | | | | | |
| | | | | | | | |
| | | | | | | | |

### Tab 3: Controlled vocabularies template – unpopulated

| Entity 1 | Entity 2 | Entity 3 | Etc. |
|---|---|---|---|
| | | | |
| | | | |
| | | | |
| | | | |
| | | | |

## Tab 2: Metadata entities template – populated

| Parent entity | Sub-entity (child) | Definition | Type | Min | Max | Cardinality | Example |
|---|---|---|---|---|---|---|---|
| Colour | | Primary colour of the image | CV | 3 | 20 | 1 | Red |
| Orien-tation | | Image orientation | CV | 2 | 10 | 1 | Land |
| UID | | Unique identifier for the image | Integer | 1 | 20 | 1 | 12345 |
| Photo-grapher | First Name | | String | 1 | 40 | 1 | Yonah |
| | Last Name | | String | 1 | 40 | 1 | Levenson |

## Tab 3: Metadata entities template – populated

| Colour | Orientation | Entity 3 | Etc. |
|---|---|---|---|
| Blue | Portrait | | |
| Green | Landscape | | |
| Red | | | |
| Yellow | | | |

# Glossary

*Bob Kasenchak and Helen Lippell*

*Words and phrases in italics refer to another entry in the glossary.*

**Aboutness**
Describes the relationship of content (e.g., a document) to the *Term* (often, but not necessarily, from a *Controlled vocabulary*) describing its primary subject(s).

**All–Some rule**
Rule of thumb for testing for valid *Hierarchical relationships* based on logical syllogisms: if all *B* is *A*, B is a valid *Narrower term (NT)* of A.

**ANSI/NISO Z39.19**
International standard for the 'Construction, Format, and Management of Monolingual Controlled Vocabularies'. See www.niso.org/publications/ansiniso-z3919-2005-r2010.

**API**
Short for Application Programming Interface, generically used to describe protocols for sharing data between software applications. In the context of taxonomy software, APIs allow dedicated taxonomy systems to share *Terms* with *Content management systems* (CMS), *Digital asset management* (DAM) applications and other consuming applications.

**Artificial intelligence (AI)**
Any of a number of processes using machines to imitate processes achieved by human intelligence. In taxonomy, often used for activities like *Content tagging* and *Term* discovery via *Text mining*. See also *Machine learning*.

**Associative relationships**
Any non-hierarchical relationship used to relate *Terms*, as opposed to *Hierarchical relationships* (BT–NT) used to construct a *Hierarchy*. Associative relationships may be generic (like RT) or specific and may or may not be reciprocal.

**Authority file**

Type of *Controlled vocabulary* used for proper names of entities (people, places, organisations, etc.). Usually flat or mostly flat, may contain alternative labels and other information for each *Entity*.

**Auto-tagging/Automatic classification**

Software-based application of subject *Terms* to documents with little or no human intervention.

**Boolean**

Generically, the use of AND, OR and NOT operators to construct short, logical statements for search queries and other text-related functions.

**Broader term (BT)**

Parent term of a given term in a *Hierarchy*. Reciprocal of *Narrower term (NT)*.

**Business case**

Document that describes the specific practical implementations for which a taxonomy project is required. The business case should be used to get agreement on resources, technology, etc., in order to do the work.

**Buy-in**

Support from *Stakeholders* and other parties in an organisation for a taxonomy project.

**Card sort(ing)**

Method for soliciting user or expert input on a taxonomy structure by asking participants to arrange concepts, utilising index cards, sticky notes or (more recently) software for this purpose.

**Classification accuracy**

Metric(s) measuring the performance of automatic *Content classification* systems.

**Content management system (CMS)**

Any number of software systems designed to store, manage and retrieve content, possibly including both text-based and other content. Compare with *Digital asset management* and *Document management system*.

**Content tagging (or Content classification)**

Application of term(s) from one or more taxonomies to pieces of content, to support *Information retrieval* or other functionality.

**Controlled vocabulary (CV)**

Umbrella term for organised lists of concepts and/or entities including *Authority files*, taxonomies and thesauri.

**Corpus**
A body of content, usually used to describe the content held by an organisation or department, e.g., to be used for *Text mining* or classified for retrieval.

**Cross-walk/Cross-map**
Relating conceptually identical (or similar) terms between two or more distinct vocabularies. Can refer both to the methodology for this activity and the resulting 'map' between vocabularies.

**Digital asset management (DAM)**
Any number of software systems designed to store, manage and retrieve non-text content, including but not limited to images and video. Compare with *Content management system* and *Document management system*.

**Disambiguation**
Distinguishing (and making unique) identical or similar terms in a taxonomy for clarity and uniqueness.

**Document management system (DMS)**
Any number of software systems designed to store, manage and retrieve text-based content. Compare with *Content management system* and *Digital asset management*.

**Dublin Core**
Set of 15 *Metadata* elements intended for adoption as an extensible universal standard to describe resources, including Title, Creator, Date and similar fields. See https://dublincore.org.

**Enterprise taxonomy**
One or more taxonomies used to classify information for a specific organisation; in addition to a subject taxonomy, enterprise taxonomy ecosystems may also include organisational taxonomies describing departmental structure, lists of relevant people and other organisations (employees, clients, vendors), content types, and other concepts useful for corporate information governance and retrieval.

**Enterprise search**
Search specific to the internal-facing content in an organisation; may include assets across multiple repositories.

**Entity**
Generally, a concept in a *Controlled vocabulary* referring, e.g., to a specific person, place or organisation.

**Facet**
Generally, any subset of terms in a taxonomy grouped together non-hierarchically; essentially a flag applied to terms as *Metadata*. Not to be confused with *Faceted taxonomies*.

**Faceted classification**
 *Content tagging* with *Faceted taxonomies*; each *Facet* contains *Metadata* describing a different aspect of an asset's *Aboutness* to support browsing or filtering content.

**Faceted taxonomies**
 A group of associated vocabularies to describe various aspects of content as controlled *Metadata*. May include vocabularies for, e.g., topic, method, location, organisation, etc., depending on the nature of the content, data or products being described.

**Findability**
 Ease of finding information sought via search or browse in an information environment.

**Filtering, search**
 Refining and narrowing of large result sets obtained via *Search* by applying additional filters to find relevant content.

**Folksonomy**
 User-generated taxonomy-like structure with little or no control imposed.

**Governance**
 Processes and procedures to maintain and continually develop vocabularies to ensure their continued relevance and utility. Can include expert feedback, reviewing content for new concepts and *Workflows* for suggestion and adoption of new terms by users.

**Granularity**
 The level of specificity described by a vocabulary in a specific domain. Taxonomists often have to decide how granular to make their taxonomy, in order to capture the right level of detail needed for live usage.

**Hierarchical relationships**
 BT–NT relationships (and their subtypes) used to construct a *Hierarchy*, as distinct from *Associative relationships*, which are non-hierarchical. The basic unit of taxonomy.

**Hierarchy**
 A tree-like structure of BT–NT relationships and the primary feature of taxonomic structures.

**Infinite loop**
 Taxonomic error that occurs when a term has been made a *Broader term (BT)* or *Narrower term (NT)* of itself. This can cause problems for applications trying to parse the *Hierarchy*. See also *Loop, infinite*.

**Information architecture (IA)**
  Broad term generally describing the design, organisation and
  construction of information environments.
**Information retrieval (IR)**
  The process of finding relevant and complete information (such as
  documents) from a repository or collection of resources; supported by
  taxonomy structures and document tagging.
**Interoperability**
  Generically, the ability of data structures to be used by multiple
  systems. Taxonomy *Schemas* are considered interoperable when they
  can be consumed and shared by disparate architectures.
**ISO 25964**
  An international standard for 'Thesauri and Interoperability with
  Other Vocabularies', with emphasis on supporting *Information
  retrieval*, and specifically to guide the choice of terms used in
  indexing, tagging and search queries. See
  www.niso.org/schemas/iso25964.
**JSON (JavaScript Object Notation)**
  Widely used open standard data interchange format; often seen in
  *APIs* to share data between *Taxonomy tools* and other systems.
**Knowledge graph**
  A *Knowledge organisation system* (often a combination of an *Ontology*
  and taxonomies) connected to content or data. Knowledge graphs
  provide additional information about a topic to end-users, mainly
  through search or browse applications. The graph is generally stored
  in *RDF*, in a graph database or other repository.
**Knowledge management**
  Broad term covering the collection, storage, management and
  distribution of information in enterprises and other organisations.
**Knowledge organisation system (KOS)**
  Blanket term for any kind of *Controlled vocabulary* used to organise
  information; including, but not limited to, *Taxonomy*, *Ontology*,
  *Authority files*, classification schemes, topic maps and *Thesaurus*.
**Linked data**
  Structured data that is (or can be) combined with other data via
  semantic queries. Foundational to the Semantic Web. When
  combined with *Open data*, linked data becomes *Linked open data*.
**Linked open data**
  Data that is both *Linked data* and *Open data*.

**Loop, infinite**
Taxonomic error that occurs when a term has been made a *Broader term (BT)* or *Narrower term (NT)* of itself. This can cause problems for applications trying to parse the *Hierarchy*. See also *Infinite loop*.

**Machine learning (ML)**
Any of a set of techniques using analysis of existing data to build analytical models. ML is considered an aspect of *Artificial intelligence*.

**Master data management (MDM)**
The system of record that holds the 'golden record', which is the most accurate and true *Metadata* for an asset. An MDM system's primary function is to provide the best *Metadata* of record to the requestor.

**Media asset management (MAM)**
Any number of software systems designed to store and manage video and multimedia files. Compare with *Digital asset management*.

**Metadata**
Data about data; data describing or providing information about other data, often controlled or otherwise machine-readable.

**Metadata, administrative**
*Metadata*, often automatically generated, describing the author, date, publisher and similar information.

**Metadata, descriptive**
Applied to a document to denote, e.g., its topic or subject, ideally from one or more *Controlled vocabularies*. See *Content tagging*.

**Metadata, structural**
Elements used to structure content into sections, such as XML elements, to define chapters, headings, series and other components.

**Metrics**
Statistical data to support a taxonomy programme by demonstrating the benefits of implementation, e.g., by measuring search efficiency or content re-use.

**Minimum viable metadata (MVM)**
Set of bare minimum information used to describe an element of content, especially where content is being transferred or shared between different systems.

**Monohierarchy**
A taxonomy with no *Polyhierarchy* in which terms may only have one *Broader term (BT)*.

**Narrower term (NT)**
Child term of a given term in a *Hierarchy*. Reciprocal of *Broader term (BT)*.

**Natural language processing (NLP)**
Any of a number of systems and processes for analysing text, including but not limited to *Text mining*.

**Navigation**
Components of a user interface in an information environment, including but not limited to web pages, providing the user with functionality to find information and other actions.

**Non-preferred term (NPT)**
Any alternative label or variant of a term; often called *Synonyms*, although other variants, such as alternative spellings and part-of-speech variants, may also be included. Useful for indexing and text processing.

**Open data**
Data that is freely, or with minimal restrictions, available for use and distribution. When open data is also *Linked data* it becomes *Linked open data*.

**Ontology**
A representation, including naming and explication of categories, attributes and relationships, of one or more domains of knowledge. Ontologies may or may not contain one or more taxonomies.

**Orphan term**
Any term with no relationships to other terms; having no parent, child or sibling terms, thus left 'orphaned' in a vocabulary.

**OWL**
Short for Web Ontology Language. Semantic web- and standards-based set of *Schemas* for modelling and storing *Ontologies*.

**Payload**
In an *API*, the actual data pack that is sent with the GET method in HTTP. It is the crucial information that you submit to the server when you are making an *API* request.

**Polyhierarchy**
A taxonomic structure that admits multiple *Broader terms (BTs)* for any given term.

**Post-coordinated term**
*Taxonomy* term that represents a single concept, usually from a single *Facet* (e.g., Size – small, Colour – blue, Category – skirts). See also *Pre-coordinated term*.

**Pre-coordinated term**
*Taxonomy* term that combines multiple concepts, especially from different *Facets*, to create a single, compound term (e.g., 'small blue skirts'). See also *Post-coordinated term*.

**Preferred term (PT)**
The canonical version of a concept in a *Controlled vocabulary*, as contrasted with *Non-preferred terms* (NPTs).

**Product information management (PIM)**
Can refer to either a system or to a process. Both of these are concerned with managing information required to market and sell products, usually across multiple channels such as websites, apps, social media or marketplaces.

**Proof of concept (POC)**
Project that is undertaken, normally with a small team, in order to explore the impact of changing processes or technology and, in the context of this book, of changing the way taxonomies are used in the organisation. It is intended to demonstrate value for *Stakeholders*, while being lower risk than undertaking a full taxonomy project.

**Qualitative**
Any measurement of type, category, characteristic or attribute, as opposed to numerically quantifiable measurements. Contrast with *Quantitative*.

**Quantitative**
Any measurement describable by numeric values, whether multitudinal (how many?) or magnitudinal (how much?). Contrast with *Qualitative*.

**Ranking, search**
See *Search ranking*.

**RDF (Resource Description Framework)**
Family of W3C data storage and interchange specifications for representing and sharing web-based information in the form of semantic triples; in taxonomy, widely used to model and store taxonomies and ontologies.

**Records management application (RMA)**
Software used to manage records, often including categorisation and retrieval as well as automating retention and deprecation schedules.

**Related term (RT)**
The most common and generic *Associative relationship* equivalent to a 'see also' note. One of the thesaural relationships (along with *Broader term (BT)* and *Narrower term (NT)*). RTs may or may not be reciprocal.

**Relevance, search**
See *Search relevance*.

**Schema**
Broadly, any model or form in which content or data is stored.

**Search**

The process of, and tools used to enable, finding content on or across websites using text-based queries.

**Search Engine Optimisation (SEO)**

The process of improving the *Findability* of a website or page in search engines, including using terms from *Controlled vocabularies* to populate *Metadata* fields for this purpose.

**Search ranking**

The order in which search results are presented to the user.

**Search relevance**

Metric(s) purporting to measure the performance of search queries by comparing a search to the results returned. See also *Search Engine Optimisation*.

**Semantics**

Term broadly describing the network of concepts and their relationships as described in a taxonomy or *Ontology*. Often specifically used to describe ontological information stored in *RDF*.

**SKOS (Simple Knowledge Organization System)**

Widely used *Ontology* for storing and representing taxonomies and thesauri described by a W3C standard.

**SKOS-XL**

Short for SKOS eXtension for Labels, an extension of the *SKOS* schema featuring additional support for describing and linking lexical entities.

**Stakeholder**

Any person or group with an interest or concern in a project.

**Structured content**

Content organised in a predictable way, usually to indicate title, paragraphs and other information, including *Metadata* from *Controlled vocabularies*; including but not limited to XML. See also *Unstructured content*.

**Subject matter experts (SMEs)**

Domain experts, often called upon to review taxonomies from their perspective.

**Synonyms**

Strictly, any two words with identical or near-identical meanings; loosely, often used to refer to any *Non-preferred term*.

**Tag**

Generically, a term from a vocabulary applied to a piece of content for the purposes of *Information retrieval*.

**Taxonomy**
Strictly, a *Controlled vocabulary* arranged in a *Hierarchy* without other fields and relationships. Broadly, the entire domain of controlled vocabularies, including their theoretical principles, construction and deployment and encompassing related structures like thesauri and ontologies.

**Taxonomy tool or system**
Application that manages taxonomy and vocabulary terms in a centralised location. Facilitates how terms may be related to each other. Connectivity point for system vocabularies.

**Taxonomy standards**
Widely accepted guides for development, maintenance and storage of *Controlled vocabularies*, including *ANSI/NISO Z39.19* and *ISO 25964*.

**Term**
The base unit of any *Controlled vocabulary*; a word or short string of words representing a single concept. See also *Entity*.

**Text mining**
Any of a number of processes used to extract and analyse text from documents. In taxonomy, text mining is used, e.g., to identify frequently occurring words and strings as candidate concepts for inclusion in vocabularies. A subset of *Natural language processing*.

**Thesaural relationships**
*Broader term (BT)*, *Narrower term (NT)* and *Related term (RT)* are the common term relationships used in thesauri.

**Thesaurus**
A taxonomy including *Non-preferred terms* (NPTs) and other attribute fields. Often used for indexing and categorisation.

**Tooling**
See *Taxonomy tool*.

**Unstructured content**
Content, including but not limited to text, lacking any *Schema* or other formal containers or markers. See also *Structured content*.

**User research**
A variety of methods and practices to gather input from users for taxonomy and *Information architecture* projects. See also *User testing*.

**User story**
In agile and other development methodologies, a way of capturing a feature, *Workflow* or other implementation requirement in the form of a standardised, user-centred request.

**User testing**
Review of a taxonomy or implementation by users for validation.

**Web Ontology Language**

See *OWL*.

**Workflow**

Broadly, any repeated sequence or pattern of activities or tasks, often facilitated by the organisation of systems and resources. In this book, workflow usually means the business and technical processes needed to manage change requests to a taxonomy.

# Index